The Hunting Gene

HUNTING – ITS PEOPLE; ITS WILDLIFE AND ITS COUNTRYSIDE

The Hunting Gene

HUNTING – ITS PEOPLE; ITS WILDLIFE AND ITS COUNTRYSIDE

ROBIN PAGE

Foreword by Robin Hanbury-Tenison

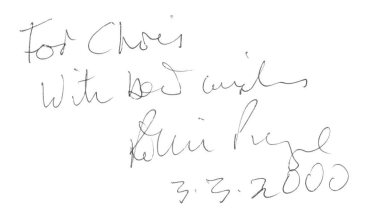

For Chris
With best wishes
Robin Page
3. 3. 2000

BIRD'S FARM BOOKS

DEDICATION

This book is dedicated to the memory of Gordon Beningfield –
artist, conservationist and friend of the countryside. He did not hunt, he gave up shooting
and fishing, but he regarded them all as important parts of the rural culture he loved so
much. He was a good man who is greatly missed by his family, his friends and all those
who love butterflies and wild places.

Picture acknowledgements

Bryan and Cherry Alexander: pp. 24, 41, 42, 54, 56, 103, 136 top, 201 top, 216, 219, 226. 'BB' (Denys
Watkins-Pitchford): pp. 51, 90, 106. Gordon Beningfield: pp 7, 73, 98. Laurie Campbell: pp. 49, 163, 209.
European Commission UK office: p. 225. Will Garfit: pp. 11, 23, 35, 47, 61, 85, 105, 139, 181, 197, 215.
Nigel Housden: pp. 2, 12, 14, 15, 22, 26, 32, 34, 38, 43, 45, 52, 72, 75, 76, 78, 79, 80, 81, 82, 83, 87, 94, 100
bottom, 101, 104 top, 123, 124, 126, 127, 133, 134, 135, 136 both, 137, 138, 143, 145, 146, 148, 150, 156
left, 158, 159 bottom, 160, 164, 165, 167, 171, 175, 178, 179 left, 182, 184, 189, 193, 194, 195, 196, 199,
200, 201 bottom, 206, 209, 210, 211, 220, 221, 222, 223, 231, 232. Robert Gillmor: p. 203. Lynda Huxley:
p. 132 left. Chris Knights: pp. 17, 57, 62, 66, 68, 71, 104, 108, 113, 115, 116, 117, 172, 183, 185 both, 202.
David Mason: pp. 55, 63, 86, 91, 109, 144. Raoul Millais: pp. 128, 129, 130, 162. Sheena McCall: pp. 64, 65,
132, 151, 155 top. Robin Page: pp. 13, 16, 33, 36, 37, 39, 40, 44, 89, 93, 95, 96, 97, 100 top, 112, 114, 125,
140, 141, 155 bottom, 156 right, 157, 159 top, 174, 179 right, 180, 187, 190, 191, 192, 196, 200, 204, 205,
212, 214, 232, 235. John Paley: pp. 99, 107, 110, 119, 121, 131, 168, 177. Dr Franklyn Perring: p. 18. Fiona
Silver: pp. 20, 21, 27, 28, 29, 54 left, 60, 100, 101, 153, 170, 186. David Tomlinson: p. 154. The Telegraph
Group Ltd 1999, London: p. 229. Rod Wilson: p. 98. The Publishers acknowledge the generous help of *The
Shooting Times* in sponsoring John Paley's illustrations.

Published by Bird's Farm Books, Barton, Cambridgeshire CB3 7AG
Distributed by Merlin Unwin Books, 7 Corve Street, Ludlow, Shropshire

Copyright © 2000 Robin Page

ISBN 0 905232 16 X

Designed and produced in Great Britain

Printed and bound in Great Britain

CONTENTS

ACKNOWLEDGEMENTS

I am ashamed to say that due to over-writing this book by many thousands of words I have not allowed myself the space to thank people in the detail I had hoped. I hope that those concerned will forgive me. My especial thanks are due to David Grayling and Rosemary Chambers for their support and encouragement all the way through this daunting project. Margaret Taylor has also been indispensable – transcribing reams of notes and hours of interviews and putting every word onto a proper computer – as opposed to my ancient Amstrad. Thanks to Nigel Housden who has accompanied me for thousands of miles and days on end to take the necessary photographs – from Norfolk to Pembrokeshire and from Devon to the Flow country we have sought to find and record the true picture of hunting as it is carried out in Britain today and to Jenny Dereham for editing a chunk of the manuscript.

Without the help of many hunts including the Heythrop, the Eskdale and Ennerdale, the Aldenham Harriers, the Trinity Foot Beagles, the Swaffham Coursing Club and the Fat Ladies Coursing Club, *The Hunting Gene* would not have been possible. I would like to thank Brian Fanshawe, David Reynolds, James Barclay, Edmund Marriage, Andrew Fletcher and Mark Miller Mundy.

In addition to Margaret and Nigel, thanks too to all the artists and photographers who have contributed to *The Hunting Gene* on spec – Will Garfit, John Paley, Sheena McCall, Fiona Silver, Raoul Millais, Bryan and Cherry Alexander, Chris Knights, David Mason, Laurie Campbell, David Tomlinson, Lynda Huxley and Dr Franklyn Perring. In addition thanks to all the authors quoted; every effort has been made to obtain the appropriate permissions.

Thanks to the Telegraph Group Ltd, London 1999 for the MATT cartoon. My apologies to Hippy, the Jack Russell, for not getting his front end into the book.

My very special thanks to Betty Beningfield for allowing me to reproduce Gordon Beningfield's painting of the skylark and also one of his photographs; also to Jim Reader who designed this book.

FOREWORD

When, in 1995, I took on the job of running the British Field Sports Society, it looked like a poisoned chalice. Hunting appeared to be doomed and morale among its supporters was very low. When the terrible tragedy of Dunblane was followed by an understandable but flawed emotional reaction against all legitimate gun users, including our highly successful Olympic teams, it looked as though shooting was doomed too. Only fishing seemed to have a reasonably secure future. And yet, as I wrestled with the intellectual, social, environmental and scientific arguments for and against all the various field sports practised in this country, I came to see increasingly how warped the public perception of them is.

As Robin Page points out in his usual astute and provocative way, there are some aspects of fishing which are disturbing, while every element in all properly conducted hunting with hounds is both humane and utterly defensible.

What should matter to us all is the ultimate welfare of each species. Because of the colossal impact we now have on the environment and the terrible damage we do to every conceivable remaining habitat, we have a huge responsibility to redress the balance. Our hunting gene is one of the best tools we have to help wildlife; not, as it is so often portrayed, to damage it. All too often, real cruelty comes instead from misguided and sentimental efforts to nurse gravely

The Skylark – *painted by Gordon Beningfield. A sign of a healthy habitat.*

injured creatures back to an appearance of health and then release them into the wild to face an almost certain lingering death.

Robin Page demonstrates again and again in this splendid book the real ways we should relate to nature. Pulling no punches, goading and teasing those with closed minds who, sadly, probably won't read it anyway, he exposes their hypocrisy and anthropomorphism. But anyone who does read it with an open mind cannot fail to be persuaded of the inescapable truth: hunting with hounds is a good and noble activity, which benefits both the prey and the rest of nature.

Robin also provokes and incites on almost every page, challenging the reader to disagree with his passionately held views on a host of diverse topics. No one will agree with everything he writes – I certainly don't – but it takes a peculiar form of self-delusion and obstinacy not to accept that his core message is right. Unfortunately, too many people still prefer to believe in Bambi.

Nevertheless, attitudes are changing. The great day of the Countryside March – when the country people came to town under the new banner of the Countryside Alliance and showed that they were gentle, polite and kind – left a message which all the hysterical animal rights propaganda and cynical political posturing cannot erase. On that day I was proud to have been a part of it all.

ROBIN HANBURY-TENISON
Chief Executive of The British Field Sports Society/
Countryside Alliance from 1995 to 1998

INTRODUCTION

At a time in Britain when hunting with hounds and dogs is under increasing political attack, this is a book about hunting. Politically incorrect it may be, but if Britain really is the home of free speech and democracy – a democracy that should safeguard the liberties of minorities – then the need for *The Hunting Gene* should be obvious to most people.

I do not hunt, shoot or fish. My close family never was part of the 'hunting set', although as a teenager I used to 'beat' on a syndicate shoot run by two uncles. I gave that up on seeing the suffering of shot deer; I gave up fishing too, at about the same time, after hooking several perch, deep into their throats. I decided that fishing was cruel. It was cruel for me, and so I decided not to take part. It was my personal, moral choice; I was happy for others who saw things differently to continue, as long as their fishing was conducted in a responsible way.

My chosen sports have always been football and cricket. Since giving up football – my last full game was at the age of 48 – my winter Saturday afternoons seem empty, apart from forays to see the village team on the 'rec', or to Cambridge United on what used to be a cabbage patch. I still play village cricket, however, and to me cricket is the greatest sport of them all, demanding skill, an appreciation of an English summer and an ability to mix with team members from all backgrounds. Cricket is a sport whose traditions run deep but, like hunting, it is currently in turmoil, thanks to a mixture of stupidity and political correctness. Over recent years cricket has almost stopped being played in our schools; school playing fields have been sold off for easy money from development, and competitive team games have been deemed politically incorrect. Oh dear, this sorry state of affairs almost deserves a book in its own right.

I have written two previous books on hunting, shooting and fishing, and never imagined that a third on hunting would become necessary. The first, *The Hunter and the Hunted*, published in 1977, concerned the ethics of country sports; the second, *The Fox and the Orchid* (1987), was about the conservation links of hunting, shooting and fishing. They were not apologies for blood sports; I have always attempted to write honestly with no desire to mis-lead or manipulate.

Indeed, I am writing this Introduction almost thirty years to the day from when I had my first article published (under a pseudonym) in a national magazine. I wrote it as a civil servant, knowingly breaking the law, because the Labour ministers in charge of my department seemed to lie in Parliament and to the media. For their apparent dishonesty they were ennobled; for my attempt to reveal the truth, as an innocent 26-year-old, I was sacked from my job and threatened with prosecution under the Official Secrets Acts.

THE HUNTING GENE

In those early books on country sports I recommended the cessation of otter hunting on conservation grounds as there were virtually no otters. I suggested that cartridges containing lead shot should not be used over wetland, because of the environmental damage caused (a Government ban finally arrived twenty-two years later, in 1999). The sport that I found most unacceptable on both cruelty and conservation grounds was competition fishing.

Now comes *The Hunting Gene*, once more driven by what seems to be the blindness and deafness of many MPs and several organisations and charities. I had no intention of writing another book on hunting – I have over a dozen books in my head that I want to write – but the outrageous claims of those wanting to ban hunting have forced me to become involved. I simply do not see why a few people should ignore the truth to achieve a political end and in the process attack others who have neither the experience nor the time to defend themselves in the media.

My departed old mother always used to say: 'Tell the truth, say what you mean and don't hold grudges.' That has been my philosophy, and it saddens me immensely that in modern politics and the media, the exact reverse seems to hold sway. Many years ago my geography master at school also had an interesting view: 'There are three sides to every argument; your side, their side, and the truth.' I have no vested interest whatsoever in hunting; all I want to do in *The Hunting Gene* is to try to establish, and describe truthfully, what happens.

As a non-hunter, non-shooter, non-fisher, I have tried to rationalise why I feel so strongly about the hunting issue; but I can find no rational explanation, apart from the fact that hunting is part of country life. It is part of rural culture, and I cannot stand, or understand, the mis-information and distortion that is spread about hunting and those who hunt. In our largely urban-dominated society, over 50 per cent of the population admits to obtaining all their information about hunting from the media – media that thrive on exaggeration, sensation and half truths. I hope *The Hunting Gene* helps to give readers a clearer and more honest picture of hunting, the countryside and the country way of life.

My one fear about the book is that some wealthy individuals or organisations may try to stop its publication. Sadly, what now passes for 'British justice' can be used to prevent fair and open discussion. The best example is the way in which the well-known crook Robert Maxwell took out libel writs and injunctions to prevent the truth emerging about his corrupt life. He achieved it because he was wealthy and the British system of injustice allows the availability of huge sums of money to interfere with free speech, right and wrong, guilty and not guilty. Robert Maxwell, an ex-Labour MP, was a fraudster on a huge scale, with friends in high places in both politics and the media, and only the magazine *Private Eye* had the courage to try and expose him.

I have attempted to explore the hunting issue honestly, and if there are any errors in the text it is because some opponents of hunting have not furnished me with all the information I would have liked, while others have not granted me interviews. Since I am trying to give an accurate view of hunting this has not been helpful.

Nevertheless, I hope *The Hunting Gene* assists those with open minds to understand the issues involved. With the countryside in crisis, understanding is wanted more than anything else – apart from positive action based on it.

Chapter One

ANIMAL FARM

william Garet.

THE HUNTING GENE

The countryside is in crisis. Farm incomes have plummeted; farmland wildlife is disappearing; traditional landscapes are facing the bulldozer, the chainsaw and the twelve-furrow plough; fields are being transformed into food production factories; the land itself is being stolen for theme parks, ill-conceived development and holiday or second homes for people who do not understand the countryside. Rural communities are dying and the sport of hunting is under constant attack. As a direct result, the whole of our rural culture is threatened, and this in a society that boasts of its multi-culturalism.

I was born in 1943 on the small family farm in Cambridgeshire where I still live. I have moved just ten yards in my lifetime, from one side of a pair of farm cottages to the other. Some people will say that such a journey will result in parochialism and a view of rural life stunted by nostalgia, the past and an aversion for change. Apparently life and politics today are about the present and the future; that is, New Britain and Cool Britannia, the mobility of labour and the global village. In 1943 there was God and the choices were about right and wrong. The new God has become the free market and the choices are not based on morality, but on 'Does it pay?'

I am glad that I have had a settled life, for it enables me to look at the present rural crisis and see it for what it is. I do not need an economist to tell me that the family farm is experiencing the worst depression since the Second World War; nor do I require a conservationist to inform me that lapwing and swallow populations are in free-fall. Because I have lived as part of the same community all my life, and because I have been close to nature all my life, I can see that both the farms and the wildlife linked to them are under immense pressure.

The farming crisis has little to do with the strength of the pound or the natural restructuring of farming. Over the years, as agriculture has gone forward technically and scientifically, 'restructuring' has taken place – thousands of farmers and farmworkers have left the land as the economics of farming have evolved. Today's looming catastrophe has nothing to do with economic evolution. It has been created entirely by political decisions to comply with the absurdities of the Common Agricultural Policy. These have linked British food production and prices with world markets and deregulated trade. Consequently like is trading with unlike, competition is being distorted in favour of the big producer and the

The landscape in crisis. LEFT: *The living countryside of traditional farming.* ABOVE: *The wildlife – dead industrialised farming of the CAP.*

producer with low labour costs. Cheapness is the market force, and family farms in high-wage, high-cost economies such as Britain are being sacrificed on the altar of Europe and the global free market.

This market has no effect, of course, on the salaries of the politicians, accountants, management consultants, lawyers and fellow-travellers who make its policies and sing its praises. The primary producers are the ones that suffer; those who produce nothing except piles of paper are the ones that prosper.

The wildlife disaster that is taking place in the general countryside is also geared to the Common Agricultural Policy. Policies have been linked almost entirely to production and the acreage in production. As a result farming has been intensified and industrialised to reap the largest subsidy harvest possible. The common birds, animals and insects that once shared the land have gone or are going – sadly, the production of skylarks gives no financial return.

Those farmers who farmed responsibly, out of conviction and with a love for their land, have been penalised; their subsidies have been smaller as production has been lower, and they are considered to be inefficient. The key words in industrial farming are 'profit', 'production', 'efficiency' and 'competitiveness'; such an outlook has taken the culture out of agriculture and turned it into agribusiness. The driving forces for farming should be 'responsibility', 'sustainability', 'humanity' and 'quality'. Today, as I write, the sounds of our own inefficiency on the family farm can be measured by the birdsong floating in through my open window, from the fields and hedgerows beyond – yes, hedgerows.

Land is disappearing under housing, factories and science parks.

The very land itself is disappearing too, as the theft of our most valuable natural asset results in whole landscapes covered in bricks, glass and concrete. The mixture of science parks, factories, executive homes and commuter hutches gives the impression of progress, boom and a rapidly rising population. The truth is that the annual population growth of Britain is a mere 0.14 per cent, according to *World in Figures* (1999), published by *The Economist*. Growth is therefore nothing more than an illusion;

Cattle help give bio-diversity to mixed farming.

in the technological revolution we are making exactly the same mistakes as were made in the Industrial Revolution. Development is simply moving the population from one part of the country to another, instead of moving the work and the new industries to where the jobs are needed. The accents I hear in the new estates and villages of Cambridgeshire are not from East Anglia; they are from Wales, Scotland and northern England, the result of firms that move in simply wanting 'Cambridge' on their headed notepaper. Property developers, assorted consultants, estate agents and skilled workers make up the complete development circus. They could have all have gone to Wigan, Liverpool or Scunthorpe where work is needed and infrastructures already exist; but 'Scunthorpe' does not read too well on a letterhead alongside Melbourne, Tokyo and New York.

New development creates short-term employment, high land prices, economic activity and, for an opportunist few, instant wealth. This is what the politicians love, for a development bonanza equals votes which in turn mean re-election. So, long-term sustainable development is ignored in favour of short-term political advantage, dressed up as 'social change', 'modernising Britain' and 'planning for the next millennium'.

THE HUNTING GENE

Bee orchids. Skipper and field scabious – casualties of 'modernising Britain'.

All these changes are gradually killing rural Britain; as farming dies real rural communities die. As families are driven away from their roots, vacant homes, development and the mobility of labour bring in a new and uncomprehending culture. People from urban backgrounds move in and a tide of urban colonialism sweeps away rural values. The new villagers can be rootless and cultureless with no sense of community, continuity or loyalty; they shop in the out-of-town superstore; they work and play away; they want street lights and dog wardens, car parks and curbstones; and their houses are just little boxes from which to commute and consume. The true countryman becomes an alien in his own land – an endangered species.

On top of all this come repeated attempts to ban hunting with hounds and dogs, the traditional sports of the countryside – sports that bind and unite whole communities right across the social spectrum. Hunting represents a living, developing, thriving culture and the attacks on it symbolise what is happening to the whole countryside. An intolerant, non-comprehending urban ethos is attempting to impose its values on people, the countryside and wildlife.

This urban attitude was described by Sir Laurens van der Post – the great writer, philosopher, conservationist and traveller – as 'the town mind'. The town mind is not limited to those who live in cities, it is an attitude of mind and can be found in rural areas too. It is based on a separation from nature which leads to an alienation from the seasons; from life, death, spring-time and harvest.

Conversely, the very presence of the town mind means that there is also a 'country mind' that can be found in people living in the town as well as in the country. The window box, the song thrush and the small tortoiseshell butterfly keep them in contact with reality and sanity.

The purpose of this book is to observe, analyse and experience hunting as it takes place in Britain today. By so doing I hope that it will help people to appreciate and understand the country way of life. If a factory closes, or new technology brings fresh work to a town, the culture of the people changes little. If rural culture dies through economic pressure, social fashion or direct political intervention, it is lost for ever. Rural cultures the world over are under pressure like never before; if we cannot look after and respect our rural

Barn owls – they are under pressure but benefit from hunting habitats.

cultures in the developed world, what hope have we of saving the customs and peoples of the developing world?

My qualifications for writing about hunting are simple. I do not hunt, shoot or fish, but I have a deep love for animals and wildlife and my abiding passion is the conservation of the British countryside and the protection of the country way of life. As soon as I could walk, I was in day-to-day contact with animals, both domestic and wild. On the farm beneath a huge and ever-changing sky, we had horses, cows, pigs, hens and ducks and in the house there were always cats and dogs. We saw new life and old life, birth and death. From a very early age I experienced laughter, tears, joy and desolation from my relationship with animals.

The newly born calves and piglets were always a delight; but then there was the orphaned calf tossed and killed by an attempted replacement mother. Piglets were trodden on accidentally by their mothers and my father would sew them up with care, patience and compassion. When the cart-horses left the farm to be replaced by tractors there was sorrow; when a donkey came there was celebration. When Judy the Labrador died, I cried for a day; I was 6.

Environmental hooliganism described as 'agricultural improvement'.

The drama of having animals has continued ever since; a cow dying of blackleg (known properly as 'black-quarter' – an infectious disease, fast acting and usually fatal, often associated with marshy ground) was sad and traumatic, as was the cow that hung on for three days after giving birth to an extra large calf. On both occasions the kennelman from the local hunt came to take the bodies away and give them to his hounds; he was part of the community and provided a service that helped us in times of difficulty. More recently my last Middle White sow inconsiderately dropped dead after visiting the boar – what a way to go – and it was the kennelman again who removed the very heavy problem.

The succession of dogs and cats, with characters and contributions of their own, have also been welcome additions to the farm. They were all working animals, but part of the family too; a wonderful cat called Nigger – then a name describing, not insulting – was a master mouser as well as a pet; then there was Jester; while currently Tumba rules the roost. Named after a huge lake in the Zaïre rainforest, where my youngest sister once worked as a nurse, Tumba is the cleverest of them all. He hunts by night, sleeps by day, and somehow has managed to avoid the menace of the nearby roads.

The dogs have been constant companions and friends too; a spaniel, more Labradors and a few Border collies. The most tragic was Foss – a collie of skill, charm and loyalty who was hit by a car and left in the road to die. She had a broken neck, and in a mist of tears we nursed her for three days hoping for a miracle, but none came. When I think of her now I still feel the pain.

Ironically, since I started this chapter my most recent dog has died, a little lurcher called Bramble who lasted for almost seventeen years. He was a wonderful companion; I do not know the psychology behind keeping dogs, but I regarded him as a friend and his passing is hard.

But the highs and lows of domestic animal ownership have been given an added focus by the birds and animals that have come in from the wild. There have been a succession of waifs and strays, casualties and characters that have given a new dimension to my relationship with animals. There have been rabbits and jackdaws, a tawny owl, a grey squirrel, a common scoter, a kestrel, a hedgehog, a heron, an assortment of foxes and, two years ago, there were even Bill and Ben the badger cubs. Some escaped, a few ended in tragedy and some were successfully returned to the wild. All have contributed to make the natural world seem even more remarkable at close quarters than it appears from field, hedgerow or even television set.

From a very early age my love and fascination for wildlife was made deeper by the books that I read. At junior school I remember devouring *The Fifteen Rabbits* by Felix Salten, the author of *Bambi*. It was the first book to make me cry; and was followed in my teens by *White Fang* and *Tarka the Otter*. With the early natural history programmes on television, nature walks at the village school and the knowledge and appreciation of my mother and father, I developed a fascination for wildlife that grew into deep concern.

It is to my parents that I owe a huge debt, for they demonstrated how farming should co-exist with the birds, flowers and butterflies that share the land with us. They were excited by the farming year, seed-time and harvest, the arrival of a new calf, day-old chicks and picking the first Early Rivers plum. But the farming year was intertwined with the natural year; they would be equally pleased by the sight of the first swallows in the spring, the cuckoo, the lapwing with her chicks, the wild roses sprawling over the hedges and the wild harvest of blackberries, sloes and mushrooms as big as dinner plates at the back end of the year.

In the 1950s and 1960s I saw the mechanical and chemical revolution that started the transformation of lowland England. It was the destruction of wildlife and landscape on a massive scale – a process that is continuing almost unchecked today. Trees and hedges were felled, old meadows were ploughed, wetlands were drained and chemicals were used with gay abandon; cowslips, woodpeckers, barn owls, bee orchids, otters and many other species all but disappeared. Despite this, the process continues and lapwings, skylarks, song thrushes and swallows have joined the spiral towards oblivion.

Over the years, because of my concern and the privileged opportunities given to me through writing, I have met some of the country's leading conservationists – Sir Laurens van der Post, Elspeth Huxley, Gordon Beningfield, Miriam Rothschild, David Bellamy, Sir

George Adamson in the year he died, with Robin Page.

David Attenborough and many more. In addition, my interest and anxiety has spread beyond these shores, as the destruction of wildlife and the environment is turning into a world-wide crisis.

In Africa the man who made the greatest impression on me was George Adamson, that wonderful old man living and working with lions. I met him several times, including in the year in which he was shot and killed by Somali bandits, and I regarded him as a friend. It was an honour to go with him to see his last litter of lion cubs. With his murder Kenya lost one of its great pioneer conservationists. He was important to me because he was involved with a process even more important than conservation – restoration, restoring both habitats and populations. He was trying to bring back to life a whole area that had been over-grazed, over-run and poached out of wildlife – and he was succeeding.

Koretta, a favourite lioness of George Adamson.

The remarkable Miriam Rothschild was leading the way in practical restoration here in England, with schemes to restore hay meadows, wild flowers, hedgerows and butterflies; bringing them all into the general countryside through sympathetic and common-sense farming, as well as with roadside schemes involving local authorities. Over the years I had numerous conversations with Sir Laurens van der Post and Gordon Beningfield about the wildlife disaster taking place throughout Britain in almost every parish; gradual practical restoration, as practised by Miriam Rothschild, seemed to be the answer.

In 1980 I went with Gordon to see the then director of the Royal Society for the Protection of Birds to urge a broader view: the protection and conservation of hedgerows, woods, wetlands and hay meadows in the general countryside and on our farms. Our pleas fell on stony ground as the RSPB was then totally committed to nature reserves and special areas – 'island conservation' – a philosophy that divided the countryside up into separate areas for farming, conservation and recreation. We wanted a living, working countryside which was seen as a whole, for people, wildlife and sensible, sensitive food production.

After years of anguish and agitation we could wait no longer and The Countryside Restoration Trust was launched in 1993, Laurens becoming the CRT's first Patron and Gordon becoming my Vice-Chairman; both were also Founder Trustees.

So the conservation of the British countryside and its wildlife has become the driving

21

force of my life – not an obsession, but a passion. Despite losing both Laurens and Gordon, the CRT has grown and now has land of its own, and wildlife is coming back as we grow quality food in an environmentally friendly way. Each working week I give half my time quite willingly and freely to the CRT; now other conservation bodies, including the RSPB, are following us in our concern for farming and the general countryside and we welcome them.

There is a peculiarity in all this, for where hunting takes place, the woods, the hedgerows, the wetland and the grass meadows remain; there is no need for restoration. The traditional hunting landscape remains rich and attractive with banks of wild flowers and woods full of birdsong; it is a living, working entity with a culture and character that goes to the very heart of rural Britain. Indeed, if I had been born on a farm in traditional hunting country, I wonder whether I would have seen the need for restoration, conservation and help for our beleaguered wildlife? All this not only makes attacks on hunting irrational and illogical; it also makes them bizarre.

Prairie land restored by the Countryside Restoration Trust.

Chapter Two

THE HUNTING GENE

THE HUNTING GENE

W hy, two thousand years after the life of Christ, ten thousand years after the last Ice Age and two million years after the arrival of man, do we still want to hunt? Opponents of hunting claim that as a pastime it is barbaric, uncivilised, cruel and degrading – but can an activity that has helped us to survive for many millennia be any of these things? Surely a pursuit that has assisted our survival for two million years must have become part of us? Within all of us there really is a hunting gene – a survival gene. The hunting gene is natural, it is instinctive, and without it *Homo sapiens*, *Homo erectus* and whoever our most distant ancestor was would not have survived when the world and they were young.

This is not just the random rambling of a simple countryman untutored in biology, zoology, physiology and anthropology; a growing number of serious scientists agree. Dr Tim Coulson, a Research Fellow of the Zoological Society of London says:

> Man has hunted wild animals for millennia. Evidence for this comes from archaeologists who have unearthed the bones of hunted animals alongside spears, arrowheads and other ancient human artefacts at sites from six continents. The archaeological evidence is also supported by man's physiology. Our saliva, teeth and the enzymes in our intestines are all adapted to aid the consumption and digestion of

The hunting gene in action in fox-hunting.

meat. Such adaption has a genetic base and will have taken generations to evolve. However, these facts alone are not sufficient to state that hunting behaviour has a genetic base – behaviour and physiology are very different. The genetics of behaviour is a young, emerging field, yet scientists have correlated several aspects of human behaviour to genes and perhaps in time, a link between our genes and hunting will be found – I for one, would be surprised if such behaviour does not have some genetic base.

It was Ron Davies MP who in 1998 said: 'We are all different. We are all products of our genes.' An outspoken anti-royal, anti-hunting MP and one time Secretary of State for Wales, this is the man who – after calling Prince Charles 'a pillock', claiming that he was unfit to be King and criticising his private life – went for a walk after dark on Clapham Common in London. What happened next nobody seems to know, because Mr Davies and the Government have not told us. The police were going to prosecute some strange people from a seedy twilight world, but suddenly the prosecution was dropped. It is likely that the revelations would have been extremely embarrassing for Mr Davies and for the Government; but we can rest assured that the dropping of the case was not because of Government interference in the legal process – that does not happen in Britain, so we are told.

All we were left with was a statement in Parliament by Mr Davies, apparently blaming his behaviour on his genes. Although he considered Prince Charles unfit to be King, our Clapham Common creeper evidently did not consider himself unfit to stay on as a Member of Parliament, and at the time of writing he is still in the House of Commons. In fact not only did he consider himself fit to be an MP, he also stood for and was elected to the Welsh Assembly.

This peculiar incident is interesting. For years politicians have been telling us that with good houses, education, hospitals, school and jobs, the behaviour and the standards of ordinary people will change. Then along comes a Cabinet Minister from the Labour Party who blames his behaviour on his genes. So education, health, status, income and affluence had all been swept aside by his genes. If the influence of his genes really is that strong, then why does that same Member of Parliament criticise hunting? For it is the hunting gene that not only helped our ancestors to survive across the ages – through heat and cold, drought, flood, fire and ice – but also set them on the path towards civilisation. At times we still respond to that venerable gene; when we look at wild, ancient landscapes, or hear the distant call of a curlew or a peregrine falcon, we are moved by feelings too deep for words and far distant from our own time – that is the stirring of the hunting gene.

Consequently, those people who condemn hunting are also condemning nature and condemning their own past. In his fascinating autobiography *Green was the Earth on the Seventh Day*, Thor Heyerdahl, the famous Norwegian explorer and anthropologist, wrote: 'If God had created nature, we ought to respect it. And if there was no God, then nature was the creator of man, and there was even more reason to respect it.' Hunting is part of nature

No hunting, no nature – just industrialised farming.

and examples of it abound, from the song thrush killing a snail to a spider catching a fly, and to a lion stalking an antelope on the plains of the Serengeti. If there is a God (and I am a convinced Christian) and hunting is wrong, then we are saying that God's creation is wrong; and if there is no God then we are dependant on nature, and hunting is part of nature. So we are saying that nature is wrong – yet it is nature that has produced us, kept us and shaped us. Even the most committed anti-hunting vegan must be able to see how hunting helped us to survive for many thousands of generations.

Part of today's problem is that with the urbanisation that passes for civilisation large numbers of people have become separated from nature; they have lost touch with the realities that helped us to survive. They cannot imagine a world without soya milk, bean sprouts and instant coffee and they seem unable to appreciate that their brave new world is recent, superficial and not sustainable.

Stephen Budiansky wrote in his *The Covenant of the Wild*: 'For two million years we were hunters; for ten thousand years we were farmers; for the last one hundred years we have been trying to deny it all.' Some believe that the great denial has only occurred in the last fifty years, but as society moves further away from the land, the seasons and nature, so the

Man the hunter-gatherer had to learn to hunt.

chorus of denial grows louder. It is based on a mixture of health food fetishes, agricultural fantasies and a muddled animal rights philosophy – in other words, ignorance.

Early man had few choices. His mind was not tormented by the options of freshly squeezed orange juice, muesli or gently poached haddock fillets for breakfast. He had to obtain food when it was available, either by gathering wild fruits, nuts, seeds and herbs in season, or by hunting for meat when his other options were out of season.

In the heart of Africa where our first ancestors probably originated there was not a constant supply of fruit and nuts. Dry seasons and wet seasons meant that food came and went. Before the advent of skills involving the use of fire it also meant that much vegetation was not palatable to the human digestive system. When man moved on, searching for pastures new, or when climate change brought prolonged ice, then hunting was the only activity that made survival possible. Man was a hunter–gatherer, and when climate made gathering impossible, hunting was the only way to provide the meat and the skins that ensured food, warmth and survival. Man became a predator and the wildlife around him became his prey.

But to hunt requires many skills and conditions. Those who describe hunting as uncivilised are simply showing that they do not understand how the civilising process began.

THE HUNTING GENE

Young Samburu warrior – the past age of the hunting gene can still be glimpsed.

Early man was confronted from time to time not only by an inhospitable environment, but also by animals that were often stronger and faster than he was, some of whom actually wanted to prey on him. Consequently he developed many strategies to enable him to hunt and hide successfully. Many anthropologists believe that what brought man down from the trees, to walk upright, was the necessity to see clearly over distances while looking for prey and to become more mobile and versatile. The ambidextrous ape became a man with a much-favoured arm, left or right, developed through using weapons and tools for throwing and lunging. The hunter had to understand his prey, he had to be aware of the seasons and interpret signs, he had to develop strategies to make the best of his opportunities and to plan, and above all he had to learn to communicate and co-operate with other members of his tribe or family. Obviously it is easier to hunt as part of a co-ordinated group than as an isolated individual, particularly when the quarry is large, fast or has sharp teeth. All this activity started social organisation too, with the men hunting, providing and sharing; and the women staying behind to protect the young, old and sick.

It was this co-operation and communication that also started the development of language and the pooling of resources. But it went far beyond the basic need to acquire food; the use of weapons gradually encouraged skill and craftsmanship as beauty and creativity became linked with necessity and practicality. Even some ancient flint hand-axes were napped in such a way that conformity and harmony were added to effective use and wood was decorated and carved, not simply sharpened.

Craftsmen in wood and stone became as important as those who actually hunted, and there is no doubt that the joys, dangers, successes and failures of hunting led to other social developments. Early artists painted in caves, on rocks and trees, depicting the hunt and the men and animals involved in the hunt; in addition, hunting almost certainly led to celebrations, dancing, singing, the telling of stories and the creation of myths.

Even today we can still get occasional glimpses of that past age, of the hunter and the hunted, of man pitting his wits against wildlife by using the skills and knowledge that nature has given him. The Bushman, the rainforest Indian and the Inuk (Eskimo) all give us tantalising visions of a past way, lingering on into the present. Some views too give us surprising pictures. It is a popular myth that primitive peoples and cultures lived in total harmony with nature and their surroundings. There was a natural balance, we were told, with man the hunter understanding that balance. It gave a romantic picture of man living in paradise, at one with his surroundings.

We now know that this was simply untrue. When man first moved into North America across the land bridge that formed between Siberia and Alaska, the animals had no fear of this new creature and were easy prey; extinction of at least thirty-three large mammal species followed because of over-hunting. Similar stories come from Australia and the Polynesian islands, where the arrival of man led to the disappearance of numerous innocent animals and flightless birds.

Hunter-pastoralists are alive and well in the northern regions of Kenya.

There is also much evidence that even for primitive man hunting became a sport. Again the popular view is that early man and primitive man simply hunted when hunger made it necessary, but this now seems to be untrue and some cave paintings seem to suggest the vibrancy and enjoyment of sport. Laurens van der Post tells a fascinating story of a Bushman hunt in the Kalahari desert. While celebrating the end of a successful hunt, with the dead oryx brought into their camp, news came of more oryx beyond the next sand dune. With ample food already, the men immediately made off for another hunt, simply for the excitement, the adrenalin and the thrill of the chase.

Gradually man the hunter–gatherer became man the hunter–pastoralist, and then the farmer. How the process started is unknown, but clearly at some stage an effort was made to secure a constant and adequate supply of food. Seed-time and harvest became the most important seasons of the year; but how and why did cultivation start? It was farming, both growing and herding, that took man further on his march towards civilisation, a march that also had devastating consequences for the planet. Today that march goes on with deforestation, over-exploitation of resources, pollution and over-population.

Perhaps a conscious effort was made to encourage favoured plants to grow near settlements or seasonal camps. Once cultivation did start, the need for wandering or following herds of wild animals ceased and home became a settlement. Perhaps too the process began entirely by accident, when spilled seed germinated and grew, and the link between sowing and harvesting was suddenly recognised. Strangely, anthropologists have noticed a sudden dip in the physical condition of early, settled man when settlement and seed-time did arrive. A predominantly seed diet, with little variation and not enough protein, led to vitamin deficiencies and disease; while the hard physical work involved in cultivation caused problems of wear, tear and arthritis in the toes, knees and lower back.

Not only does this reinforce the importance of protein-rich meat in early times, but it also emphasises that much of modern vegetarianism is based on affluence and the ability to purchase fruits, nuts and vegetables from all over the world, in season and out. Such luxury was clearly beyond the stunted, physically damaged early farmers; and whether such a modern choice is based on a morality-founded lifestyle or is simply a middle-class fashion statement driven by affluence is open to question. As a former vegetarian, I believe that most First World vegetarianism can seldom be called sustainable or sensible.

With the domestication of cattle came a ready source of high-protein food; but again how the process started is shrouded in mystery. Did early man take in species which he found he could tame and exploit for food? Did he find abandoned or orphaned young animals which then developed into domestic stock, or did the evolutionary process encourage some animals to seek out and choose man? By some such strategy food, shelter and protection were obtained and goats, sheep and cattle became domesticated. So the origin of the domestication of animals seems to be a case of take your pick – choice, genetics or chance? Certainly many attempts have been made, unsuccessfully, to domesticate some animals that have remained wild. Efforts have been made through the ages to farm red deer, fallow deer and wild boar, and these are continuing today, yet whenever the creatures escape they quickly revert to the wild. In contrast, reindeer or sheep left out in the wild for half a year can be herded and lose nearly all their wildness almost instantly.

So cultivation and herding led to food security, or almost, but even with farming and folding the diet was supplemented by hunting; the hunting gene persisted. Often, too, the domestic animals became the hunted animals and action had to be taken to protect stock from wild animals. The shepherds watched over their flocks, and the sower went out to sow; the Biblical time span follows the change from herding to farming and the Bible is almost a holy farming handbook showing the transition from pastoralism to agriculture. It also shows people totally in touch and in tune with nature. When critics claim that Christianity is out of touch with modern life, in reality they are saying that they and modern life are out of touch with spirituality. Many of the Biblical parables, stories and incidents are related to the seasons, nature, farming and the most basic facts of life; it is from these things that modern man has become separated.

As hunting continued, so its sporting element increased, with entertainment joining or replacing necessity. The Assyrians, Babylonians, Egyptians and Greeks all hunted, often with hounds and running dogs. Xenophon the Greek historian, writing four hundred years before the birth of Christ, was the first to write in detail of the theories and skills involved in hunting. He was followed by Plato, who wrote: 'There can be no more important kind of information than the exact knowledge of a man's own country; and for this as well as for more general reasons of pleasure and advantage, hunting with hounds and other kinds of sport should be pursued by the young.'

Hunting in Britain from farming's earlier times was to supplement the supply of meat from domestic animals and to provide a break from the routine of growing crops and minding flocks. When the Romans arrived they were impressed with the hunting dogs used by the wild tribes they both encountered and subjugated. The dogs were admired for their ability to follow scent and also to point at their quarry. By the time of the Anglo-Saxons every free-born man had the right to hunt his land or enter the forest to bring something back for the pot. It was the Normans who changed all this and who sowed the seed for much of today's anti-hunting prejudice.

Coursing dates back to the time of the ancient Egyptians.

THE HUNTING GENE

Hunting continues to take place in many forms. Ferrets are still popular.

After 1066 hunting ceased to be available to one and all; it became the reserve of royalty and the nobility, with harsh Forest Laws protecting their privilege. Hunting and the royal forests became the playthings of the aristocracy and woe betide anybody who stepped out of line, or set a snare line. And so hunting developed on two levels: the hare, the deer and the fox were hunted by those who had; deer, rabbits and birds of all kinds were poached by those who had not. At both levels skills and traditions were developed and the hunting gene continued to make its presence felt across society.

Hunting went through good times and bad. Oliver Cromwell frowned on it as representing privilege, corruption and idleness; but after the passing of the Commonwealth horses and hounds quickly returned. With the advent of railways and tarmac-adamed roads the popularity of hunting boomed among the rich, and the hedges of the enclosures added to the thrills and spills.

Through the twentieth century hunting continued, from the poshest fox-hunt for sport to the lowest farm labourer with his ferret hunting rabbits for the pot – and, at the time of the First World War, still catching sparrows in nets along the hedgerows for sparrow pie. Today the hunting gene can still be seen in hunting, shooting and fishing. With political, social and economic change the base has again broadened. Now people from all walks of life hunt, and the democracy and availability of hunting is almost as it was before the arrival of William the Conqueror.

But as hunting and society have changed, the hunting gene shows itself beyond those who hunt with hounds, shoot or fish. Surprisingly it can be found in schools – in the form of attention deficit syndrome; it is a syndrome more suitable for hunting than studying and shows itself in an aroused state of alertness and an inability to concentrate on non-physical things for any length of time. This is the hunting gene surfacing, as behaviour that would have aided survival in a primitive society. In today's society it is seen as a disorder, although a current school inspector says:

> It is easy to cope with, in theory. The fact is that boys need more physical activity in school than girls. That is why games and sports are so important for boys; it gives them a physical outlet. Now, it is politically incorrect to say that boys and girls are different and so they have to stay in their desks all day. Their lack of physical activity shows itself in worse behaviour in class, and anti-social behaviour once out of school. Yes, it could be called the hunting-gene, as it was the men who once had to hunt.

Because of the way in which society has changed and free speech has become restricted, I cannot give that school inspector's name.

The hunting gene emerges in other spheres as well. Our television sets are full of films showing in graphic and violent detail hunts involving people, from cowboys and Indians (American native people) to police thrillers and gangland wars. The theme is always the

To some people, global warming is a less important issue than a fox being chased over a muddy field.

The Hunting Gene

The hunting gene in action – horse, hound and bike.

same: criminals, heroes and beautiful women are being hunted – the hunting gene is everywhere, providing entertainment and vicarious thrills.

The strangest twist concerning the hunting gene is difficult to understand. Although it is clear that hunting helped us as a species to move towards civilisation and progress, it is now obvious that other forces have taken us beyond progress, turning yesterday's civilisation into today's 'syphilisation'. After scaling the heights to become civilised, we are now being encouraged to tumble back down the other side in what could be terminal decline.

Incredibly, despite the vast number of social, environmental and international problems, all man made, there are still people and opportunist politicians who think that the hunting gene in its country context must be attacked and outlawed. In other words, chasing a fox across a muddy field is more unacceptable than global warming, wildlife calamities, rising crime-rates and sexual and social deviation. If attacks on hunting continue then Cool Britannia will rapidly become Fool Britannia.

Chapter Three

THE HUNTING PARTNERSHIP

William Garfit.

THE HUNTING GENE

The journey from hunter–gatherer to what passes for modern, sophisticated, civilised man or woman has been a long, hard one. At some stage along that path we met two animals who came with us and helped us on our way. Without their help our journey would have taken far longer and perhaps we would never have reached where we find ourselves today. Our companions became our friends, for the horse and the hound joined us in a unique hunting and working partnership that even now continues to flourish.

Of course, there are numerous other examples of birds and animals working together with man. The beasts of burden are obvious – elephants, camels, oxen and many more – but hunting relationships also became widely established. In many parts of the world falcons, hawks and eagles fly from gloved fists to pursue game in what some falconers believe is the world's oldest hunting partnership. In China cormorants are used to catch fish for their owners and in Britain ferrets have been used to flush rabbits for many generations. Australia once boasted the most astonishing union: for about a hundred years until the early twentieth century, wild Killer whales helped local fishermen to round up and harvest Southern Right whales as they passed by on migration. The unfortunate Right whales were so named because of their slow speed; they were 'right' to hunt.

The pack of Killer whales would herd their victims into a bay and then attract the local fishermen to finish the business. One whale, Old Tom, would actually tow one of the whaling boats by a rope, wearing a groove in his teeth as he did so. The whale's skeleton, complete with worn teeth, can be seen at the Eden Vale Museum on the New South Wales coast. The method was almost like sheep dogs rounding up sheep for the shepherd. Both the Killer whales and the fishermen benefited. The Killer whales were allowed some of the kill and the fishermen had the rest. It was an astonishing relationship involving completely wild animals – co-operating because they gained from the practice. Despite being such an amazing story, it is one that seldom seems to be retold; I wonder why?

But although the various hunting partnerships are important and interesting, the

The man and horse partnership has been vital to both and a fundamental factor in the history of Britain.

partnership between man, horse and hound is unique. The uniqueness stems from the bond that can build up between man and horse and between man and hound or dog. It is a bond that goes beyond a simple working relationship, and can become a real partnership based on trust, respect, emotion and even love.

Of the two animals, the horse has been the most important in helping us in our achievements. It has assisted us in war and peace, in work and play, and it has helped us to widen our horizons. It is even true to say that the horse was fundamental in the way the inhabitants of the small collection of islands called Britain helped to shape and change the history of the world, enabling travel, exploration and conquest.

If historians and archaeologists are right, the planet once had far more horses than people and the horse, in various shapes and sizes, inhabited vast tracts of land. Fossil remains suggest that its ancestors thrived

The third party to the partnership.

through many ages and on several continents. Then suddenly disaster struck and the horse retreated or disappeared; the Americas became horseless and remained so until the arrival of the Spaniards.

What created the problem is not clear, but probably a dramatic climate change caused the horse almost to suffer the same fate as the dinosaur. Some managed to hang on in remote regions of southern Russia and the Ukraine, and it was there that domestication occurred – to the benefit of both horse and man – between five thousand and six thousand years ago. The nearest relative to that early wild horse is Przewalski's horse and that too was saved while on the edge of extinction. It really is wild and virtually untameable and it exists today mainly in a number of animal collections. I have seen it at Port Lympne in Kent, where a healthy breeding herd has been nurtured by the remarkable John Aspinall. As we drove away from the enclosure on the day of my visit, the stallion galloped alongside, separated from us by a simple fence, its eyes rolling, its ears back and flat and its lips curling back from its teeth. If the first domestic horses came from similar stock it is hardly surprising that domestication arrived so late.

Once the horse had joined the list of domesticated animals, it spread quickly across Europe, Asia and Arabia. It was used for riding and pulling carts and chariots for war and peace; chariots were used widely in Ancient Egypt and Mesopotamia and the horse became a symbol of power, wealth and intimidation.

In Britain the horse – or, more accurately, a Celtic pony that resembled today's Exmoor pony – was firmly established, it is thought, by the year 2000 BC, and remains have been found in as remote a place as Orkney. With the arrival of the Romans, the Saxons and the Normans, other breeding lines came in. It seems that the more northern horses became larger and heavier, the southern Arabs became lighter and faster, and gradually in Britain various crosses of the two were bred according to need.

The horse became part of everyday life, being used for work, war and sport. Ponies were needed for pulling and carrying; and ancient pack-horse bridges can still be seen, built with low walls so that the panniers were not impeded. Larger, heavier horses were required for war, to carry men in armour; and faster, agile horses were wanted for hunting and racing.

So the horse helped us to work and trade, to fight and to play. We learnt to control it and steer it, to shoe it and doctor it. We needed the horse to carry our loads, pull our carriages, fight our battles and play our games. It became deeply rooted in our culture and we owe it an immense debt of gratitude. In good times the horse did well; in bad times when food was short and work still had to be done it suffered. In warfare its losses and suffering do not bear thinking about.

The annual National Shire Horse Show at Peterborough still survives.

A view of Appleby's traditional horse fair.

With careful breeding, the heavy horse brought about a colossal agricultural revolution and for two hundred years the Shire, the Clydesdale, the Suffolk and the Percheron were the power on the land, and a close bond was forged between the horseman and his horses. I regard it as a great privilege to have been born at the end of Britain's pastoral age when real horse power was still in every parish. We had Diamond and Dolly on our small farm, a Shire and a Clydesdale. I can still remember my father lifting me up onto that broad chestnut back as Dolly pulled the water cart to the cattle in the meadow. I seemed to be a huge distance from the ground.

I remember too the day at harvest when she found it hard to pull the trailer loaded with sheaves across the rutted ground. Soon afterwards she was loaded into a lorry and the stable became empty apart from memories and sadness; a Fordson Major tractor stood in the tractor shed and a new, harsher age was ushered in.

Fortunately the bond struck between the old horsemen and the heavy horses remains and there are still farmers, breeders and enthusiasts keeping the old strains and traditions alive in both Britain and the United States. Each year I go to the Shire Horse Show at Peterborough, which is a living tribute to those wonderful animals from our past.

Because of the importance of the horse in work and play, horse sales and horse fairs were often the highlights of the rural year. Some of these still flourish too, the most famous one taking place each June at Appleby in Cumbria, on the edge of the Pennines. Horses, dealers, diddicoys, farmers and gypsies arrive from all over this country and Ireland, and

the sales and deals have the ring of medieval bartering, complete with 'luck' money. Other habits arrive too and the local garage clearly states 'fifty pound notes and Irish punts not accepted'. Illegal races are sometimes held along the A66 and trotting races take place on the Tuesday of the fair.

Gypsies and farmers are not the only ones who still worship the horse; with flat racing, steeple chasing, gymkhanas, eventing, show jumping, polo, carriage driving, long-distance riding and dressage, the horse's popularity is as high as ever. But if it were possible to communicate with horses, which horse would be the happiest or the most fulfilled? Without a doubt that would be the hunter, a horse bred over the years to run and to jump.

Hunting creates an astonishing relationship between horse and rider. The rider does in theory retain an element of control over his mount, but the horse itself begins to return to the wild. The transformation from riding horse to hunting horse is remarkable; a lone, bored horse becomes transformed. On seeing and hearing other horses, ears become pricked, eyes search and the horse suddenly feels vibrant and alive; it is again part of the herd. It watches for the hounds, it listens for the horn and it gallops with sheer joy.

The life and mood of the hunter is best summed up by Professor Roger Scruton, the hunting philosopher, in his book *On Hunting*. He writes:

> Only one kind of horse gets the most out of being a horse and that is the hunter. Alone among domesticated animals the hunter has the chance to run with the herd – fit, well fed, and carefree – over country cleared of his natural predators. No equine joy matches that of running side by side with other horses, immersed in the great tide of species-life and excited by the baying of hounds.

The hunter and the rider provide part of the hunting team, and it is the hound that completes the partnership.

Our relationship with dogs, the family *Canidae*, goes back twice as far as our attachment to horses and the emotional bond is far stronger. In many cases today the dog really has become 'man's best friend' and as a result dog numbers and the pet industry are booming like never before.

The story starts about twelve thousand years ago; the first dog remains found mingling with man's date back to then. That first domesticated 'dog' was almost certainly related to the wolf. This should not come as a surprise, for the wolf is still quite easily tamed, but not domesticated; John Aspinall has demonstrated this many times by walking with his captive wolves and playing with them. Sadly, the ancestor of all domestic dogs has been demonised though exaggerated tales of harassment and horror as cowboys, loggers and trappers plodded their way across North America. In addition the howl of the wolf has been used for years to add fear and trembling to films about vampires and the residents of Transylvania.

Strangely, the howl of the wolf now provides confirmation of the long family tree of the domesticated dog, for in every hunting kennels in Britain hounds will sometimes 'sing'. They will howl in unison like a choir of canine crooners and even after twelve thousand years they are transported back into the life of the pack. But, unlike the wolves outside Dracula's abode, the 'singing' hounds are not sinister; their discordant notes are said to be a sign of contentment.

The ancestor of the domestic dog: the wolf.

THE HUNTING GENE

All dogs, including foxhounds, retain some wolf characteristics.

There are thirty-eight species of *Canidae*, including the dog. Other members of the family include the wolf, the red fox, the coyote, various jackals, the dingo and the African wild dog. Interestingly, according to scientists, there is less difference between the DNA of wolves, coyotes and dogs than there is between the assorted ethnic groups of human beings – who, it is claimed, belong to a single species (*The Domestic Dog and its Evolution, Behaviour and Interactions with People*, edited by James Serpell, Cambridge University Press, 1995). So from the wild wolf and a number of crosses with near relatives, nature has presented us with an astonishing four hundred breeds of domestic dog.

Again, how the domestication process was set in train can only be a matter of speculation. Perhaps wolf puppies were taken into captivity; some may have then returned to the wild, others may have been eaten or killed for their fur, but a few may have become tame; the bond was forged and the remarkable partnership between man and dog began.

The domestication process could have started another way, however. In a remote African village I have seen both domestic and feral dogs that survive entirely by scavenging. They steal bones and the leftovers of cooked casava and millet, and they scavenge anything they can from the village cattle, goats and hens. They are scrawny, scraggy animals that are shown no love, and if they approach too close at meal times missiles will be thrown at them to make them retreat. Yet the dogs stay on; they find their lives easier and the food supply more secure than if they went back to the wild. Perhaps this happened to the wolf; in hard times it may have begun to scavenge around the edges of human shelters and settlements and gradually have been attracted closer, until some individuals got drawn into the circle completely.

Slowly, from the opposite perspective, it was realised that the dog could be of use and so those best adapted for a particular purpose were kept. They bred and the habits and features which gave them a use became more marked with every generation. Individual breeds gradually developed. Those early dogs were almost certainly used for guarding, herding and hunting, causing the status of the dog to improve. The first hunting dogs would have been used for flushing and, later, chasing and killing at bay. Soon man realised that he had an ally to help him in the hard task of survival. The traits developed for hunting gradually developed into adaptations for sport, and long dogs relying on speed and sight became popular as well as those that hunted by scent.

Over the centuries have come remarkable stories concerning our relationship

Sheepdogs have adapted from hunting to herding.

with dogs, incidents involving acts of incredible loyalty, devotion, courage and love. So much has the partnership developed that it is possible to feel almost as much affection for a dog as it is for a person. The poet W.H. Davies summed up the situation well:

> Still do I claim no man can reach
> His highest soul's perfection,
> Until his life from day to day
> Deserves a dog's affection.

Consequently, some of the most enjoyable times are shared with dogs and it follows that some of our saddest and most traumatic days are caused by dogs. I still miss my little dog, quite unashamedly. After such a long and close relationship the final decision was difficult. Life just became too hard for him. He stumbled, he fell, he whined, he slept, the vet came and he was gone. I buried him in my favourite meadow, close to an ancient hedge where I shall join him one day. The 'may' was just bursting into flower and, as I dug, with tears rolling down my cheeks, willow warblers, skylarks and blackcaps sang.

Today there are an astonishing number of working dogs, all with their own highly tuned skills, characters and physical features; there are pointers, retrievers, guard dogs, guide dogs and dogs that pull sledges; there are dogs that listen, dogs that search for drugs and criminals and those lost in avalanches; there are dogs that flush grouse, kill rats, hunt mink, herd sheep and follow the scent of people, foxes and marauding lions; there are long dogs, short dogs, heavy dogs, fast dogs, brave dogs and wimps; but all of them make life easier and more interesting for their owners, admirers and friends.

The skills are remarkable and highly tuned in some breeds: a retriever swims across a swollen river after a fallen duck, an Alsatian brings down a violent prisoner on the run and a falconer's pointer 'freezes' to indicate the presence of grouse. All demonstrate the change and the achievement that have been reached in partnership with man.

Saluki lurchers, dogs with very ancient roots, at Appleby.

44

Grand Bleu de Gascogne, one of the oldest breed of hounds.

Inevitably, for me one of the best dogs is the Border collie. Not only is it remarkable because of its skill, agility and obedience when rounding up sheep, but also as it works it shows its ancestry. When the wolf hunts, it freezes as it sees its prey; when it is successful it stalks, runs and kills. When a Border collie rounds up sheep, it freezes as soon as sheep are seen; it stalks, it runs and then it drives, holds or separates. The hunting instinct is still there but the killing instinct has been modified into herding.

Like the horse out hunting, the most natural dog – and possibly even the happiest dog – is the hound. It is allowed to live again as a member of a pack; it has security of food and shelter and from time to time it is allowed to hunt, almost as a wolf or an African hunting dog, and almost wild. Hounds know when they are going to hunt; they are alert, excited and anxious to go. As they peer from the hound trailer or the lorry they are all eager anticipation, and then they look to the huntsman, the leader of the pack.

The feelings of loyalty and admiration between the hounds and the huntsman are mutual. Most huntsmen really do love their hounds and the emotional link runs deep. They care for them, feed them, breed them, walk them, exercise and hunt them, and when their active lives are over they put them down. They experience happiness, pride and deep satisfaction and they feel great sadness when the partnership with a faithful old hound comes to an end; it is like losing a friend.

Before writing this book, I had never seen the actual day-to-day management of hounds or watched them hunt at close quarters. Now that I have, I understand why so many huntsmen and kennelmen cannot imagine any other occupation. A ban on hunting would break a unique relationship, and there is no doubt that it would also break a number of fine and dedicated countrymen.

The lineage of the modern hound is a long one. With the arrival of the Normans came their sports and their hounds: bloodhounds and blue-mottle Gascons, the main ancestors of the foxhound. The Gascon's line could be traced back to the seventh century and the Bishop of Liège in the Ardennes. His monastery was dedicated to St Hubert, who became the patron saint of hunting.

In Britain the Gascon was known as the Talbot, which was crossed with the English hounds so highly praised by the Romans. Once crossed, the Talbot's hybrid vigour made it the ideal hunting hound, which was then selectively bred to hunt stag, fox and hare.

So the hunting partnership is complete: huntsman, horse and hound are uniquely joined together. To see the drama of a hunt streaming across an open English winter landscape remains a moving experience. It is aesthetically pleasing and close to nature, and it holds an ancient raw but beautiful attraction. Once it was seen as part of the countryside and of country life; then suddenly outlooks began to change. The change coincided with the arrival on the scene of Bambi.

Chapter Four

ENTER BAMBI

THE HUNTING GENE

Bambi was the creation of Felix Salten, who wrote *Bambi, a Life in the Woods* in German in 1923. In 1928 it was translated into English and became popular as a children's book, but it was in 1942 that its fame swept across the world. This was when the words were turned into pictures and *Bambi* the feature film appeared as Walt Disney's first full-length cartoon movie. It was a film that had far-reaching consequences, and on television and video the legacy of *Bambi* is still reaping huge dividends, both in the form of money and of animal rights.

Bambi came into the world as a little cuddly fawn who could already reason and speak English. He had large, soft brown eyes and an expressive face and his birth was greeted with wonder by Thumper the rabbit and a host of little furry friends. The bluebirds sang and the greenwood rang as happiness and joy swept through the secret forest.

The opening sequence is of a woodland paradise with an angelic choir singing in the background. The wise old owl comes home at dawn and the little cuddly squirrel wakes up and stretches just above him. Is there conflict, and are they depicted as predator and prey? Certainly not; from the very first scene they have ceased to be animals and have become in the minds of most filmgoers, including me, furry and feathered little people. I must have seen the film when I was about 5 in the late 1940s; it is a story of great sadness and great happiness and its impact, both commercial and psychological, was enormous.

Indeed, even now the influence of *Bambi* can be found in the most unexpected places. In the third sentence of his report 'The Behavioural and Physiological Effects of Culling Red Deer' (1997), Professor Patrick Bateson of Cambridge University writes: 'If you wept as a child at the death of Bambi's mother, you know what it is like to be hunted.' It is a rather strange beginning for what purports to be a serious scientific report, particularly as Bambi's mother was not hunted at all, she was shot.

The commercial success of the film showed quite clearly that cuddly little Bambis and Thumpers would open purse strings. At the same time, by turning wildlife into people, animals were given some of the same values and moral judgements as human beings. To look into large doleful eyes surrounded by warm soft fur inspired desires to have and to hold, not to kill and to eat. What was once regarded as venison and survival was now seen as Bambi, a cuddle and companionship. The great separation from nature, with help from the silver screen, had begun; it was anthropomorphism Hollywood-style.

I have nothing against films for entertainment only and I have thoroughly enjoyed the video of *Bambi*, at least ten times; but, sadly, serious wildlife films have picked up on the Bambi theme. Even the most savage predator on the African plains now tends to appear as 'Old Flop Ears', and when she kills or captures prey and eats it alive the voiceover informs: 'And now babies Spot, Whimper and Lone can have a tasty meal and they will survive another day under the hot African sun.'

Not only does the Bambi syndrome affect images of animals, it applies to real animals too. This is best summed up by Stephen Budiansky, who in his book *The Covenant of the Wild* writes: 'The favorite animal in a survey of visitors to the National Zoo in Washington D.C.

A roebuck instantly activates the Bambi syndrome in many people.

was the giant panda, typically described by zoogoers as "cute, cuddly and adorable." It actually is solitary, ill-tempered and aggressive, but never mind … Mere facts cannot compete with perception.'

What made the impact of *Bambi* far greater than it would otherwise have been was the fact that the film arrived at the same time as the great agricultural revolution. The end of the Second World War heralded huge changes on the land; advances in technology, chemistry, biology and botany meant that farming was transformed. Fewer people were required in the fields; real horse power was replaced by mechanical innovation and farm labourers became more like minders than workers. Men and women left the land in their thousands. Consequently a country in which virtually every child had a grandfather, aunt, cousin or some relative on a farm or living in a village became a country in which the vast majority of the population gradually lost touch with its rural roots and so lost touch with nature too. The country became something out there, beyond the town, beyond suburbia. It turned into a place that was full of dirt, cockerels that crowed at inhospitable hours, cows that dirtied the lanes and slow-witted yokels who spoke with strange rural accents. It remains one of the great scandals of our time that rural accents are regarded as a sign of dull-witted ignorance, while urban accents – particularly from London – are deemed acceptable.

THE HUNTING GENE

The process of separation from the land continues even now and with farming in the financial doldrums, thanks to the Common Agricultural Policy, more families are about to have their rural roots severed. The process has left Britain with almost the smallest rural population in Europe and its rural culture is threatened as a direct result.

Even so there are increasing numbers of people whose lives have gone full circle; they again live in the country, but they commute to work and live urban lives in rural surroundings. In many areas the genuine country person, living and working in the country, has almost become an endangered species – as rare as a rainforest Indian.

As a consequence, our relationship with animals has changed fundamentally. Fifty years ago, for most country people the partnership between man and beast was a working one. One hundred years ago that applied to townspeople too, as horses were the main source of pulling power for transport and delivery; about the only leftover of horse transport today is the brewer's drey, which is more of a publicity gimmick than a commercial solution.

Although the relationship was a working one, that did not rule out real emotional attachment. The great heavy horses worked better if they were decently fed, well groomed and treated with appreciation. Clean, well-fed animals were healthier, calmer and easier to handle. Animal husbandry was not based on sentiment but on respect.

Beyond the farmyard, this relationship spread into the wildlife of the countryside too, and it was normal for farmers, farmworkers and their friends to try for rabbits, hares, pheasants, partridges and wildfowl in season. They wanted – needed – to kill their quarry for the cooking pot, but they had regard for it during the close season; wildlife was part of their lives and traditions and linked to the country year. It was common to see men carrying guns or snares down the street, with dogs at their sides and hares or rabbits slung over their shoulders. Such a sight did not warrant a second glance. Today in some areas the countryman carrying a twelve bore and a rabbit is looked upon as a manic serial-killer loose in the street. He receives stares, not glances, and the expressions of suburbia range from fear to disgust. The unspoken thought is: 'How could that sadistic man kill our beautiful wildlife?'

The practical relationship between man and animals benefited both. It was accepted that where there was life there was also death; where there was health there could be sickness; where there was activity there could be accidents and injury. It meant that practicality and honesty tempered sentiment; that some young animals would die through weakness, injury or disease; that a favourite animal could break a leg or simply get old. Decisions would have to be made concerning life and death – to prolong a struggle or shorten suffering.

Now separation has occurred the reality and practicalities of life and death have become clouded. Most people no longer *work* with animals, they live with them as companions, or see them while on a day out at the zoo. With the current plethora of pet programmes on television, anthropomorphic fables are passed off as serious natural history and, with an infusion of animal rights into many programmes, including the news and current affairs, the Bambi syndrome now reigns supreme. Animals, budgerigars and even snakes and stick insects have become little people with their own characters and rights. Animal illness and injury are looked upon with horror, while what is often ignored is the fact that long and elaborate veterinary treatment does not just extend life, it may prolong suffering that the creatures in question cannot understand.

This does not mean that people who can see through the Bambi syndrome are without love for animals. It means that their relationship with animals is based on reality and practicality, and not on a lie. Over the years I have cried bucketsful of tears for animals and birds – wild and domestic. During the course of writing the first four chapters of this book I have not only watched my much-loved dog die, but I have witnessed two real wildlife dramas that have involved me emotionally.

For the last three or four years our small farmyard has been swallowless. The decline of swallow numbers has been steady and unrelenting. From a figure of fourteen nests when I was a boy, the farm finally has no swallows. I believe that there are two reason for the decline. It has been caused by fewer insects being available for food through the use of farm sprays and by the tidying mania of some farmers, which has led to fewer nesting sites being available.

Why should this worry me? The swallow is only a bird, and a predator at that. But it is a remarkable bird; it is small, fast and attractive, and each year it undergoes two huge and incredible journeys. It flies several thousand miles north from Africa to breed, and then it flies back again to avoid the perils and lack of food in our winter. The disappearance of our swallows was an immense sadness; for countless years the swallows were a talisman of summer – then suddenly they were gone. This year a pair returned late, on 29 May. We did everything possible to persuade them to stay, even to the extent of providing mud for nest building. Finally, without using the mud, they stayed, laying their eggs in an old nest in the eves of the barn. When it was clear that incubation had started I was happier than if I had won the lottery. Sadly, however, the story has a tragic ending. For no obvious reason the female died on the nest, while apparently incubating her eggs. Each night for three weeks afterwards the male loyally perched by her, before finally leaving.

At the same time, on the CRT's land, a pair of mute swans arrived for the first time and built a nest at the edge of the brook. Each time it rained I worried in case the water would rise and the eggs would be ruined. Several times I went to see her sitting patiently after rain, with the water just inches from her. Then a storm came at about the time incubation should have been completed. There was lightning, thunder and at least an inch of rain. The next

THE HUNTING GENE

The mute swan survived with her six cygnets.

morning the entire nest was gone – lifted up and floated away. I looked for the swans, but there was no sign of them. I felt the loss personally.

Six weeks later I saw the two adults, not far from the nest site, with six cygnets, all doing well; they must have got them off, in the nick of time, just before the storm. Again I was pleased; not because the swans were little white feathered people, but because two wild, vulnerable birds had succeeded in very hostile circumstances. No animal rights helped them to succeed; on this occasion they had been lucky – so had I.

Animal rights have arrived on the back of both *Bambi* and the change in our relationship with animals, and as a direct result the issues concerning farming, hunting and working with animals have been clouded. I can not abide cruelty, but misrepresentation and misinformation are just as unacceptable.

It is because I have always had animals that I respect them and it is because of my relationship with both wild and domestic animals, great and small, that I find the whole concept of animal rights absurd. The issue of rights, and animal rights in particular, is based on fantasy. How can anything – whether animal, vegetable, mineral or human – have a right, or even rights? We are all marooned, drifting on a spinning planet in a galaxy, in a universe, in infinity, with our whole concept of the creative process hampered by the fact that the human mind is locked into time, and we cannot, it seems, understand anything beyond that dimension.

So, in a world where there is disease, pestilence, natural disaster and man-made catastrophe, how can anybody or anything have rights? How can there be a right to employment when new technology and man-made economies create unemployment? How can we have a right to good health when diseases are endemic? How can anybody have a right to a home if there is an earthquake or a hurricane? As far as reality dictates, there is no such thing as a right, but we do have responsibilities. We have a responsibility in settled, affluent times to create work, hospitals and shelter for the benefit of us all.

We also have responsibilities towards animals. We should always treat them with due regard, and to those that work with us or for us we should show kindness, sympathy and understanding. Towards those that compete with us or that we use for food, we should show respect and we should make sure that they die with dignity.

There can be no illusion – rights without responsibilities do not exist. So animal rights really do equal animal fantasies. Those spreading the myths and the politics of animal rights are usually people who have little experience of working with, or looking after, animals – domestic or wild. They live in an anthropomorphic world, separated from nature, in which not only their pets but even the wildest of animals are turned into good, furry little people.

Because of the never-ending stream of pet, vet and animal hospital programmes, the situation is getting worse. It naturally follows that any animal seen to be killed deliberately, particularly out in the open, is – according to the animal rights lobby – being subjected to cruelty. Death cannot be seen or recognised, hence even 'slaughterhouses' become 'abattoirs' to soften the reality.

Some of those who shout the loudest about animal rights come from the world of show business and depend for their publicity on the press. They claim the moral high ground by not only campaigning for animal rights but also often for vegetarianism too. It is ironic that many of the photographs that help to sell their message depend on gelatine, used in the manufacture and processing of the film. Gelatine, of course, comes from cows, dead cows; so often the message of soya-powered animal rights and non-killing is proclaimed through the help of slaughterhouses and killed cattle. We need to be told when these blatant double standards are to be eliminated by using 'vegetarian' camera film.

The power and potential income available for animal rights was first shown in the early 1980s during campaigns to stop the culling of seal pups. The seal is the perfect Bambi syndrome animal. It has eyes far bigger than Bambi's and its cries, caught on a cold Arctic wind, could almost be mistaken for those of a child. There may have been a case for stopping the killing of some seal pups, or for more controlled hunting, but the pictures were emotive: doleful eyes, crimson blood on pure white snow, wicked hunters – the Bambi syndrome was activated on a massive scale. Money poured in and real political pressure was put on governments. Models and actresses (usually vegetarian), in non-renewable, simulated fur, strutted the streets of New York and London as the bottom fell out of the seal-skin market.

THE HUNTING GENE

To help it on its way the centralised superstate of the European Union banned the importation of seal skins, to huge popular acclaim.

Those worst hit were not the great fashion houses – who were able to turn to other wares – or the commercial hunters who had other strings to their seasonal bows, but the traditional, indigenous Inuit hunters, living just above subsistence level thanks to the money received from the sale of seal skins. The hunters still killed seals as they were their main source of food, but the skins were now unsaleable and went to waste. Virtually their only source of cash in a money-driven world had been taken away. Animal rights charities made millions; First World ego-tripping celebrities occupied the new moral high ground as long as gelatine-dependent cameras were present, and the Inuit people were plunged into poverty. A proud, self-sufficient people was forced to depend on handouts.

What made the situation worse was the fact that the commercial hunters and the Inuit were hunting different kinds of seal. The commercial hunters were killing the young of Harp seals that pup in colonies – so

A subsistence Inuk hunter – badly hit by the seal skin ban.

it could hardly be called hunting – and initially the numbers killed meant that their activity was not sustainable. The Inuit were hunting the far more numerous Ringed seal. In the main, they really did hunt; they hunted the adult seal for its meat, to feed themselves and their Husky dogs. Because of the numbers involved their activity was entirely sustainable; it was their prime source of food, and the sale of skins for hats and clothing simply allowed them to live slightly above subsistence

level. The complete ban on skins imposed by the EU caused the price of a skin to fall from £35 to £2.30. A mixture of emotive propaganda, carefully arranged photo-opportunities and political expediency devastated the already low living standards of an indigenous people. Even when the end result became known, there was no public apology from the charities concerned or from the EU, and the Inuit became a forgotten, marginalised people.

It was clear that, thanks to the Bambi syndrome, animal rights had become more powerful than human rights. The seal had its place in nature – catching fish. The Inuit did not have their place in nature – catching seals; although they had been doing it for generations. Incredibly, animal activists, separated from nature, could not see that the Inuit were part of nature and part of the natural cycle. What could the Inuit do instead: hunt polar bears – the other seal hunters of the Arctic? The fat of the polar bear is already so full of heavy metals that drift up to the Arctic in ocean and atmospheric currents from the industrialised West that, according to EU regulations, it is almost classifiable as toxic waste! Sadly for the Inuit too, polar bears are covered in fur and have lovely eyes.

Those who saw beyond the hype of the seal campaign were not impressed. The Rev. Howard Bracewell was working with the Inuit at the time and he does not mince his words:

> I was living and working with the Inuit, or Eskimo people as they then were known, in the high Canadian Arctic on Northern Baffin island and the islands further north. We lived through that period when seal skins became bad news and, no doubt, due to much emotional lobbying in Europe by many who had probably never seen a seal, let alone a subsistence family, seal hunting was suddenly out. Fine for those who kill seals for fun and monetary gain. But when it destroys a cultural economy as it undoubtedly did, and I know because I was there, it is sick. How many who brought about this ban still eat beef, pork and poultry, and wear leather? I speak *not* as part of the pro-hunting lobby, but as one who has lived with people who did, and still do kill to live.

Bryan Alexander, the well-known writer and photographer, who has worked extensively among the indigenous peoples of the Arctic, agrees:

THE HUNTING GENE

The anti-sealing campaign has probably done more to destroy traditional Inuit culture than anything else in the past thirty years. The message coming from animal rights organisations in the south was that it was wrong to hunt seals and other fur-bearing animals. When you belong to a hunting culture like that of the Inuit, and you depend on hunting for food and winter clothing, that is a tough message to take. Many of them didn't have a choice.

Even today 'Greenpeace' is a dirty word in many native hunting communities across the Arctic. What I find breathtaking is the ignorance that exists among animal rights groups, many of whose members have lost touch with nature and live in the cities that are responsible for polluting the once pristine Arctic environment. Toxins from their cities are poisoning the very animals that they are trying to protect, the same animals that the Inuit depend on for food. For them to dictate to the Inuit on how they should live their lives is amazingly arrogant.

During the winter of 1980 I lived with an Inuk hunter called Ituku and his family at an isolated camp in North Greenland. One February day, we had been out seal hunting on the frozen sea for twelve hours at −30°C and had come home empty handed. The news on the local radio that evening included a piece on the anti-sealing campaign. 'Could you visit Brigitte Bardot and explain to her that we *need* to hunt seals,' Ituku said to me in a concerned voice. 'She doesn't understand anything about how we live here.'

The whole philosophy of animal rights takes numerous strange and unfathomable turns. Many of those opposed to fox-hunting, and even a minority of conservationists, claim that the fox in Britain has no natural predator. But what about man? For thousands of years the fox competed with man and is still doing so. As a result foxes were killed to reduce that competition, as well as to provide warm fur for clothing. It was natural competition, natural predation and part of nature's cycle. It is a mystery that as society becomes more secular, so man is taken out of nature and set apart – when logic suggests that he should be seen more clearly as a part of nature. My position, as a Christian, is simple: I believe that we are a special part of nature, but at the same time we live our lives with the rest of creation in the natural world.

In exactly the same way, man has competed with some birds of prey for hundreds of years, particularly the sparrowhawk and the hen harrier. I have had sparrowhawks take bantam chickens, and it is clear that the hen harrier acquired its name because it 'harried' hens. In 1544 a naturalist called Turner wrote of the hen harrier: 'It gets its name among our countrymen from butchering their fowls.' At that time there was no game shooting and so the hen harrier was not persecuted by game interests – which is the popular fallacy – it was removed by the crofter and small upland farmer who was having his poultry stolen. So the 'persecution' of the hen harrier should, properly, be called 'competition' with the hen harrier. Because of this competition, the hen harrier was pushed to areas where it did little damage. As a result lapwing, golden plover, curlew, redshank, dunlin and red grouse did extremely well in the uplands; *their* main predator, the hen harrier, had been driven out by *its* main predator, man. With the knowledge gleaned since 1544 it should be possible to devise a system of continuing control, allowing hen harriers in some areas and golden plover, lapwing, curlew and red grouse in others. But no, such a scheme seems to be too simple, or it is politically incorrect.

The sparrowhawk – beautiful but lethal.

THE HUNTING GENE

For reasons that defy logical explanation, hen harriers cannot be controlled. A scientific survey, the results of which form the basis of the Langholm Report (1997), clearly showed that hen harriers damage grouse populations. (The report conveniently ignored other birds such as lapwing and golden plover.) But even before the report was published, the RSPB announced that it would not tolerate any control of birds of prey. So a position was taken, based not on science, bio-diversity or conservation but on conservational correctness, emotion and a desire not to confront the real issues.

Similarly, sparrowhawks are currently causing mayhem among songbirds. A breeding pair of sparrowhawks will eat approximately 121 lb (1 cwt 9 lb) of 'mugged' songbirds a year. If all the birds taken were sparrows, then our 30,000 pairs of sparrowhawks would account for an incredible 66 million birds a year, equalling 18 million blackbirds or 3.3 million pigeons. In 1961, when sparrowhawks received legal protection in Britain, the population was a fraction of what it is today and the sparrow and songbird population was considerably higher yet, incredibly, conservationists state that the decline in songbirds is due alone to 'habitat loss and agricultural chemicals'. The real reasons for the decline of our bird populations are habitat loss, agricultural chemicals *and* predation. The simple way to prove this would be to study the songbirds of two areas – one with sparrowhawks and one without. But scientists seem reluctant to undertake such a study.

The curlew – badly damaged by predation.

So, while the crow, magpie, hen harrier, sparrowhawk, fox and mink populations are doing very well, thank you, some conservationists are sitting back and watching the lapwing, curlew, golden plover and water vole heading for extinction – in the name of conservation. With man taken out of the natural cycle, predators run riot. The talk is of a natural balance when the whole of our landscape is unnatural and so the wildlife populations are out of balance.

Some conservationists also insist that the number of predators are controlled by their prey. This avoids the fact that some predators, such as the sparrowhawk, have preferred prey. Consequently lapwing or snipe (as in the Ouse Washes) can be hit hard. Yet once the lapwings and snipe have gone, the sparrowhawk simply switches to something else. Contrary to popular conservation mythology, when this happens extinction, or near extinction, can be caused by predation. This seems to be confirmed by Professor Robert May, an ecologist at Oxford University. Writing in *Nature* ('Thresholds and Breakpoints with a Multiplicity of Stable States', number 269, 1977), he suggests that once the population of a prey species drops below a certain level, it is in the 'predator pit' and an adaptable predator can prevent it from recovering. It achieves this by switching its focus to another prey species, so keeping its own numbers high. The small amount of predation it exerts on the species in the 'predator pit', when the opportunity occurs, is still sufficient to prevent its numbers building up sufficiently to allow recovery. Thanks to those misguided conservationists who will not control predators, birds such as the lapwing and curlew are well and truly stuck in the 'predator pit'.

But why won't conservation bodies publicly support predator control as a conservation tool? This is 'population management' – control – not extinction, to help threatened species and encourage bio-diversity. So, it would seem, we are back at Bambi; we must not kill predators because it will upset members and lose us money. The illusion of nature's balance is the safe way of avoiding offence.

Another element is also present; for some reason man seems to revere predators, although no psychologist can tell me why. Deer can be shot to stop them eating orchids, but predators must be left alone. Yet when man himself acts as a predator and kills, howls of outrage follow.

The human fascination with predators extends to Africa, where lions, leopards and cheetahs are held in high regard. Every visitor wants to see a 'kill', which is considered to be the highlight of any safari. Years ago I too wanted to see a kill, but then I changed. At one time I had been naïve enough to believe that 'there is no such thing as cruelty in nature'. Africa cured me of that illusion and I can still see in my mind hyenas at dawn, bellies distended and jaws dripping with blood. Behind them was black grassland, burnt in a bushfire; and from the ashes shone countless white bones, old and new, revealing nature's killing fields. Nature might not have cruelty, but it does not have compassion either, it is about survival and has no feelings whatsoever. Later, as I left the Kruger National Park, I saw lions almost at the conclusion of a hunt. I did not stop but drove on. Soon afterwards I wrote:

THE HUNTING GENE

Muscles, sinews – tense, taut.
Power – springing, running, leaping.
Claws – clutching, tearing, holding.
Frenzy – dragging, falling, dying.
Feeding – growling, purring,
    sleeping.
The wind whistles in the thorns.

I called it 'African Death'.

A sort of animal rights cult has grown
around the memory of George Adamson.
He was a good man, a former hunter–
gatherer, who went out shooting and
collecting wild honey; in later life he
became a conservationist and lover of
animals in a practical way. He had hornbills
and ground squirrels join him at his

George Adamson, a practical conservationist.

breakfast table and his understanding of the African bush was greater than that achieved
by any gaggle of PhDs. I saw him with his lioness Koretta in a wonderful relationship, and
the work he did in reintroducing lions to the Tana river in the Northern Frontier District of
Kenya was important because it showed that it could be done. Why should his work now be
confused with animal rights? To feed his lions George had to shoot antelope, the beautiful
lesser kudu, impala and the graceful gerenuk and he had to buy camel meat. The life of the
lions depended on the death of other animals, not in a natural way but almost against nature.
If his lions had rights, what about the rights of the lesser kudu and the camels? They
obviously had none. For George Adamson, and for me, this was not a problem, but it should
be remembered that for every saved predator there is a lot of suffering and a lot of death.

So it is in this muddled and separated atmosphere of animal rights that hunting in Britain
takes place. It is seen through an atmosphere of delusion, distortion and misrepresentation,
in which the visions of Bambi and Thumper skip happily through sunlit glades. In reality the
hunting process is about as close to nature as it is possible to be, but in an age of separation
most people do not see dead animals, and so they equate death with cruelty. They see furry,
cuddly little people being chased by fierce dogs and barbaric huntsman. They believe that all
nature lives in harmony and shares a natural balance in Bambi's happy wonderland. Hunting
offends this mirage and they take their anger, self-delusion and environmental illiteracy to
Parliament, demanding political action and legislation. There, the cynical, the politically
correct and the ignorant see wonderful opportunities for personal promotion and self-
advancement.

Chapter Five

THE RUNNING HARE

William Garfit .

THE HUNTING GENE

When the word 'hunting' is heard, most people immediately associate it with fox-hunting, but the animal whose antecedents go back the furthest as a creature of the chase is the brown hare. The hare is a wonderful animal with a natural history that still retains much mystery and an oral history that has created myth, legend and folklore. How the hare arrived in Britain in the first instance is part of the puzzle; some people claim that it was introduced by the Romans but it is far more likely to have arrived unaided at the end of the last Ice Age. Its present range is huge, spreading across Europe eastwards to central China, and southwards to the semi-desert areas of Africa. It is assumed that the brown hare reached Britain from the east, as forest was cleared and grassland and farmland replaced woodland. It has been introduced to Australia, New Zealand, Chile, North America and to several islands off the British coast.

In the north – in higher, colder areas – its numbers decline and it is replaced by its cousin the mountain hare. Although smaller, the mountain hare is just as attractive as the brown. In winter its coat turns white, aiding its survival. When the snow arrives and stays, its camouflage is perfect – even without snow its white, coat can be concealed in long heather, making it difficult to locate.

Hare today – hare numbers are recovering.

Further north still, there is the Arctic hare. Whether it is a sub-species in its own right or simply a mountain hare that stays white for the whole year round, not even the scientists can agree upon. The fact that the Arctic hare, living well above the Arctic Circle, stays white the whole year through makes it very unusual indeed. Virtually every other bird or beast that turns white in winter reverts to normal in summer – the ptarmigan, the Arctic fox and the stoat. As for the poor stoat, it is its brief, seasonal white dress, plus black tail, that make it a much-sought-after prize. To put it poetically:

> An animal I know is very forlorn,
> It's cursed by all gamekeepers as being base born,
> They trap it, and shoot it, and say it is vermin,
> Then they flog it to royalty who wear it as ermine.

Fortunately for the Arctic hare, it has no black markings to add to its attractiveness. Less fortunately, in the middle of summer its white coat can make it very conspicuous when browsing in short vegetation.

Until quite recently the hare was one of Britain's most common animals. In fact, before 1880 when the Ground Game Act allowed tenant farmers to kill rabbits and hares on their own land, the hare had reached almost plague proportions.

When I was a boy, hares were a common sight in East Anglia and during a normal walk around the farm several hares would be flushed. The difference between a hare and a rabbit is easy to see: the hare is larger and faster, with long back legs; at times it seems rather neurotic, not quite knowing whether to run, lope or even sit down. In March the apparent neurosis turns to total madness and they will run in circles,

The survivor: a brown hare sheltering in snow.

jump and box – becoming genuine mad March hares. To the trained eye the hare is surprisingly easy to pick out in long grass or cereal crops; it often sits up to see what is happening, the black tips of its ears clearly showing. In the deep mid-winter it does the exact opposite; it crouches low against the wind and the cold, driven snow.

During the course of the farming year we often used to find small leverets. Leverets are simply young hares, so-called from infancy to late adolescence. A few years ago, when my brother was showing a zoology student from a university around the farm, he mentioned the scarcity of leverets. 'What is a leveret?' the future scientist/conservationist asked. 'A sort of rat?'

The gestation period for a hare is just forty-two days, and the doe can have up to four litters a year. The summer, from March onwards, is the most common and favourable time for the female to give birth, but surprisingly – and totally in keeping with an animal that has a reputation for mystery – pregnant females have been recorded in every month of the year. Another oddity is that it is possible for the doe to become pregnant again while already pregnant (this is known as *superfoetation*) and the two pregnancies will continue side by side without influencing each other.

Another unusual habit is *refection*, which means that hares use their own droppings as a food source. Many plants in a hare's diet are hard to digest, so this method of dining out aids digestion. The first droppings are wet and quite dense; when eaten again the resultant droppings are much drier and lighter and they are ignored as food – any temptation of a third snack is overcome.

On one occasion when I was small and the corn was still being cut with a binder, my father found a tiny, newly born leveret under a sheath of wheat. It was beautiful; unlike baby rabbits, which are born blind and naked, leverets are born fully furred and wide eyed. The temptation in those days was to keep one for a pet, but the accepted wisdom was that leverets were too highly strung to make good pets and so we always left them where we found them. When some neighbours ignored the common view, all seemed to go well – until the unfortunate animal chewed through the electric lead of their television set.

The fact that small leverets can be picked up at all is due to one of the hare's great defence mechanisms – its ability to crouch low and rely on its stillness and colouring to provide camouflage. Jim, the old First World War veteran who worked on our farm, had a simple way of telling a hare from a clod of soil: 'As a clod is approached it gets bigger, as a hare is approached it skulks and gets smaller.' He had several sayings about 'Sally', asserting that 'winter wheat should cover a hare in March' and that 'ten hares eat as much as a sheep'. Sally was the common country name for a hare in our area; in other parts the hare is sometimes called Sarah or Puss –

possibly because of the cat-like way it washes its face and whiskers. It is always referred to as 'she'.

In Jim's time there were many beliefs, superstitions and oral traditions that were alive and well. It was widely believed that pregnant women should not eat hare for fear of a miscarriage. This was based on the fact that the hare seems to have a greater volume of blood than many other animals, causing hare meat to be dark while that of the rabbit is pale. The meat of a 'bucking' hare was said to cause stomach trouble, and if a hare ran through a village street it was thought there would be a fire.

It was considered lucky to carry a hare's foot; it was not quite so lucky as a rabbit's foot, but the hare had the benefit of additional medical properties. That belief went back a very long way. In December 1664 Samuel Pepys wrote in his diary:

> I have never been in so good a plight as to my health in so very cold weather as this is, nor indeed in any hot weather, these ten years, as I am this day, and have been these four or five months. But I am at a great loss to know whether it be my hare's foote, or taking every morning a pill of turpentine, or my having left off the wearing of a gowne.

The following month, in January, he had evidently left his hare's foot behind, for on feeling unwell he had to touch a companion's:

> It is strange how fancy works, for I no sooner almost handled his foote, but my belly began to loose and to break wind, and where I was in pain yesterday and tother day and in fear of more today, I became very well, and so continue.

THE HUNTING GENE

At the time of Pepys, because of the hare's strange behaviour, rolling eyes, rising and falling ears and its March madness, it was commonly believed that a witch could turn herself into a hare.

Strange to relate, there is a modern story that gives the hare (or rabbit, depending on the version) a remarkable piece of insight. A little blind hare was hopping along to its form (the scrape where hares lie up) when it bumped into a little blind toad. The toad put out its front leg and said: 'You've got big floppy ears, you've got nice soft fur, you've got sweet little twitchy whiskers; you must be a little leveret.'

The leveret was most impressed and put out its front paw to feel the toad: 'My,' he said, 'you are very, very cold; you are extremely slimy; and you've got a great big mouth – you must be a land agent.'

The natural history of the hare has always been the subject of debate. Old Jim maintained that when a leveret had a white spot in the middle of its forehead, there were three in the litter. About the actual birth there was disagreement; some old farmworkers claimed that the doe gave birth to all the leverets at once, with the fully active leverets immediately able to disperse for their own safety; while others thought that the doe gave birth singly in different parts of a field or hedgerow. In much the same way, some claimed that the female fed her litter one at a time to reduce the risk of predation, and others suggested that the doe called the young up and fed them all together.

Chris Knights, who has produced some of the photographs in this book, knows the answer to the riddle of the leverets' birth. He has witnessed it. He is a remarkable man; apart

from being a Trustee of the CRT, he farms some nine thousand acres in Norfolk – not bad for an 'ol' Norfolk boy' whose grandfather was born in a hen house. In addition to farming and producing millions of vegetables every year, he is one of the best practical naturalists and most talented wildlife film-makers in the country. While making a film on hares for Anglia Television's *Survival* programme, he and a friend, Terry Andrew Arthur, witnessed the birth of leverets. Terry may well have been the first person to film a wild hare giving birth. Both he and Chris film only truly wild animals, through a mixture of patience and wildlife knowledge. They both regret that much modern wildlife filming involves the use of tame or captive animals. Chris was excited by the birth: 'The leverets can walk straight away and the next night we could only find one about fifty or sixty yards away. The doe gives birth to all the leverets in the same place, and then dries them all off very quickly.' There were four in the litter, one of which was born dead. Astonishingly, no sooner had the doe finished giving birth than a buck hare arrived and tried to mount her until he was boxed away.

Even professional naturalists cannot solve all the mysteries concerning the hare. Chris Knights believes that the female calls up her young for feeding, but Robert Burton – another of the CRT's Trustees and the author of *The Daily Telegraph*'s long-running 'Nature Notes' column – disagrees. While researching the Arctic hare, he watched a doe feeding no fewer than eight young at the same time. She did not call up her young; they arrived before she did at what seemed to be a pre-arranged place and waited patiently until she appeared. With daylight in Arctic Canada for the full twenty-four hours, she arrived at intervals of exactly eighteen hours and twenty minutes. Occasionally a leveret arrived late; when that happened it missed its feed.

Among old countrymen there are numerous views about how best to catch a hare. Most agree that, as the hare's bulging eyes are situated almost at the side of the head, the animal has all-round vision. One novel way of capturing 'Sally' was apparently to circle her in ever-decreasing circles. The hare would be so distracted that she would not run off and a coat could be thrown over her. Another version was said to be the method foxes use: to approach cautiously from the front since hares spend so much time looking behind them. The best way of catching a hare was never agreed, but once a hare was caught – usually shot – jugged hare was generally acknowledged as being a sumptuous meal. We regularly ate hare from harvest time until their March madness set in. With carrots and onions all simmering in the pot, and parsley and thyme stuffing balls and red-currant jelly as part of the feast, it was – and is – delicious.

In addition to crouching low in their forms and sitting tight, hares are famous for their speed. Through countless generations of fleeing from enemies the hare has evolved into a sprinter of repute. Astonishingly for such a small mammal, she can reach 35 m.p.h. in short bursts and her agility at speed has ensured her survival in a potentially very hostile world. (Various 'experts' claim speeds varying from 30 m.p.h. to 50 m.p.h.; 35 m.p.h. seems about right to me.) On occasions she seems to run simply for the joy of running. As William Wordsworth wrote:

THE HUNTING GENE

All things that love the sun are out of doors;
The sky rejoices in the morning's birth;
The grass is bright with rain-drops; on the moors
The hare is running races in her mirth;
And with her feet she from the plashy earth
Raises a mist; which, glittering in the sun
Runs with her all the way, wherever she doth run.

The sign of a fast farm dog has always been its ability to 'turn' the hare, to make the hare change direction in an attempt to avoid capture. Years ago we had a dog that would make a hare change direction on a sixpence. The Labrador would sometimes overshoot or cartwheel with her legs tangled and the hare would continue on her way. Watching the chase was entertaining in its own right, and it is this fascination with dogs chasing hares that is the basis of the oldest form of sport, coursing – running dogs and following the hare by sight. Normally it is not an equal contest as the hare's ability to jink and change direction makes her a very successful survivor.

The sport of coursing dates back to at least the time when the Pyramids in Ancient Egypt were being erected; there are murals of the period featuring long-dogs chasing hares. These were the forerunners of the greyhound, the saluki and the lurcher – gaze hounds that pursue their quarry by sight. The love of long-dogs has spanned time, class and geography. The Roman and Norman noblemen loved long-dogs, but so did the lowly Saxon cottagers. The lurcher has been the traditional dog of the gypsy for centuries. In 1208 King John accepted '10 leash of greyhounds' in lieu of money for a fine. Shakespeare was familiar with coursing; he gave Henry V those famous lines at the Battle of Agincourt:

I see you stand like greyhounds in the slips
Straining upon the start. The game's afoot …

By 1522 'poor Pussy' was being hunted by so many people for 'their disport and pleasure' that she received greater protection from Henry VIII. By 1692 it was illegal for the poor to own a greyhound; for the wealthy to own a good coursing dog was a sign of status – perhaps this is the origin of the lingering folk memory that still triggers such a hatred of coursing.

My early encounters with a lurcher involved someone at the other end of the social ladder, the local gypsy. It was said that wherever he and his dog went at night the hare population plummeted. When I walked my little lurcher along the road for the first time, seventeen years ago, 'gypsy Jim' was passing on his bike. He was so taken aback to see me with the dog that he almost crashed. He liked what he saw and offered me £25 there and then in cash – I had no hesitation in declining his kind offer.

At about the time I acquired Bramble, in 1982, we had no hares on the farm and there were few in the parish. The local hare population had fallen from being plentiful to almost extinction in just a few years. When I was writing *The Hunter and the Hunted* in 1977 I went to see a hare shoot on a nearby estate. On the day I attended, 450 hares, 12 pigeons and 10 rabbits were shot; over the 3 days of the hare shoot the tally was 1622 hares, 44 pigeons and 16 rabbits. By the time I wrote *The Fox and the Orchid* in 1987 the hare population had been devastated and we had not seen a hare on the farm for four years. I had a traditional gypsy running dog with nothing for him to run after.

The catastrophic fall in the hare population all over Britain was so dramatic and startling that I seriously thought about arguing for a ban on hare coursing and hunting – not for reasons of cruelty but on conservation grounds as there were simply not enough hares to hunt. It did not take the greatest intellect in the world to guess the reasons for the decline and the scientists of the Game Conservancy quickly came up with the causes. Strangely, now that hare numbers are again picking up, more scientists are 'working' on the hare as part of the Government's Biodiversity Action Plan, although most of the work has been done previously. It seems that much of the skill of science today is not a matter of solving environmental problems, but of locating and obtaining funding. The aim of the Action Plan is to double the present eight hundred thousand spring population of the brown hare by the year 2010.

The crisis for the hare began when the seeds were first sown for the current farming disaster – that is, in 1973 when Britain joined what has become the European Union. All the policies of the Common Agricultural Policy were designed to increase production. Those who increased production fastest made the most money; 'money', 'productivity' and 'efficiency' were the key words. 'Sustainability' and 'responsibility' did not feature in the language of the Eurocrats, and are still absent today. In lowland Britain the pace of ripping out hedgerows, draining water meadows and ploughing every possible square inch of land reaped its reward with artificially maintained prices. If you did not plough, you did not reap the full financial reward.

As a direct result of this mindless industrialisation of agriculture, environmental considerations had no place. The destruction of farmland wildlife accelerated and a degree of pollution from agro-chemicals and nitrates became accepted as normal. As an indicator species of a healthy environment, the hare became scarce or even locally extinct. With intensified cultivation and a constant stream of chemicals the hare and leveret were under greater threat. Despite the amount of land planted with cereals, there were times when the hare had virtually no food. At the end of harvest hundreds of thousands of acres of stubble were burnt and then ploughed – they became hundreds of thousands of acres with absolutely no food for the hare. A once common animal became an absentee.

Even when stubble burning was banned – because of smuts on middle-class washing lines and in swimming pools, rather than needless carbon dioxide emissions – the chopping of straw and immediate ploughing brought no improvement in the hare's food supplies.

In 1992 the system of EU subsidy changed to an Arable Area Payment. Grain prices were allowed to fall but were compensated for by a payment based on the amount of cultivated land. Consequently all those who had ploughed every square inch were rewarded; those who still had grassland and woods received no money for their non-productive areas – in other words, good, traditional mixed farming was financially penalised.

In livestock areas the situation for the hare was no better. With headage payments for breeding cattle and sheep, livestock numbers rocketed. There were EU quotas, but the quotas enabled farmers to increase their herds vastly; the sheep population increased by 40 per cent to forty million in just a few years. More grazing mouths meant less cover for hares and more trampling feet threatening leverets. With more animal mouths to feed, some farmers turned to making almost continuous silage, cutting their grass fields at regular intervals from April to November. The forage harvesters cut to within an inch of the ground at running speed, mincing all leverets and ground-nesting birds – lapwings, curlews and partridges – as they went. As if all this were not enough, the intensification of farming was accompanied by a dramatic rise in the number of certain predators, particularly the fox, crow and magpie. The brown hare seemed doomed.

The hare would have disappeared completely from the general countryside if it had not been for two sections of the farming community: those who were taking part in country sports and those who, like us, had made the choice to follow environmentally friendly farming rather than greed. The hunters and shooters retained their wetland, their hedgerows and their grass meadows. It was soon clear that the habitats left for the pheasant and the fox were also good for a wide range of flora and fauna, including the hare. On the farms where country sports take place hare numbers are now almost back to pre-EU days.

Research by the Game Conservancy shows that grass margins in arable fields, beetle banks to break up large areas of cereals and grassy hedgerow bottoms all provide the hare with food and cover. When the Game Conservancy took over an arable farm in Leicestershire and immediately put in grass margins and cover crops, controlling predators as they went, the almost extinct brown hare came back quite literally in leaps and bounds. Since then the Countryside Restoration Trust has achieved the same rapid and startling return amid the prairies of Cambridgeshire, bringing wildlife back almost overnight by sensible and sensitive farming, including restoration to traditional meadowland.

In 1992 'set-aside' also considerably helped the hare. Due to the absurd and ill-thought-out Common Agricultural Policy, the EU managed to produce huge mountains and lakes of surplus food. After paying vast sums to induce farmers to bring land into production, it then paid them large sums to take land out of production. Set-aside was exactly that; it was land set aside. Farmers were paid not to cultivate it. The few remaining hares found havens of peace and weeds (food) and a dramatic recovery began.

Although Chris Knights's main love is wildlife, he also shoots. His farm has to make a living for himself, his family and up to eight hundred workers. Although he farms vegetables intensively, he has grass margins and areas of heath left for wild flowers and butterflies, and he even has an ancient drove road running across his land with rough grass on both sides of the track.

A nesting stone curlew stands up to a lamb.

Many East Anglian farmers would have ploughed up the old sheep trail for extra production – he preferred the production of birdsong and wild flowers. In addition to having a thriving natural habitat, he unashamedly controls foxes and as a result he has healthy populations of ground-nesting skylarks, grey partridges, oyster catchers, ringed plovers and lapwings. He also has one of the highest densities of breeding stone curlews in Britain. If, in the spring, the stone curlews arrive on a fifty-acre field before it is sown, they get the field rather than Chris getting his intended carrot crop.

It is said that bio-diversity – the achieving of a variety of habitats and species – is one of the main aims of conservation today and that is exactly what Chris Knights is doing. The hares love his land: 'In 1990 we bought 2500 acres and there were probably three hares on it; now, with a bit of grass, cover and predator control we have hundreds – my keeper took out thirty foxes in the first month.' Chris is not a courser himself, but he allows coursing on his land. He explains:

> The Swaffham Coursing Club is the oldest in the country and when I bought the land they asked me if they could carry on. I am not a fanatical courser, but I'm not opposed to it. If you get a lot of like-minded people interested in hares, then it's better for the hare.

THE HUNTING GENE

This was confirmed on another Norfolk farm, owned by Mary Birbeck whose passion for many years has been coursing. The highlight of her life was when in 1973 one of her dogs won the Waterloo Cup, the major coursing event in Britain. She has two thousand acres, including three hundred acres of woodland, about ten miles as the marsh harriers fly from the Wash. They fly inland to hunt on her farm as it is so rich in wildlife. She says:

> To have hares you have to have a nice farm, and you have to think about them as you farm. You have to leave them something to eat. I leave good headlands, and the stubble is left for as long as possible. I love the hares first, then the English partridge and then the pheasant. My gamekeeper is not allowed to set a snare, in case a hare gets in one.

Her gamekeeper took me around the farm. It was remarkable; she was farming her two thousand acres with hares as her prime concern, just as the Countryside Restoration Trust farms for wildlife in general. Around each field there is a thirty-yard strip of set-aside and at the heart of the farm is a large area of grassland, alive with skylarks and yellowhammers. Many of the hedges are wild and unkempt, full of cover and food for both birds and insects. The sheer number of hares on her land indicates a healthy farm and an environmentally friendly system of farming. The farm is managed by a famous company of land agents who are forever trying to persuade her to become 'more efficient'. Yet her type of farming ought to be regarded as the way forward for healthy agriculture and her hares and her sport are by-products of a sensitive farming system. The fact that the hare is an indicator species, helping to indicate a healthy countryside by its presence, should make coursing an acceptable part of country life; wherever there is organised coursing there are hares – it is as simple and as logical as that.

Greyhounds coursing at an organised meeting.

How and why coursing should have moved away from the aristocracy and gentry is easy to see. For generations work on the land was hard. Modern, pampered critics of the countryside forget that electricity, piped water, tractors and combines have lightened the load of country living for only two or three generations. Before then anything that provided relief from the hard daily routine or provided entertainment from the land was welcomed. When a farm dog took off after a hare, it was a break and it was entertaining. When a hare raced away with two lurchers or greyhounds, one against the other, yet another dimension was added. Who had the best dog? Which dog made the hare turn first? The killing became irrelevant, but when a kill was made it was welcomed since it meant meat on the table at a time when farm wages were low and meat was a luxury.

Gordon Beningfield's portrait of Bramble, my little lurcher.

Even today, with virtual-reality computer games, anthropomorphic television programmes and most people working away from the land, when people see a dog chasing a hare they find reality a compelling diversion. One recent Boxing Day, after hares had returned to the farm, I was walking over our biggest field with my nephew and his wife – she is a pleasant girl, but urban born and bred and against 'blood sports', which have never formed part of her life or experience. Suddenly a hare exploded from her form and Bramble took off at speed. Even at the age of 12 he was fast and everything in his running seemed to express joy. Gradually he closed the gap. The hare turned in an instant and Bramble applied his brakes; they didn't work and he lost yards. He continued half-heartedly and then gave up; the hare accelerated away. Every week, or even every day, she would have a similar run – against a dog, a fox or a tractor – and she had won another race to survive. 'That was exciting,' Tracey said with a genuine smile of pleasure.

'Yes,' I agreed, 'and do you know what you have just been watching? Hare coursing.'

I did not get Bramble as a coursing dog. He was bred by a wonderful old countryman, Monty Christopher, the retired head gamekeeper at Sandringham. I met Monty several years ago while I was writing *The Wildlife of the Royal Estates*, and he has become a good friend. He comes from the old school of keepering; he is an excellent naturalist, knowing the names, natural history and folklore of nearly all the birds, flowers and fungi he comes across. He is an expert singer of folksongs too, accompanying himself on the mandolin. The more he refreshes himself with a certain frothy brown liquid, the more the tunes sound the same.

He wanted to breed a lurcher that looked like a miniature deerhound and arranged for a Norfolk lurcher bitch to meet a Bedlington terrier dog. Bramble was the happy and delightful result. Inevitably, once I had him I gained immense pleasure from watching him run. He ran and teased the farm's Labrador puppy; he would run at Rinty, swerve by him and was never caught.

When you have a dog as fast, fit and agile as Bramble, it is only natural to want to see him run as he was bred to run. Once when I was driving the wheat trailer towards the combine at harvest time, a rabbit got up and Bramble leapt from the tractor and caught it within a few bounds. That made me want to see him chase a hare – not to kill it but to test his speed and agility. Then a woman phoned, inviting me to see some deerhound coursing in the Fens, where they still had plenty of hares. Bramble was over-awed – not by the hares but by the deerhounds, three times his size. It was wonderful to see two deerhounds running neck and neck and all the hares getting away. When it was Bramble's turn, he kept his eye on the huge deerhound and not the hare.

As hares gradually returned to the farm, Bramble saw his first local hare; he simply gazed in disbelief. He must have been 8 or 9, and he had only chased rats, rabbits and foxes before. When the hare got up from under his feet, he just stood and watched as if to say: 'What on earth is that?'

There was coursing in our family several generations back. My great-grandfather and his friends and relations always went coursing in the Fens on Boxing Day. A cousin, many times removed, still possesses a screen woven out of reeds. Behind it the 'slipper' with two dogs stood, concealed.

My first coursing invitation in preparation for this book came out of the blue, from a garden designer in Hertfordshire. She runs an unofficial coursing club and invited me along, knowing that I had a little lurcher. Her interest in coursing started by accident. She was offered a lurcher but initially refused it. Finally she succumbed and took the dog. It was a mistake, as she immediately fell in love with all lurchers and has owned them ever since. 'I was hooked,' she told me, 'and if possible you should use your dog for what it is bred. I hate the idea of people having spaniels, or sheepdogs, in flats, unable to do the work they were bred for. I don't like killing hares, but I love watching my dogs work.'

She calls her club the Fat Ladies Coursing Club because most of those taking part are middle-aged ladies just a little wider and rollier than average; many are housewives and secretaries. There is even someone who works in an animal refuge but who believes that coursing is kind to the dogs and good for the hares. The club has a few male members – including Ted Walsh, a legend in the long-dog world as an authority on whippets, greyhounds, lurchers and hares. His coursing days are over but he still attends the Fat Ladies

Under New Labour. LEFT: *Civilised behaviour.* RIGHT: *Uncivilised behaviour.*

meetings if he can, photographing the proceedings as the women and their dogs walk off and joining them in the pub afterwards for lunch.

On the day I went with the Fat Ladies a farmer heavily into country sports, but vigorously opposed to abortion, was present. He was equally against hare shooting:

> I love shooting, but I have not shot a hare for fifteen years. They say that four hares eat as much a sheep and so you can have too many hares on your land. Coursing hares is infinitely less cruel than shooting; people are so opposed to it because they don't understand that in coursing the hare is either killed or it gets away. A hare shoot can be hideous carnage with hares wounded, maimed and experiencing great suffering – I won't do it.

There was a doctor too, who claimed that people were much more difficult to deal with than animals; and there were two young men in the prime of their lives. Justin and Andrew are male strippers able to course during the day as they work mainly at night. They both live on the edge of London as it is handy for work, and they both enjoy watching their dogs work. Andrew's wife was with him:

> I'm a town girl really, but a country girl at heart. I used to be anti-hunting, anti-everything because I did not understand it. All I could see was a little fluffy animal.

The Fat Ladies Coursing Club of Hertfordshire.

> Now after going with Andrew I understand it, and enjoy it, although I still don't like seeing a kill – but that is only a small part of it.

While watching Justin course, I was watching barbaric, uncivilised behaviour, according to New Labour. When seeing him strip in front of three hundred screaming women and then being woman-handled and almost eaten alive – quite literally – I suppose I was watching civilised behaviour.

The coursing meeting was held on gently rolling land on a famous shooting estate in south-east Cambridgeshire. It was overcast and damp, but even in early December it smelt of autumn. As the coursers spread out in a long line across a field of winter wheat a flock of whistling golden plovers flew overhead. Two handlers and their dogs walked slightly ahead of the others as they began to cross the field; this was 'walking up' coursing.

Normally, the garden designer is mild mannered and good humoured, but if anybody got out of line she barked out an order like a sergeant major. It is important that any crouching hares are flushed properly and that the line remains straight. After one hare got up and was about eighty yards ahead, the two lurchers were slipped. Some hares seem to hear danger first while others see it; whether through sight or sound this hare immediately accelerated away. As the lurchers closed in, the hare turned at right angles. A jink, a swivel, and she was away along a grassy bank towards a wood, the dogs well beaten. She had never been in danger and knew exactly where safety could be found.

THE RUNNING HARE

The lurchers at the meeting were a wonderful variety of long haired and short haired, large and small. There is no such thing as a pedigree lurcher. They are a mixture – mongrels – involving anything that combines speed and intelligence; so a greyhound, lurcher or saluki can be crossed with a terrier or even a collie to combine brain with speed. On a field of stubble, brain and speed were obvious in both dogs and hares; hares were everywhere and several ran off unchased as there were simply too many. The favourite direction was towards a small wood, over which three buzzards were floating on the wind. Buzzards in this part of Cambridgeshire? I was amazed. Tom Reeve, a gamekeeper of the old school on an adjoining estate, told me that he enjoyed hearing the buzzards: 'They've been around for three or four years now. I love to see them as they are such graceful, beautiful birds. Modern farming does far more damage to wildlife than they do. I suppose we have two or three pairs on the estate and perhaps ten pairs in the whole area.'

The number of hares was remarkable; out of fifty-three seen, only eighteen were coursed and six killed. Each time a hare was caught Justin or Andrew ran to make sure it was dead. I did not see a single tug of war between two dogs, a situation so loved by the antis and cameramen who want sensation rather than factual representation.

On one course a little lurcher went tumbling as the hare jinked. She rolled and stayed down, yelping and crying out. She had dislocated her front right foot. The doctor carried out both the diagnosis and the cure; he gripped the leg and snapped the joint back into place with little fuss. The dog was taken home to a warm hearthside and I heard later that she had made a full recovery.

It was an astonishing morning. The hares were turning and running straight and strong, knowing where safety lay in a strip of maize or the wood. The dogs pursued with pace, grace and agility. Coursing is a fusion of beauty and tension; the dogs running, the hares jinking; muscles and motion in a symmetry of movement, balance and speed. Filmed in slow motion with music to back it, the scene would look as beautiful as a cheetah running down prey on the African plains. I have seen that too and experienced exactly the same emotions.

Ironically, that evening I watched a wildlife programme on television about wolves. A wolf was shown coursing and catching Arctic hares; it was depicted as something natural, beautiful and humane. I am always on the side of the pursued, but the pursuit is a drama, a passion, a conflict of life and death. Time stands still. Each course seems to last half a lifetime – the chase, the turn, the tumble, the pursued is away; the pursuer slows to a trot and stands looking without focus. Cheetah, wolf, lurcher or greyhound – how long has it lasted? Only forty-five seconds. Where is the hare? It has reached the safety of the wood.

Then comes a kill; the hare is caught within 150 yards. Was she old? Was she ill? By the time Justin arrived, still fully clothed, she was dead; there was no long suffocation, like a cheetah with a gazelle; no eating through the stomach of the living prey, like a wolf with a deer. It was life and death settled in seconds.

The Fat Ladies – and the male strippers, the doctor, the farmer and their dogs – had enjoyed their morning and forty-seven hares were none the worse for their experience. They would meet other foes – stoats, foxes, dogs, even feral cats – most days. The lurchers curled up in a variety of boxes, on rugs, blankets and bean bags, while the coursers sat down to a meal of venison cooked in red wine. According to anti-hunters another degrading, barbaric activity had taken place in the countryside. Quite how or why what I had witnessed could be described in those terms leaves me baffled and confused.

Then came another invitation to see more lurchers, at a single-handed competition deep in the Lincolnshire Fens. It was astonishing: a gathering before dawn at a hotel for breakfast, with a dress code imposed which ensured that all those present wore a jacket and a tie. The coursing rule was one dog against one hare, and a dog that caught and killed a hare proceeded to the next round. Despite the huge prairie fields, again most of the hares got away, about one in six being caught. It was a fascinating event, with an even greater mixture of people than the earlier meeting; there was a solicitor, a greengrocer, a taxi driver from Burnley, a dog warden from Manchester and many more. There was also a reformed poacher, with no fewer that one hundred convictions for poaching with long-dogs. He claimed to be as pure as the driven snow now. Poaching in the area is still a problem and several fields close to the coursing area had large notices announcing 'Beware Dog Wires', implying that trip wires had been erected to stop unwelcome, illegal coursing.

Some of the dogs at this meeting were saluki crosses and were referred to as 'desert dogs'. 'Salukis are the dogs that have been coursing for thousands of years. It all started in the deserts of Arabia,' I was told. It was said that one dog had recently been sold to an Arab for

Single-handed coursing in the Fens.

£10,000, to be taken back to Saudi for desert coursing.

Two particular courses were remarkable; the first lasted for about three minutes and the dog was run to an absolute standstill by a fit, fast hare that turned, jinked and went through its repertoire several times before running off into the distance. Another hare ran casually to the bank of a dyke and paused. The lurcher continued closing in at speed. The hare calmly made its way down the bank and disappeared, leaving the dog baffled and confused. The hare had simply gone into a drainage pipe, a trick she had obviously used before and would use again. The worst coursing that day was in the garden of an isolated house surrounded by bushes. A sparrowhawk chased a blackbird into a dense conifer hedge and then sat on the rooftop waiting patiently for the bird to reappear. I frightened the songbird mugger away.

The Greyhound pub in Swaffham.

The next coursing event I attended was more highly organised. It was run by the Swaffham Coursing Club; dating back to 1776, it is the oldest coursing club in Britain. (There are twenty-four greyhound coursing clubs in Britain today, as well as four clubs for whippets, one for deerhounds, one for salukis, and about fifty lurcher clubs.) The original Swaffham club was started by the nobility and gentlemen land owners; now it is made up of a complete social cross-section. In the 1800s the popularity of the sport was shown by the fact that the Greyhound pub in the middle of Swaffham had standing room for over 140 horses. The coursing rules at Swaffham are almost identical to those drawn up for the original club. The death of the hare is almost irrelevant; it is the pursuit that is important and points are awarded by a judge for the dog that turns the hare and follows the jinks and turns with the greatest skill.

For the first morning of the Anglia Cup it was cold and misty with a slight frost. There were not 140 horsemen attending, but there must have been that number of cars, vans and Land Rovers, together with a van proclaiming 'The Sizzling Sausage' to provide refreshment for the five hundred or so people present.

It was a remarkable scene – way out in the heart of rural Norfolk, with a banner draped over a hedge proclaiming 'Swaffham Coursing'. There were farmers, farmworkers, game-keepers, a crab fisherman from Cromer who doubles as the coxswain of the Cromer lifeboat

ABOVE: *Chris Mead enjoying the coursing.*

BELOW RIGHT: *The beaters have a rest at mid-day.*

and two Scottish students studying wildlife conservation who had driven through the night to get to the meeting. One had a lurcher at home that he ran at rabbits; he had become hooked on coursing. His friend was from Skye; it was his first experience of coursing. He said: 'I don't have a problem with it. It's all to do with conservation and the right habitat for the hare.'

There too was the unmistakable figure of one of the most respected conservationists in the country, Chris Mead of the British Trust for Ornithology. His reasons for being there were quite simple:

I live close by and I'm very interested to watch the dogs working. They are bred for it and they are not endangering the hares. The hare is a valued part of the environment wherever coursing takes place. I don't think it is cruel; over four or five hundred yards the hare is either killed almost instantly, or it virtually plays with the dogs and gets away. If I was a hare I would much rather be coursed than shot.

For the day's coursing, the first of three, seventy-five beaters worked their way in a large arc through the surrounding fields to drive the hares slowly onto the coursing field. Behind the hedge was a slipper in a fine red coat, using a Land Rover as extra cover. Once the hare to be coursed had a lead of about one hundred yards he slipped two greyhounds simultaneously from a double leash. The crowd, including one bookie, stood along one side of the field with stewards along the other side to retrieve any killed hares.

As we waited a hare loped up the field towards the beaters, while a little group of French partridges moved in the opposite direction. Unlike the Fat Ladies Coursing Club where the dogs were watched for fun, this was competitive coursing. One dog

The slipper releases (slips) two greyhounds.

wore a red collar and the other a white. A judge sitting on a horse for better vision would declare the winner by waving a red or white flag, and the winning dog – the one adjudged to have persued most expertly – would move through to the next round. Malcolm Cock, another Norfolk farmer, was getting nervous about his dog – as was John Bromiley, a full-time greyhound trainer from the Fens specialising in coursing dogs. He trains a number of superb-looking greyhounds but, peculiarly for a coursing follower, he claims to be almost a Buddhist. As the sun warmed and anticipation grew, a number of cameramen – still and movie – assembled to get pictures of running hares. Chris Knights and Terry Andrew Arthur were among them.

The first hare appeared on the field, loping through the hedge and apparently quite unconcerned. When she was a hundred yards into the field the slipper released the dogs. A man in plus-fours began commentating on the course down his mobile telephone to the owner of one of the dogs, in Oxfordshire. The greyhounds ran after the hare with astonishing speed and grace; Sally was immediately aware of the pursuit and accelerated away. The dogs were almost on her – a turn and a jink and the greyhounds had overshot. With one sprawling, they closed again and once more at the very last second the hare jinked, almost with an air of arrogance. Again the dogs stumbled, giving the hare twenty yards. She then ran straight and hard towards the small wood in the corner; one dog gave up and the other ran on half-heartedly, well beaten.

The next course was astonishing; a hare came through the hedge and after a hundred yards the dogs were slipped. They tore off fast and straight, ignoring the hare totally, just racing each other. After three hundred yards one of the dogs stopped and looked for the hare; the other

The hare turns … and gets away.

dog kept running simply for the joy of running – the hare was already safe. There were many hares gradually being driven forwards behind the coursing field. 'Look at them,' one old boy commented, 'they're running round there like a flock of bloody sheep.' When the next hare appeared he got excited: 'Goo on ol' hare – git away – git away into that wood,' and it did.

The most spectacular course involved one black and one white greyhound. On release the white dog ran like the wind as the hare continued loping along, thinking about whatever hares think about on a February morning. It simply did not change its speed or its direction; it was in the world of approaching March madness, or thinking of newly planted trees with attractive bark to strip. The white dog seized it at full speed; both hare and dog rolled over three times in a spectacular cartwheel and the hare was killed instantly without fear or suffering of any kind. During the whole day seventy-seven hares were seen; forty-eight were coursed and thirteen killed.

My final day's coursing was at the Waterloo Cup, held at Altcar near Liverpool. It is the most famous coursing competition in the world and for many years it was the most important sporting and gambling event in Britain. In 1874 it attracted a crowd of eighty thousand and in 1871, after Master McGrath had become the first greyhound to win the Cup three times, both the dog and its trainer were granted an audience with Queen Victoria at Windsor Castle. The event still attracts up to ten thousand people, including several hundred from Ireland who sample English Guinness and lay bets with one of the dozen bookmakers present.

Over the three days of the Cup there were 108 courses with just 14 hares killed. Like me, Clarissa Dickson Wright, the famous television cook, attended the first day and is quite untroubled about how her employers, the BBC, view her attendance. She said:

> It is a sport I have long been interested in. I grew up partly on the South Downs where there were a lot of hares and coursing; when the coursing went, the hares went too. It is a very subtle sport and it is traditional. The Grand National was born to amuse the crowds that had gone to the Waterloo Cup. It is not barbaric.

Before hitting the television screen, she was a successful junior barrister and views the threat of anti-country sports legislation as a backward step.

> If you disagree with someone, the way forward is by rational argument. I have yet to find any anti who will have a rational argument on coursing; banning people is not the way to proceed. If you use legislation to curb people's freedoms, instead of increasing them, you get into a situation similar to the one Germany found herself in 1939. Hitler was the last man to ban foxhunting.

'I say, chaps, you are naughty.'

Sadly, there were overtones of the Third Reich at the Waterloo Cup. Several thousand people were attending to watch a traditional country event, but halfway through the day about a hundred antis, surrounded by the police for protection, were allowed on to the site. Some of the men wore balaclava helmets and, at the front, two protesters carried plastic caricatures of Prince Charles and Camilla Parker-Bowles in hunting dress. The group stood and hurled insults and abuse at passers-by and the police simply watched. 'You fucking paedophiles,' 'You pieces of fucking shit,' were screamed with venom and hatred. 'You fucking scum of the earth, we don't want you on the earth,' 'You fucking perverts' – the breadth of their vocabulary seemed to match their knowledge of hares.

In a public place men and women were allowed to hurl abuse, protected by the police who made no move to caution or stop them. Such behaviour would not have been tolerated outside the British countryside. If a foul-mouthed balaclava-clad individual went into a gay club, to a Premier League football match or to the Notting Hill Carnival shouting 'You fucking paedophiles', he or she would be arrested immediately, charged and given a prison sentence. Evidently abusing country people is allowed. Some policemen are embarrassed by what they have to allow. As one serving officer told me:

> It has nothing to do with the law. We have instructions from above; we have to treat these people with kid gloves. This means that we are selective in our use of the law – it is politics interfering with the rule of law. This should not happen in a democracy. In truth most police officers would like to sort these thugs out. They are not interested in animal welfare, they just enjoy the violence and the abuse, and most of the time we just have to watch them.

The Hunting Gene

Those opposed to coursing claim that the sport is cruel and that if hares need controlling they should be shot. This is a strange claim. For this chapter I decided not to visit a hare shoot as the memories from experiences in 1977 are still vivid. Hare shoots are terrible; hares running at 35 m.p.h. are difficult to shoot and up to 30 per cent are wounded, with limbs broken and even shot off. A suffering hare screams like a child and the images and sounds simply bear no comparison with coursing. Hare coursing is not a regular sport for me, but I cannot call it cruel. I have no hesitation in calling organised hare shoots cruel, although they can sometimes be necessary.

Television must take some of the responsibility for the twisted logic surrounding coursing. Whenever a coursing film is shown, it is always of two dogs pulling a live hare in different directions. In witnessing well over one hundred courses for *The Hunting Gene* I did not see one tug of war. Shortly before starting this chapter, I watched the BBC News. An early item covered a train crash in India, with dozens of bodies lying on the ground. Then came a section on coursing. The newsreader warned: 'And now comes an item on hare coursing. Some viewers may find the following pictures distressing.' Predictably enough, the item included some old film of a hare tug of war. I have never seen a film of a hare shoot shown on television. In 1998–99 at legal greyhound coursing meetings, 238 hares were killed out of 1611 courses taking place over 90 days; it is thought that between 500 and 1000 times that number are killed each year on shoots.

Opponents claim that hare coursing is like cock fighting and bear baiting. Again that is peculiar logic. Bear baiting and cock fighting involved captive animals in restricted conditions (usually in towns). Coursing and hunting involve free wild animals living in open countryside with a high chance of escape. In fact, the nearest current sport to the old fighting sports is stocked lake fishing. Live fish are put into a restricted area of water; they are then caught on barbed hooks. The longer each fish fights, the more the fisherman enjoys it. It is ironic that after Labour's election victory the first anti-hunting Bill was introduced by a fisherman – Michael Foster. He declined to be interviewed about fishing for this book. There are nearly four million fishermen in Britain, many from traditional socialist backgrounds. Unsurprisingly, Labour claims it has no ethical problem with fishing.

Because of the contribution it makes to the conservation of the brown hare – a wonderful animal – legal coursing should be acceptable. The question of whether it is cruel is clear cut. In 1976 a House of Lords Select Committee was set up by the then Labour Government to report on coursing. It concluded that the amount of cruelty in coursing 'is less than 1% of the amount caused by hare shooting' and that the ethical question should be left 'for the individual conscience and not for legislation'. Nothing has happened since then to change the situation, apart from the ever-increasing hype and hypocrisy.

Chapter Six

THE HUNTED HARE

THE HUNTING GENE

In addition to being chased by long-dogs – gaze hounds – pursuing by sight, the brown hare is hunted by hounds, hunting through scent. Again this is an ancient sport, dating back to before the time of Christ.

Certainly hare-hunting has been taking place in Britain for hundreds of years. Elizabeth I was said to be a keen follower of beagles – small hounds whose followers try to keep up on foot. Even in days when wildlife was more plentiful and hunters had a greater choice of quarry – deer (fallow and red), wild boar, fox and hare – the purists preferred hare-hunting. They believed that the brown hare was the noblest of quarries, being both fleet of foot and clever. Thanks to the hare's habit of running in large circles, she also gave followers the best opportunities for watching the hounds work.

Until writing this book I had always taken the phrase 'watching hounds work' with a pinch of salt. I had assumed that simply being out in the open countryside and being part of the chase were two of the most important elements of hunting, and that watching hounds work was a minority aspect included to aid respectability. During the writing of *The Hunting Gene* I have been closer to the hounds and those who breed and look after them than ever before, and I have learnt that watching hounds work is undoubtedly part of the fascination of hunting.

On a good scenting day the hounds will work together as a unit; on a bad scenting day the pack will perform more as individuals. Those with good noses who are keen hunters and who find scent will 'speak'; the other hounds will go to them – and even depend on them.

Those who know each hound are not simply looking at a pack of hounds hunting. They are watching individuals perform, and they are comparing their skill and tenacity with those of earlier hounds. The whole process of hounds finding scent, losing scent and casting for more scent is both a fascinating process and an attractive spectacle.

The circle run by the hare usually makes the hunting of the hounds easier to follow and hare-hunting does offer a strong element of watching the hounds work – it can be compulsive to watch any working dog doing its job well, whether Border collie, pointer, retriever, guard dog or even guide dog.

A poem by Wilfred Scawen Blunt (1840–1922), 'The Old Squire', sums it all up. It is a long poem that starts and finishes with the following verses:

I like the hunting of the hare
Better than that of the fox;
I like the joyous morning air
And the crowing of the cocks.

I like the hunting of the hare;
New sports I hold in scorn.
I like to be as my fathers were,
In the days e're I was born.

Another lover of hare-hunting and coursing was that great writer and pamphleteer William Cobbett (1763–1835). He hated the power of the Establishment and the privilege of the aristocracy, but he hated cant and hypocrisy even more and defended hunting as vigorously as he defended farming and rural communities. He preferred hunting to shooting, for 'the achievements are the property of the dogs'.

The North Norfolk Harriers being exercised.

The Hunting Gene

Today there are 73 packs of beagles and 11 packs of Bassett hounds, all followed on foot; plus 16 packs of harriers – hounds larger than beagles but smaller than foxhounds and usually followed on horseback. Beagle and Bassett packs cover most of England. Some of the harrier packs hunt both hare and fox.

The first hounds I ever saw were beagles; they are attractive little dogs. Although many packs are private there are a number attached to public schools; one is linked to the Royal Agricultural College at Cirencester and the Ampleforth beagles have a close association with the famous Roman Catholic college at Ampleforth. A number of packs are linked to army camps – there is an Army Beagling Association – so a hunting ban could criminalise members of the armed forces.

My local pack is the Trinity Foot Beagles, with close ties to Cambridge University. The kennels are in my parish and a succession of kennel-huntsmen have always played their part in village life. The son of one of the earlier kennelmen is my jobbing builder and lives in the High Street, and the most recently retired kennelman lives in the old people's bungalows.

During my childhood the beagles could be seen almost every day. In the summer they were exercised along the parish roads, with the kennelman and whippers-in accompanying them on bicycles. The whippers-in do exactly what their name suggests. They have whips – not for hitting, but for helping to control the hounds. On the day of the most exciting exercise I was woken up at 7 o'clock in the morning by the sound of beagles in full cry; they were streaking along the road by the farm chasing a surprised-looking golden retriever. The dog came to no harm but the kennelman's pride was severely dented. Now, due to increased traffic, the whole pack would be severely dented if it were exercised on roads.

At feeding time on a windless day the hounds could be heard barking in every corner of the village. They still can, leading to a village newcomer asking Paul Smith, the current kennelman, to feed his hounds later in the morning 'as dogs barking at 7 o'clock in the morning is much too early'. Paul is from a mining background near Stoke and only arrived in hunt service following the closure of his local pit – an act of political vindictiveness and economic illiteracy under the Tories. Now he finds a Labour government just as ignorant, just as vindictive, just as uncaring and just as keen to make him unemployed once again.

He loves working with hounds and came to the Trinity Foot Beagles from the Fitzwilliam Foxhounds. His liking for hounds is so great that at his wedding several hounds joined him and his bride at the altar. The Rev. Jack MacDonald performed the wedding service; before the start of each beagling season he blesses the hounds.

From the very early days until recently, both the Trinity Foot Beagles and the Cambridgeshire Foxhounds have been important locally. The hunts have collected fallen stock – livestock that has died on farms through illness, injury or even old age. It has meant that farmers have avoided the problem of digging large holes for burial and the hunt kennels have received free meat for their hounds in return. It was a system that worked well and benefited both farmers and huntsmen. Nothing was wasted; until the time of BSE any fat or offal not fit for the hounds was sent away in evil-smelling containers to be made into

The Trinity Foot Beagles keen to start.

cosmetics. What any Romeo was actually kissing when his lips lingered on those of a heavily made-up woman was anybody's guess – it could have been cow's udder, pig fat or even ram's bottom.

Today a hunt dealing with dead animals must incinerate all waste, which means that some hunts can no longer afford to offer the service as incinerators are expensive to buy and to operate. The result is that the Trinity Foot Beagles are now fed on biscuits. Most of the local foxhound packs, however, still eat meat and the service of collecting fallen stock can be arranged. The hunts will also put down injured or dying farm and wild animals, another invaluable help both to the farmer and the conservationist – as well as being humane for the animal concerned.

During the writing of this book one of my own old ewes went off her feet. It was my fault: I get too sentimental with my sheep and treat my small breeding flock as pets – complete with their own names. I had let the old girl get too old. Another Paul, the kennelman of the Cambridgeshire Foxhounds, arrived quickly and shot her at close range. It saved Leah suffering, it relieved my anxiety and it re-emphasised the close links between hunting and farming.

It is both tragic and ironic that during the course of writing this chapter the markets for new calves and old sheep have disappeared completely in some areas and farmers unable to sell their stock have even found it impossible to give their animals away. At a time when a growing chorus of MPs and animal rightists were chanting 'Ban Hunting', MAFF (the Ministry of Agriculture, Fisheries and Food) issued a statement advising farmers to have their stock put down humanely by the local hunts.

There is no doubt that a ban on hunting would seriously affect the welfare of farm animals as there would be nobody on hand to deal quickly with injured or dying stock. Injured wild animals – particularly deer – would have nobody to follow them up and put them out of their misery. At the present time it is estimated that about half a million domestic animals are taken by hunt kennels each year. The alternatives are to leave animals to suffer, to turn a blind eye or even to tip carcasses illegally into rivers and streams – an easy and cheap form of disposal.

It is a strange fact that although the Trinity Foot Beagles have always been part of the village, until recently few locals actually hunted with them. Even now I have only followed them for the purposes of writing. It would never have occurred to my father to have attended a meet. As a working farmer he had neither the time nor the inclination. If he wanted to watch a dog chasing a hare, in the normal course of land work one of the farm dogs would soon oblige.

Each year in early autumn he would be visited by two 'young gentlemen' from the Trinity Foot Beagles – the Joint Masters – asking permission to hunt his land. Each year he would happily give his consent as long as he was notified of when the local meet was to be held. If he was out in the fields then he would sometimes be entertained by the events. Usually there were so many hares that the pack would split and there would be little groups of beagles running in all directions. A long way behind came the panting young gentlemen and young ladies, sometimes using language as colourful as their glowing cheeks. The safest animals on the farm on days like those seemed to be the hares.

Today things have changed. The Trinity Foot Beagles still have strong links with the University – going back to 1862 – but is a private pack. It has students following and a Joint Master who is a postgraduate molecular biologist, but academic work is now higher on the University list of priorities than it was in 1862 and locals and keen hare-hunters form the nucleus of the hunt. The Senior Joint Master is Stephen Lambert, a former Master of the Heythrop Foxhounds and the current racecourse manager at Stratford racecourse.

He is an old student of Magdalene College at Cambridge and still hunts with the Heythrop. He greatly enjoys beagling: 'It is wonderful to see the hounds work. It is a good, natural form of hunting and the hounds work hard. The followers are lovely people too and it is less demanding than foxhunting.' Another Master is a London accountant, Patrick Eggleston, whose wife attended Sidney Sussex College. The whippers-in include a student, a civil servant from my own village and Malcolm Garlick from Newmarket – he is involved in the transportation of racehorses to all parts of the world, ensuring that they travel safely, without stress.

One of the most interesting followers, and a former whipper-in, is the Rev. Jack MacDonald. He is the Dean of Gonville and Caius College. Until arriving at Cambridge his background was entirely urban and sub-urban; he had no link whatsoever with country sports. His main interest was, and is, theology; he attended a Roman Catholic

March madness.

school in Manchester and then trained for the Church of England, serving first as a curate in Peckham, south London.

He has no doubt that he was 'provoked into field sports' on arriving at Cambridge. 'They were being attacked in an irrational way,' he says:

> I've always voted Liberal, and I don't like the idea of majorities tyrannising minorities. I came across a lot of it in Peckham, involving race and colour. In Cambridge I came across the same thing involving hunting. It is abhorrent that the urban majority should just arbitrarily decide, without really thinking about it, that a certain activity is atrocious and criminalise it. So I took up hunting to make a statement.
>
> Hunting is not bloodthirsty. Death is not the primary aim, the main joy is in being out of doors, seeing hounds work, seeing them follow a line, having access to the countryside and talking to other people – it's all very 'civilised'. In watching a kill you are seeing hounds do what comes naturally to hounds – the hare is either killed in milliseconds, or it gets away. It seems to me to be much more cruel to wing a pheasant with a gun than to hunt with a pack of hounds.

> Part of my interest is that there are so many moral implications – in a wider sense it is our relationship as human beings with other animal species. I think that hunting is the least controversial way of humans relating to animals. I have more misgivings about factory farming and keeping pets in towns.

As a Christian philosopher, he has views which have an understanding and a conviction that shame most politicians:

> It is very dangerous for people to say that we must abolish the distinction between animal welfare and human rights – that we treat humans and animals without any distinction. Does this mean we give voting rights to primates and human rights to foxes? Those who believe this tend to play fast and loose with human rights; the sort of person who says we want proper human rights for foxes tends to say the foetus can be disposed of without any problem; a disabled person can be disposed of by euthanasia with no problem.
>
> Hitler abolished hunting with hounds; he did not want furry animals killed, but was happy to gas six million Jews. I find the moral smugness of the anti-hunting lobby utterly repellent.
>
> The Christian view has always been that there is something special and unique about *Homo sapiens* – we are made in God's image. We share a mental life, a life of morality with the creator of the whole universe. That sets our dealings human to human apart from our dealings human to animals. That is why I don't mind eating rump steak. We cannot lose the point. We cannot start treating animals as if they are humans. A fox does not have the same mental and emotional life or the responsibilities as humans. Being part of the image of God, we should have a proper and compassionate regard for other species. I don't see hunting as assaulting this at all. People out hunting have a deep respect for the environment and the natural world that God has given us. So I am a clergyman who sees no incongruity at all in saying 'I am a Priest of the Church of England and I take part in field sports.'

It is a strange fact that although the ethics of hunting are almost the same for hare, fox and deer, for some reason hare-hunting does not seem to attract the outrage of the antis in the same way as fox-hunting. It is sometimes called 'the forgotten field sport'. Not only is it forgotten; often it is not understood – one old anti-hunting Labour MP a few years ago demonstrated his ignorance by saying: 'I think hunting beagles with packs of dogs is very cruel.' Amazingly, when the anti-hunting Foster Bill moved into Parliament, a commentator from the BBC's Natural History Unit claimed 'Intensive agriculture and hunting has had a dramatic effect on the [hare] population and nobody knows how many hares are left in Britain.' Apart from again revealing the BBC's animal rights agenda, this was nonsense. The population of the hare was known, and it was known to be increasing. Only about 1500 hares are killed by legal hunting each year, which is insignificant as an influence on the total hare population. Perhaps a programme should be made about the Natural History Unit – it could be called *Programmes or Propaganda?*

My first day out with the Trinity Foot Beagles was remarkable – I could not find them. The meet was supposed to be on the edge of the Cambridgeshire Fens, deep into diddicoy country. The landscape was cold, bleak, overcast and empty. The fields were mainly sown with winter wheat and there was no sign of life – no farm work, no diddicoys, no beaglers and no hares. The diddicoys had been and gone – there were piles of hedge clippings dumped along one drove road – but the hounds were not to be seen. The kennelman insisted later that he had been out and enjoyed a hunt. How do you lose beagles in the flat open Fens? I did – quite easily.

For my second attempt to follow the beagles I went even deeper into the Fens, to a field near Earith that is still flooded each winter when frost threatens, to allow Fen skating. The meet took place at the bottom of a long drove road. A handful of followers, all non-students, were out. One elderly gentleman handed me a flask. The contents were warming and welcome on a cold day; the sun shone but the wind carried a freezing edge to it. Heavy black clouds were building up in the west and the followers had a number of choices: follow, watch from cars or a mixture of both to keep near shelter. The huntsman and whippers-in had no choice.

Foot followers and beagles pause for a rest.

THE HUNTING GENE

The rainbow makes a dramatic impact over the Fens.

The hounds were cast. It is an attractive sight to watch hounds searching for scent at the start of a hunt. A hare ran off, out of a ditch, heading north; another was running south. Suddenly a hound spoke, the others joined it and they were away, fourteen and a half couple of hounds following a strong line. They quickly disappeared, as did the huntsman and whippers-in. The retired kennelman stayed by the hound van – as did Paul, the present kennelman, with one eye on the threatening clouds and the other on the direction of the disappearing hounds.

The sky blackened still more and rain started, a few large spots at first and then a deluge. I retreated to my car, the kennelman reverted to the van to find the hounds. The rain stopped and the sun returned, casting the clouds with a new deeper blackness and creating a spectacular rainbow. The hound van returned – without the hounds. The kennelman had helped the huntsman to stop the pack hunting a deserted marina through which the hare had cleverly run.

Soon hounds were back, only half hunting and half searching. Off they went again and the rain returned. We sheltered in an old disused barn that a pile of pellets revealed to be a perching place for a barn owl. This did not surprise me as part of the hunt was taking place on a farm well known for its conservation interest. Along several of the drove roads silver birches have been planted and many have nest boxes attached, inhabited in the summer by tree sparrows – now one of Britain's rarest farmland birds. The farm also has a healthy population of corn buntings, another increasingly rare farmland bird. It seemed to confirm the view that many practical countrymen see no conflict between hunting and conservation.

The hounds hunted in a huge circle and by the time the sun had returned they were running over winter wheat. There was no sign of the hare, but soon they were off again in full cry. I started to follow, but mud was sticking to my boots and my jeans were getting wet and muddy. The hounds came round hunting in a large circle once more. This time they hunted beyond the winter wheat and onto a field of recently harvested potatoes. Occasionally a hound would speak, to be joined by several others. But nothing could be found. Patrick, the huntsman, was convinced that the hare had simply 'clapped' down in the soil and the hounds may even have hunted over her. As dusk turned into darkness, the

Wet underfoot for paws and boots.

huntsman blew his horn and the hounds all came to him. Although soaked several times, the followers all claimed to have enjoyed their day, as had the hounds; the hares had all survived.

I went next with the Trinity Foot Beagles to gently rolling farmland east of Cambridge. I had a pleasant stroll in the countryside; I had several interesting conversations and, yes, I saw the hounds work again. I learnt that hunting in Wellington boots was far from sensible as wet soil builds up, making walking difficult. Huntsmen are often mocked because of their dress, but light boots and socks up to the knees are more sensible than Wellington boots and jeans. The coloured coats and socks are sensible too as they help to distinguish the huntsman and the whippers-in from the rest of the followers.

One of the followers was a Northumberland girl from a farming background studying ecology and animal behaviour at Anglia Polytechnic University. She gave an interesting insight into her course of study: 'The majority of people on my course are townies, vegetarians and against every field sport. They do not understand and do not know what goes on. They see everything through rose-tinted spectacles. They are doing the course because they like looking at animal programmes on television or they are into domestic pets.'

The hounds streamed off into the next parish in full cry and the kennelman and hound van roared off to keep them away from roads. For the next three-quarters of an hour, either I or the hounds were lost. Eventually I heard them again and briefly saw them. They killed a hare, it was said, in the next field; but like most of the followers I did not see it. To them and to me it had been a pleasant day in the open country. Was it cruel? In the pattern of the hare's normal life with the disturbance of predators and road traffic, it was just another day. I saw nothing I could equate with cruelty.

THE HUNTING GENE

Whether or not it is cruel, some ask if hare-hunting is necessary. Does it have to be necessary? It is not necessary to eat strawberries in January or wear Armani clothes in July – but some people choose to do so. At the root of hare-hunting is the choice to do so or not to do so – a matter of personal morality. Hares can do damage to farm crops and to many young trees, and an element of population control is necessary in some areas. Hare-hunting does not have the impact of shooting, but it does not have the wounding or suffering of shooting either. I found nothing unacceptable about beagling, but if I am honest and I had a choice, I would prefer to watch a football match.

Shortly after one experience of beagling I switched on the television. Quite by chance it was the children's programme *Blue*

Peter. The announcer was saying that one of the *Blue Peter* dogs, Bonnie, would be retiring. 'She's retiring to the country,' she said, 'where she will be happy chasing rabbits.' The BBC considers it to be a state of happiness for a dog to chase a rabbit, but politically incorrect for a dog to chase a hare.

The other form of hare-hunting involves the use of harriers. Harrier packs cover some spectacular country and I was tempted to follow the North Norfolk Harriers or the High Peak Harriers in Derbyshire, as both cover wonderful countryside. The followers in both places are warm, friendly people too.

I decided, however, to follow the Aldenham Harriers, whose kennels are close to Markyate in Hertfordshire. My reason was simple and personal. For several years my good friend Gordon Beningfield, the artist and Vice-Chairman of the CRT, had wanted me to go with him to a meet of what was his local hunt. He did not hunt and gave up shooting and fishing, but as a painter, conservationist and countryman he appreciated the contribution hunting country makes to both landscape and wildlife. In addition he enjoyed the company of people who hunted, shot and fished; many of his friends from ordinary backgrounds either hunted or were car followers. Sadly, Gordon became ill, but in 1998 we arranged to go to the New Year meet of the Aldenham Harriers. Bad weather came, the meet was cancelled and we never had another opportunity.

The countryside around the Aldenham kennels explains why Gordon Beningfield regarded hunting as so important. Most of the farms and estates in the area are involved with

Young and old enjoy their sport. LEFT: *Young beagler, Hugo Topping.* ABOVE: *Retired huntsman of the Trinity Foot, Jack Calder.*

shooting or hunting and the landscape reflects their interest – an interest which in the case of the Aldenham Harriers dates back to 1878. There are woods and meadows, hedgerows and copses, and there is a hidden countryside that seems to be in another world from the M1, Luton Airport and Hemel Hempstead.

There are woods with holly, ash, beech and hazel. There are bluebells, birdsong and butterflies, and there are bridleways and tracks that take you into the heart of the country. There are badgers, silver-studded-blue and marbled-white butterflies and skylarks singing. Gordon was convinced that without the habitat for hunting much of this wildlife would be gone. The land left for fox, pheasant and hare gave so much more and as an artist he loved it.

His friends hunted. They included Derek Christopher, the local policeman. Rod Wilson, the local forester who supplied Gordon with logs, and who followed in his Land Rover. Gordon knew and liked Graham, the kennelman, who had been in hunt service all his working life. Derek Christopher, now retired, is a smiling, friendly man and the epitome of what a local policeman used to be – living, working and playing in the local community. He was brought up in north Barnet: 'I was a town boy but I started riding when I was 15 or 16 and enjoyed it. When I left school I went into stables and started hunting with the Enfield Chase. It was tremendous – some people ride to hunt, and others hunt to ride – I rode to hunt.'

Once in the police – the third generation of his family in the force – he still hunted twice a week:

> I was only an ordinary policemen and we had one horse. I used to hunt in the morning, then my wife would come in the car, and we would swap, so that I could be on duty by 2.00 p.m. That kills the myth of having to be wealthy to hunt – if you want to do it badly enough, you can, even if the effort is huge.

He loved hunting hares with the Aldenham Harriers, but most of all, he sys, he enjoyed 'the friendship and association. It is so important in hunting; you make friends, you are all of a like mind and you enjoy the countryside and the atmosphere – what more could you ask

Attractive hunting country in Hertfordshire.

for?' Although he no longer rides – he used to point to point – he is still an active member of the hunt and believes that hunting should be a matter of personal choice. 'But in any case,' he says, 'I think roads and development will cause a natural contraction of hunting. We also have to regulate ourselves – self-regulation would be a good thing.'

Rod Wilson, another of Gordon's friends, is an ordinary forester who likes following hounds – hare or fox, the Aldenham Harriers or the Vale of Aylesbury Foxhounds – in his Land Rover. The story of Rod Wilson is a tragic one and illustrates how hunting people – whether following on horse, foot or in cars – get virtually no protection from the law while simply doing what they want to do. They can be physically and verbally attacked, sometimes by thugs wearing balaclava helmets and wielding clubs and baseball bats, and there are numerous examples of the police just standing by and watching. It is rural terrorism of the worst kind, usually carried out by visiting and violent urban gangs.

While following the Vale of Aylesbury Foxhounds one day, Rod was so savagely attacked by men wielding clubs and wearing balaclavas that he ended up in intensive care in Stoke Mandeville Hospital with a fractured skull. It is said that two policemen were nearby; they simply sat in their Panda car and watched. Shortly afterwards Rod's mother died of a stroke caused by stress and anxiety. Nobody was, or has been, arrested. Rod is simply an ordinary countryman who liked watching hunting. His mother was just a good hard-working countrywoman. Nobody could have cared less about their fate. There was no outcry, no public enquiry, no questions in Parliament, just silence – yet the unprovoked attack would have done credit to the Hitler Youth Movement of the 1930s. Rod has almost recovered but nothing can bring back his mother or erase his trauma. Tragically, in a free country all hunting people, whether on bikes or horses, realise that one day it might be their turn. In effect this is rural terrorism, yet few MPs speak out against it. It is odd that in hunting out hunts and attacking huntsmen and hunt followers, many antis and saboteurs are demonstrating that they too have the hunting gene – they enjoy their hunt. What they condemn in others, they justify in themselves.

As far as the Aldenham Harriers are concerned, the threat of violence is tragic for it is a friendly, happy hunt. Those taking part vary from high-flying business consultants to working farmers and housewives. It is multi-cultural too; it boasts a Turk, a Norwegian and an Asian among its members. Alp Arikoglu sums up his feeling for hunting well:

> I've been in this country for forty years and come from a farming family in Turkey. Hunting gives me great enjoyment, social life and an understanding of the countryside – all good things. I feel a country person now – I love it – rural people are identical wherever you go in the world. I still have a share in our family farm in Turkey. Cruelty? The antis do not understand and have no idea. What is worse they won't come and find out either – or listen. In hare hunting the lead hound kills and mostly it is the weakest hares that are killed – with shooting you just shoot anything. I regret all the English things that are disappearing – the way of life; the sense of humour, the tolerance of each other, and the easy-going life-style – respect – they are all going. I fear for my children's future.

A Turkish incomer has a clearer view of rural life and a greater understanding of English values than many of our urban-based politicians.

The Aldenham Harriers form a community within a community. All year long there are events and occasions: dinners, a hunt ball, a harvest ball, a sponsored ride, a puppy show, a barbeque and many more. They even have a beginners' hunt to welcome in new youngsters – at the most recent one it was an experienced rider who fell off and flattened his bowler hat.

At two meets of the Aldenham Harriers I experienced the same problem as with the beagles. I could not keep up. With the hunt taking place on horseback, walking was impossible. Being over farmland, even my Fourtrak had to stick to farm tracks while most of the

hunting seemed to be over the next hedge. Rita, a retired hunter, and her terrier follow each meet on foot, but I simply lacked her knowledge, anticipation and stamina. At the attractive village of Ayot St Lawrence the hunting always seemed to be round the next corner and I saw very little. The most significant part of the meet was driving to it – through industrialised farmland almost cultivated up to the road itself, where obviously no country sports or conservation interest featured in the farming plan.

At the next meet in Bedfordshire the same message was clear. To get to the meet I drove by desolate fields, some of which were wall-to-wall Brussels sprouts. It was a wildlife desert compared to the estate where the meet was held – with hedges and woods, grass margins and shelter belts. It was primarily a shooting estate with hare-hunters welcomed. Again it was difficult to see the action. Graham, the whipper-in and kennelman, reported one hare 'chopped' in rape before it

Kennel huntsman Graham Hughes wearing the green jacket of the Aldenham Harriers.

The green jacket is not worn for September hunting.

had time to run. That is another advantage of hunting – a hare may be old, injured or even suffering from spray poisoning; if it is, then the arrival of the hounds spares it an uncomfortable and stress-filled end.

The only sensible option was to ride with the hunt to see it as the mounted followers see it. Riding is more difficult than it appears and I had not ridden for eight years. Hunting for even the most competent rider has an element of risk, and it is properly described as a 'risk sport'.

Since I first rode to hounds for *The Hunter and the Hunted* in 1977, I have only hunted six times – all journalistically. When I rode with the Fernie Hunt for the *Daily Telegraph* twenty years ago I had several spectacular involuntary dismounts and I still have a bent little finger from a break I received during one of my falls.

It also has to be said that horses can be both difficult and ill-mannered. My first hunt still lingers in my memory; it was with the now disbanded Cambridgeshire Harriers and I was smartly dressed in a donkey jacket and my mother's gardening trousers. I was on a small horse and as I left the commercial stables I was following a large horse, with my nose level with its rear end. For the first twenty strides it let out a long, loud fart, each blast leaving me desperate for sweet-smelling fresh country air.

So it was with genuine trepidation that I decided to ride again. My first refresher course was on the mechanical horse at the Newmarket Horseracing Museum. I foolishly mounted it in jeans, and the galloping action plucked all the hairs from the inside of my thighs. Then, after three hour-long lessons, I took the plunge.

The Joint Master and huntsman of the Aldenham is Ian Pierce. He is an affable farmer who farms over eight hundred acres, some of it rented. He was happy for me to hunt and arranged for me to borrow a horse, assuming that there would be no jumping. There was one slight twist to the arrangement. Last year Kate, the horse, had belonged to Ian and he had hunted hounds from her; this season it was owned and hunted by Val Barr, the Field Master, a farmer's wife. This meant that for two years Kate had been at the head of the hunt. It is the Field Master who decides when and where the mounted followers ride so that they do not impede the huntsman, the hounds or the whippers-in. There are cardinal rules in hunting, the greatest is *never to overtake the Field Master*.

The day of the hunt started in darkness. It was a beautiful morning with only the second frost of autumn; the stars were clear and a new moon was shining brightly. Dawn was breaking as we arrived at the field of the meet; frost was white on the grass as horses were unboxed and prepared. The excited hounds were let out of the hound trailer and there was an air of anticipation. It seemed a different world from the M1 and the A5 which we had briefly experienced on our journey to the middle of Hertfordshire. It was autumn hunting, hunting before the season had properly started, to get the old hounds into the swing of things and to show the young hounds how it should be done.

I mounted Kate; at 16.2 hands I seemed a very long way off the ground. A lady rider smiled at my obvious lack of confidence: 'Don't forget to roll as you hit the ground,' she said helpfully. Margaret Taylor, who computerised this book, drove me to the meet and showed her confidence in my ability by taking her riding boots and hat with her, expecting to have to retrieve the horse when I was left hanging on a hedge or sitting in a puddle.

Ian blew the horn and the hounds moved off with him. Kate's ears and eyes were following the huntsman; she was keen, one of the herd, and twenty similarly excited horses followed the hounds.

With the frost intensifying just after daylight, my feet were cold. The hounds moved on fitfully — working, searching, speaking by hedgerows and across stubble. It was certainly a crash course in galloping as Kate wanted to be in her rightful place — at the front. It was

Hunting is a dangerous 'risk sport'.

exciting too, with adrenalin flowing in me and the horse. There were hooves pounding, mud flying, horses all around and the hounds were in full cry. It was genuine excitement, the thrill of the chase intensified by the simple desire to stay on Kate and survive.

The hounds checked and a hare ran towards us. Nobody 'hollered' – that evidently is saved for protest marches. 'We don't do that often,' it was explained. 'We want the hounds to do the work.' The hare ran past us in silence and veered through the hedge; a skylark began to sing a solitary dawn chorus. The hounds were still hunting fitfully in the cold, but the sun was up and the whiteness was gradually melting into green.

We were off again after a different hare. Kate was straight into a gallop with her speed turning the breeze into a gale on my cheeks. We stopped; there was a fence – what should I do? I didn't want to fall. My heart sank. Three riders galloped and jumped and then the inevitable happened: the Master's old horse made the decision for me. She did what she would have done normally and took me along with her. She galloped and jumped; there was a clatter – we had demolished the top of the fence – but we had landed and I was still on board. Only five of us jumped. The others chose caution. 'Well done,' the smiling lady said, 'I am most disappointed, you are managing to stay on.'

There is only one problem with jumping into a field – you have to jump again. The exit was over wire. Kate looked after me once more and I did not even crush that part of my anatomy that I was expecting to crush.

It was a wonderful morning. As we stood still in the corner of a field with the horses and hounds steaming, I thought of Gordon Beningfield and a lump came to my throat. He would have loved this traditional scene: the horses and hounds, the first hints and tints of autumn on the hedgerows and on the leaves of the trees, the ripe hedgerow harvest of blackberries, sloes, hips, haws and hazel nuts. He would have loved the brown hares too, and the landscape that had helped to preserve them. I felt quite emotional for the friend I missed, at the season he loved, in the countryside he fought for.

We hunted again with hounds in full cry. They flew into a wood and there they killed. Suddenly it was quiet and we did not see the kill – we heard its silence.

Puppies Quainton and Quaker on Ian Pierce's farm.

The sun was warm and Kate carried me safely down a steep bank into a large field of stubble. Hounds went downhill in pursuit of a hare; they were gaining with every stride as the long back legs of the hare make running downhill difficult. The slope then curved gently upwards, and as the angle changed Sally's speed increased and she gained distance from the hounds. A mere twenty yards had become forty yards and then she was through a hedge with the hounds trailing back, but still in full cry.

To the east a fox ambled along a boundary fence and made off unhurriedly; to the west hounds were still hunting, and then came more silence. Soon Ian and his hounds came back and he blew his horn for home. Astonishingly, the hare had got away – another fox had been found and the harriers had switched to fox, marking Reynard to earth.

We trotted back to the field of the meet and it was only then that Kate overtook the Field Master. We had seen nine hares – four and a half brace – one brace had been killed (one chopped in rape) and three had been hunted and got away. I dismounted, grateful to have survived. A lone hound left the pack and sought out Val Barr, it nuzzled her and she stroked it enthusiastically; it was a puppy, Cricket, who had lived on the Barrs' farm during the summer for puppy walking and wanted to renew a friendship. It had been a beautiful, dramatic, euphoric and yet sad morning for me.

It had been memorable too. I had seen one of my favourite animals hunted; I had been with friendly people following a hunt; I had witnessed the ancient hunting partnership in action; I had felt the sun on my back and the wind on my face, and smelt the damp, fruity scents of a changing season. I had been part of an event – even a ritual – centuries old, and my part had involved tradition, history and my personal choice, something that should be above and beyond politics.

Chapter Seven

A Hunting We Will Go

William Garfit

THE HUNTING GENE

When it comes to writing about the realities of fox-hunting, I am in a strange position because I do not hunt. When it comes to writing about the fox, my difficulties are increased still further as I have always been fascinated by foxes and regard them as one of my favourite animals. Yet the deeper I look into man's relationship with animals, and the more I see the pressures building up in the British countryside, then the more I am convinced that hunting is good both for the fox and for the living and working countryside. In loving the fox and appreciating hunting, I am in a similar position to Jorrocks, that larger-than-life huntsman created by Surtees, who said: 'It arn't that I loves the fox less, but that I loves the 'ound more.'

We have had years of seeing wildlife decimated by development, road construction and the industrialisation of agriculture, and have heard this destruction described as 'progress' and 'efficiency'. Hunting actually gives wildlife and landscape some respite; it gives them a reason for remaining, for being. There is no contradiction in that. In conservation jargon, hunting provides a mixture of habitat management and population management in which the fox is both controlled and preserved. This is a conservation combination fully understood in most countries – but apparently not in urbanised Britain, where all wildlife issues appear to be dominated by the Bambi syndrome and political correctness.

My fascination with foxes began when I was a child with tales of Brer Fox and Chicken Licken. Then came that wonderful story *Wild Lone* by 'BB' – Denys Watkins-Pitchford. It is a privilege to have three of his original woodcuts as illustrations in this book. Fiction turned to fact when the Cambridgeshire Foxhounds met at the pub next to the village school; our headmistress would troop us all out to watch as the extraordinary partnership

An original woodcut of a huntsman by 'BB'.

prepared to hunt. I loved the horses and the hounds, but all day long, as the distant sounds of the horn floated into the classroom, I hoped that the foxes would get away. To our headteacher the meet at The Hoops did not create a problem. It was part of the rural year, alongside nature walks, the harvest festival and picking wild flowers for the village flower show. Hunting was natural, it was normal, it was part of country life.

But where were the foxes? On walks around the farm and in games around the parish we never saw a fox. Although we did not see them, stories of their craft and cunning abounded. One day a degree of reality dawned. Dead and dying hens greeted my father when he went to collect the eggs. By the time I saw them they had been laid in a row outside the hen-house. Some were just mauled and dead. Some were headless – a well-known sign of a visit by a fox. On a small, traditional mixed farm it was a real loss.

But despite this I still did not see a fox. The hunt continued to meet in the village once a year. There must have been some foxes about, but we never saw them. The foxhounds even hunted our land if scent or inclination brought them to our side of the parish – that is until a gate was broken and not repaired, so they were banned from setting foot, hoof or paw on any of our fields. Our vet was one of the Masters and it took him a new gate and much sweet talking before my father finally relented.

The reason for the shortage of foxes was quite simple, and it extended to most of Britain. Along the High Street, and in cottage gardens all over the parish, people kept hens so they could produce their own eggs. At the first sign of a fox, snares would be set and shotguns left at the ready to deliver 'lead aspirins'. As a result foxes were very few and far between. Crows and magpies received a similarly hostile welcome from all poultry keepers – to see a magpie was a rare and memorable occasion. Before myxamatosis devastated the rabbit population, and before the banning of the gin trap in 1954, rabbit trappers also accounted for wandering foxes as a fox visiting a rabbit snare-line reduced the trappers' potential income. Any fox avoiding those hazards had gamekeepers to worry about.

I did not see my first fox until I was well into my teens. It was in cover on the far bank of the brook. I was so astonished, and thrilled, that the image lingers in my memory even now, as clear as if it were yesterday. Since then I have seen hundreds of foxes and I get a surge of enjoyment on every occasion. They are beautiful animals – intelligent, keen, alert – and it is easy to see how they arouse the Bambi

THE HUNTING GENE

reaction in those who do not understand the complete cycle of life and death, both inside nature and outside nature. Since the day I first saw one I have watched them hunting along hedgerows, pouncing on voles in long grass, attempting to pluck low-flying pigeons out of the air, stalking rabbits and stealing our poultry. I have written a book about them – *A Fox's Tale* – and even a poem:

> Eyes searching the darkness
> For light and movement, slow enough
>   for death,
> Ears piercing the stillness
> For sound and padded since, the
>   whereabouts of life.
> Nose scenting the air
> For the hidden patterns of the night.
> The fox returns.
>
> He stands alert, surveying time,
> Head cocked, enquiring, listening –
> Brush combed by a sudden breath of wind;
> Beauty and knowledge are combined with speed,
> In ruthless harmony
> The fox moves on.
>
> He passes into darkness
> As cloud restores the night;
> A pheasant calls in warning, of footsteps that bring fear;
> The air sighs.
> Beneath the trees a shadow hunts, time freezes and a rabbit dies;
> A dog barks as moonlight falls on bloodstained grass.
> The fox has gone.

I have had foxes as pets too and they have been a joy. Inevitably, as with all animals taken from the wild, my foxes have created periods of great happiness and times of intense sorrow. I have cried bucketsful of tears for them, but I am glad that they have been part of my life. I have vowed never to have another animal taken or rescued from the wild. If a lost or injured cub appears I expect I shall change my mind, just as I did two years ago when two distressed badger cubs were found lost and hungry in a prairie field of wheat. I fed Bill and Ben up almost too well and they escaped before they were ready for release back into the wild. I hope they survived.

Since the days of fox scarcity, their numbers have recovered in a quite astonishing way. With most people now buying their eggs from shops and supermarkets and with few rabbit trappers trying to make a living, two huge pressures have been taken off the fox. In addition to this gamekeepers' numbers have tumbled: from 22,000 in England, Wales and Scotland in 1900 to 4000 today. Consequently the fox has few enemies and little competition over huge areas of Britain. In a truly wild world the fox population would be limited by the natural food available; something approaching a 'natural balance' would be achieved. This balance would be struck during winter, when the very old, the very young and the inexperienced would find it hard to survive because of the limits on food.

Now, however, there is little winter hardship. There are dustbins, bird tables, food put out for livestock and powerful machinery allowing cultivation in January and February – providing the foxes with supplies of worms – mean that winter mortality has plummeted. To make matters even better an estimated 220 million vertebrates are killed on our roads each year, from red deer to wrens, giving scavenging foxes a high-protein diet of fresh meat the whole year through. This supply of good meat is available to crows and magpies too, allowing high populations of these predators and scavengers to survive the winter. In a natural balance, our declining songbirds and endangered farmland birds would start their breeding seasons in the spring with few predators to worry them; now as they try to breed predator numbers are

A fox cub emerges from woodland.

unnaturally high. In many areas fox numbers have never been higher both in country and in town; and the 'predator pit' has become an important reality for many endangered species. The more food there is available, the smaller each fox territory needs to be; so the population soars.

The high density of urban foxes leads to another wildlife evasion. Townspeople complain that foxes are living under their garden sheds, that their cats are being killed and eaten, that fox earths are unhygienic and cause a health hazard; then foxes are cage-trapped in large numbers, before being transported into the countryside and released. In other words, townspeople refuse to accept the responsibility for the management of their own foxes and simply pass their problem on to other people and to other foxes. Foxes are territorial. Urban foxes dumped in the countryside get a hostile reception from the resident foxes; they get a hostile reception from farmers, conservationists and gamekeepers too, and many semi-tame animals are shot and snared as they wander around strange territory.

For years various organisations have denied that the dumping of urban foxes takes place, although the fact of fox release has been obvious to those of us who live in the countryside. In 1999 a wildlife liaison group in Cambridgeshire actually advertised for a friendly farmer, with a farm of about three hundred acres, who would allow fox releases to take place on his land. Apart from the fact that a farm of three hundred acres would only provide part of a single fox's territory, resulting in the released foxes immediately moving into the surrounding area – why are town foxes moved anyway? Country people are repeatedly being told that foxes are harmless and need no control. If this is really the case why do urban local authorities, animal refuges and private individuals capture their own foxes and move them into the country? If foxes really are as harmless as the Bambi lovers suggest, perhaps the answer is that country people should trap their foxes for release into the towns?

One of the oddest cases of fox release occurred at the RSPB's Minsmere reserve in Suffolk when a member of the public released a family of almost full-grown cubs in the car park. All the RSPB will say is that shortly afterwards the fox cubs 'disappeared'.

Another strange incident occurred in Croydon in 1997. A mother saw a fox on her pram, in the garden, looking at her small baby. Anti-fox hysteria filled the tabloid press for a few brief days. Ironically, although the fox was almost certainly just investigating the pram and the baby was quite safe, all manner of dangers and foxy threats were built into the incident by the very people and journalists who normally argue that foxes cause no damage to farm stock or wildlife – babies are obviously different. The incident was resolved when the local council announced that the fox had been safely caught in a cage-trap, described as being 'humane' – of course. Immediately the fox shock/horror story was forgotten – it was yesterday's news.

I phoned the council, however. 'What happened to the fox?' I asked. At first I was told that it had been released into the countryside. 'Why?' I asked. 'If a fox is considered a danger to urban babies – isn't it likely to be a danger to country babies?' Suddenly the story changed. The fox hadn't been released at all, because it might be dangerous. 'Then if it is dangerous,' I asked. 'has it been killed or are you going to kill it?' Over a period of three weeks I tried to get a straight answer from a number of officials about the fate of one urban fox; I tried in vain. When country people openly control foxes they are criticised. When one urban fox caused a problem a shroud of secrecy and misinformation was floated into place.

Misinformation is at the heart of the hunting controversy. Many urban opponents of fox control, having already forgotten the story of the Croydon pram, insist that foxes cause no damage or no problem and rarely kill. Anybody with no knowledge of foxes would assume from that propaganda that the red fox's main diet is cucumber sandwiches and profiteroles.

The truth is that the fox will eat whatever is available in season and whatever takes its fancy out of season. It is a mixture of killer, carnivore, scavenger and omnivore. It will eat hens, pheasants, lapwings, curlews and avocets; as well as rats, mice, small deer, hares, lambs and even reindeer calves. In addition it will eat worms, beetles, blackberries, plums and apples – evidence of these delicacies has been found in the droppings of foxes. As well as all these, my pet foxes have all been extremely partial to sponge cakes and chocolate.

I had my first pet cub, Cassius, when he was only a few days old and his eyes were still shut. He was born at least ten feet from the ground in a hole in the trunk of an old elm. He grew into a beautiful animal, alert, playful, graceful and greedy. From a standing position he could jump onto the sideboard without knocking anything off, just to see if chocolate was being hidden on top of it. He was never fed raw meat, yet as he grew he would stalk and attack any living thing smaller than he was – and many ducks and hens much bigger. At first he mauled and then he killed, and once he had got a dead hen in his mouth he would put his ears back flat, and he would squeal and bite rather than give up his prize. Although he had been brought up in exactly the same way as a puppy, and indeed with a puppy, the urge to kill was deep within him and could not be controlled. Neither could he be house trained. He finally ran off at the season of the year when the air is full of romantic scents for young dog foxes and he was shot in a neighbouring village. Again my tear count ran into thousands.

Another pet fox, a rescued cub, grew into a superb specimen. Sidney was large and had a wonderful coat. He too escaped and disappeared. Early one morning all the hens in the deep-litter shed were becoming hysterical. Rinty the Labrador went mad at one of the hen-houses and I caught a fox in the beam of my torch under the shed. I carefully lined it up in the sights of my .22 rifle and was about to shoot when it moved. It had a blue collar; it was Sidney, obviously surviving very well in the wild. I allowed him to escape and never saw him again.

Many opponents of hunting give misinformation on fox damage to livestock, either as a result of ignorance or as a deliberate effort to mislead. They claim that if a fox raids a

Rusty, the author's pet vixen.

hen-house 'it is the farmer's fault' – for not having a fox-proof shed. The truth is that a fox is very resourceful and if it sets its mind on poultry, sooner or later it will succeed. We have had some foxes pull out wooden boards to get into the hens and others have squeezed through the smallest gaps in windows to get a free meal. Many people advocate free-range hens; we have had hens, ducks and a goose taken in broad daylight. If hens and guinea fowl roost up trees at night they are still not safe; we have had hens last seen perching in plum trees fifteen feet above the ground disappear. Old country tales suggest that a fox will walk in circles beneath a tree containing roosting hens or pheasants, and sooner or later a bird will get dizzy and fall to the ground. It is a fact that a now-retired RSPB warden once saw a fox chasing its own tail and behaving in a peculiar way, until an inquisitive blackbird ventured too close and became an instant snack.

Fox problems come in spasms. On the farm we will have periods of time when foxes do not bother us, either with the poultry or the lambs, although from the smell and droppings it is clear that they visit the farm regularly. Then we will get a spate of trouble: an old fox finds easy pickings; or a fox simply acquires a taste for poultry or a first lamb, taken while the ewe is busy giving birth to a second.

The odd hen would not be missed – although when a fox gets into the hen-house and just takes one bird, it inevitably picks one of our few guinea fowl. I have no doubt that, just like us, individual foxes have dietary preferences. Unfortunately, however, foxes may also engage in surplus killing, and a whole hen-house can be wiped out in a single night. Some scientists say that this is the fox killing to store food for the future. Foxes do store food for the future – we often find hen's eggs buried in the garden – but surplus killing is usually done for fun.

Surplus killing is not a trait limited to foxes. Mink are notorious mass murderers and even birds of prey will kill for fun when food is plentiful. When redwing and fieldfare migration is in full swing along the Scottish valleys in the autumn, peregrines have been seen to stoop and kill after they have just fed. Well-fed kestrels hovering over a harvest field will kill mice and voles and simply leave the bodies of their victims. A friend who is a safari operator in Kenya, Joe Cheffings, has seen lions that have just fed kill a wildebeeste that has had the misfortune to wander into the pride. The lions then used the body as a toy, rolling on it in lethargic play before leaving it for the vultures.

I suppose some scientists would call all this killing 'hunting behaviour induced by an audio-visual response mechanism' rather than 'fun'. They do not appear to have any behavioural jargon for 'fun' as it applies to foxes. I have seen a vixen and cubs chasing hens and throwing the fluttering bodies up into the air, like a bitch and her pups with a ball or a rag. They were having a wonderful time and there were dead and dying hens everywhere.

The worst case of surplus killing I have come across involved the CRT's tenant farmer. Tim Scott had ninety-three juvenile ducks and geese killed in a single night and only one was taken and eaten. On another occasion he lost forty ducks and twenty hens inside a hen-house, including five rare red-breasted geese and five Hawaiian geese – one of them a favourite hand-reared goose called Jenny. The value of the killed ducks and geese lost in a single night was well over £1000. He has never replaced his lost birds; in a non-gamekeeping and non-fox-hunting area the risks and the threat are too great. At one time the area was hunted by the Cambridgeshire Foxhounds, then came the M11 motorway and hunting became too dangerous. With hunting gone the foxes were not pushed away from the farms and barking dogs now have little deterrent value. In fact on one occasion I looked out of my bedroom window to see our then Labrador Tinker straining on her chain, barking hysterically, with a fox simply sitting ten feet away, watching with interest.

For the purposes of this book I could have used a variety of pictures of birds and beasts – adults and young; wild, tame and domesticated – killed by foxes, to illustrate both the destruction and the threat, 365 days every year. I decided, however, not to include shots of dead animals; the hunting argument is already distorted by the absurd films and photographs of dead animals used by hunting's opponents. I did not want to follow along the same emotive trail. It has often puzzled me. If pictures of dead animals are always shown when the BBC and other channels cover hunting; why are shots of slaughterhouses not shown in

A roe deer kid – at risk from foxes.

cookery programmes, or pictures of clear-fell forestry used when discussing household furniture and DIY?

Some fox apologists claim that foxes will not take lambs, stating that even newly born lambs are too big. The fact that foxes take adult brown hares, considerably faster and heavier than lambs, makes a total mockery of this claim. While researching for this book I came across an instance of a fox being seen with a roe deer kid – about the same size as a lamb.

THE HUNTING GENE

If a fox will take a young deer, why won't it take a lamb? Fortunately for the roe deer kid in question, a forester intervened and rescue followed; despite its ordeal the kid made a good recovery in a wildlife refuge.

Alan Smith, who with his wife Tilly keeps reindeer in the Cairngorms, lost an even bigger reindeer calf. A few years ago a fox killed a three-week-old calf weighing twenty-four pounds, and another calf was taken this year. Despite having large antlers, the cow reindeer actually defend their calves with their front feet, by stamping. A fox will try to lure the cow away from the calf and then dart in for the kill.

The high fox population is a major contributor to annual damage to wildlife. Because of a combination of foxes, crows and magpies, lapwings have almost ceased to breed in Wales and there are numerous ground-nesting birds that are in serious trouble because of foxes. It was in Wales too that foxes virtually put paid to Britain's largest colony of its rarest tern, the roseate tern. Until 1990 nearly two hundred pairs nested on a small island off the coast of Anglesey. Then a mixture of fox and peregrine harassment forced the birds to leave – they now breed in southern Ireland. In days gone by when predation pressures increased, birds and animals could move to neighbouring areas in the hope that suitable habitats away from problems could be found. In over-crowded, over-populated and over-developed Britain this is no longer possible. If a lapwing or a roseate tern flies over the next hilltop there is now a new town, a motorway, a golf course or a marina preventing respite. For the roseate tern the only solution was to fly across the Irish Sea.

Over recent years the Game Conservancy has carried out research that shows conclusively that fox control helps both the brown hare and the English partridge. On his Breckland farm Chris Knights is proud of having the highest density of stone curlews in Britain, because of a combination of population management (fox control) and habitat management. He has no doubt that without any fox control he would have no stone curlews, ringed plovers, lapwings or even partridges.

Nearby, Aubrey Buxton (now Lord Buxton) lives on the Norfolk farm once owned and written about by Henry Williamson, author of *Tarka the Otter*. He is a naturalist of international standing, and

A Cairngorm reindeer calf with its mother.

114

when running Anglia Television he started the famous *Survival* series, which helped to spread the wildlife and conservation message world-wide. He also helped to start the careers of many now-famous wildlife photographers and film-makers – including Chris Knights.

Three years ago Aubrey Buxton realised a conservation dream. Behind the seawall between Stiffkey and Blakeney he created thirty acres of freshwater marsh. In three years he has attracted just over thirty pairs of avocets and in the last breeding season they successfully reared over thirty chicks, not one, as far as is known, being lost to predation. Again, he believes that in addition to providing the right habitat predator control is one of the reasons for his success.

A bittern in danger of being bitten.

Avocets are also now breeding inland for the first time in the Ouse Washes at the Welney reserve of the Wildfowl and Wetland Trust. In 1999, the fourth year of breeding, over twenty pairs successfully reared between thirty and thirty-five young. In 1997 there was failure when foxes ate all the eggs. The Wildfowl and Wetland Trust is one of the few conservation bodies both honest enough and sensible enough to be quite open about the need to control foxes, mink, crows and magpies.

One bird receiving much publicity at the moment because of its endangered status is the bittern. The bittern loves reed beds and efforts are being made to create more suitable habitats for it. However, none of the major conservation bodies running high-profile campaigns to save it can be heard saying publicly that foxes and mink also like reed beds. One of the reasons for the demise of the bittern is not loss of habitat but loss of life; mink and foxes see them in a slightly different light from conservationists – yes, the bittern is getting bitten. At the RSPB's reserve at Minsmere, one of the last places for breeding bitterns in Britain, the first four clutches of eggs in 1999 were taken by mammalian predators. Two were taken by mink and the culprits for the other two were not confirmed. (Foxes?) Fortunately successful trapping followed and, out of eight more nests, six were successful and thirteen young fledged.

One Norfolk wildlife warden has no doubt about the importance of controlling foxes. Regrettably his name cannot be given, for even some organisations that demand predator control on their reserves want to keep the fact away from their subscription- and donation-paying members. He says:

Vulnerable nesting birds. ABOVE LEFT: *An avocet.* ABOVE RIGHT: *a common tern.*

Personally I believe that predator control is the most important thing we do. If we did not control foxes on this reserve we would not have anything, and that would be true on all the major nature reserves along the North Norfolk coast. English Nature, the Norfolk Wildlife Trust, the National Trust and the RSPB all control predators, they have to – it is good management. I have known a fox take as many as twelve avocet clutches in a single night, and on Scolt Head a few years ago tern numbers were decimated by foxes. I use a mixture of shooting and snaring – checking my snares twice a day. If ever snaring is banned we will be in serious trouble here. Because of the vegetation shooting can be difficult. In fact it is so difficult that wounding rates can be as high as 50 per cent. On this reserve I spend more time looking on the ground for signs of unwelcome visitors than looking in the air for birds.

His reference to Scolt Head is interesting. For years the island, owned by the National Trust, was famous for its tern colonies. It was managed by a traditional Norfolk countryman from a gamekeeping background. When he retired Scolt Head management was 'modernised' by ecologists and experts in 'environmental management'. Foxes ran riot and for several years the tern colonies, among the most spectacular in Britain, were empty. Now that predator control is again being undertaken by a Norfolk man, from a traditional gamekeeping family, foxes are being targeted and the terns have almost returned to their former numbers.

When things were at their worst, the West Norfolk Foxhounds volunteered to go over to Scolt Head to find the offending foxes and mark their earths, but political correctness was

North Norfolk tern colonies have been disrupted by foxes.

put before conservation need and the offer was refused. When a fox problem arrived at the Peakirk Wildfowl Trust, just outside Peterborough, causing the loss of wildfowl and flamingos valued at over £3000, a similar offer was made by the Fitzwilliam hounds. The offer was accepted and ten hounds (five couple) quickly solved the problem.

Because the fox threat is so obvious to countryman, farmer and practical conservationist alike, the argument should not be about the need for fox control, but about how to apply fox control. Those who claim that the fox does no damage are speaking out of almost total ignorance or political mischief, or they are doing it simply to attack country people – which is a subtle form of racism.

There are numerous ways of killing foxes, both legal and illegal – snaring, trapping, poisoning, gassing, shooting and hunting. It is estimated that at the beginning of each spring there are about 240,000 adult foxes, producing 425,000 cubs. About 100,000 are killed on the roads each year, 80,000 are shot, possibly up to 50,000 are killed using terriers, 30,000 are snared, 10,000 are probably killed using lurchers and about 16,000 are killed by hunts. Surprisingly, on the website of the League Against Cruel Sports there is a peculiar reinforcement of the anti-fox-hunting argument: 'If fast running dogs such as greyhounds or lurchers were used to hunt foxes, the whole thing would be over in seconds, but then there would be no "sport".' This makes the League's opposition to hare coursing very hard for me to follow – killing foxes with lurchers is evidently humane, but killing hares with lurchers is inhumane? It confirms the muddled logic of many of hunting's opponents.

Gassing and poisoning are both illegal, but out of desperation some people still do both. In my view these methods are cruel and indiscriminate and may kill other species of wildlife. Astonishingly, at one time some opponents of hunting advocated gassing. It was a case of 'If you can't see a death it becomes acceptable.'

Snaring may cause suffering; and if the snare breaks while still attached, horrendous injuries may result. In both snaring and cage-trapping stress levels can be high, with the animals injuring themselves as they struggle for release. Any animal in the wild attempts to put a 'flight distance' between itself and a perceived threat. Once it feels safe and the flight distance has been achieved, flight will cease. The fox, the hare or the deer will stop running and stress will be minimal. While running is in progress stress will be small; it will only be in the last few seconds, when the animal realises that the flight distance cannot be maintained, that a degree of *stress* may turn to *distress*. All wild animals in cages will feel distress at some stage.

With shooting the risks of wounding are obvious. I have seen the body of a running fox jolt at the impact of a 12 bore shot, but it has kept running and escaped. What follows can be gangrene and a long slow death, or partial recovery and a fox that finds it easier to raid farmyards than hunt wild food.

Wounding rates for foxes vary considerably depending on the skill and the experience of the shooter. I believe that in the hands of experts, the wounding rate for shotguns is about 25 per cent and some gamekeepers will admit that the rate with high-velocity rifles is as high as 15 per cent. Consequently amid all the talk about cruelty and humanity, barbarism and compassion, I believe that for the fox the method involving the least stress is hunting with dogs. The fox is either caught and killed or it gets away – it is as simple as that. The pre-capture pursuit interval, when stress may turn to distress, is about two minutes' long and the actual kill is almost instantaneous.

Twink Allen, professor of equine reproduction at Cambridge University Veterinary School, believes that there is little stress in hunting:

> It is difficult to define stress. There is stress and distress. Stress is when we exert ourselves physically and we become increasingly stressed, but we adapt to it and put up with that type of stress. Similarly foxes and deer are well adapted physiologically to be able to run and evade being caught. They cope with the stress well. In a hunt, as one animal chases the other, I am confident in my own mind that the fox is not more stressed than the horse or hound until very close to the time when it is going to be captured – then it turns to distress. The same happens to an over-ridden horse who is at the end of his tether, as at the end of a long steeplechase or Grand National; the point must be reached where stress becomes distress. But I do not believe the hunted animal feels distress until very close to the end because it always thinks it can get away. It maybe lasts thirty seconds, but even then you cannot put human thoughts and feelings into wild animals. As a vet, I can justify hunting easily. The level of stress is so infinitesimal compared with the distress inflicted on animals by humans, and inflicted

on animals by other animals in the wild; by comparison hunting is utterly and totally immaterial.

In my experience the least cruel and sadistic people are farmers and hunting people who know and understand animals. We should also remember that the horse and hound are both athletically specialist pack animals, and they enjoy doing what they are doing in a pack, whenever they get the chance to do it. The fox on the other hand is a loner. He is an athletically competent, clever loner. He knows how to hunt and goes backwards and forwards and plays with the hounds – I've seen it. And he knows about scent; when it is a good or bad scenting day. On a bad scenting day he messes about and on a good scenting day he goes like hell.

Some claim that it is unnatural to hunt or pursue a carnivore with a carnivore. In the wild many species of carnivores dislike rivals and will chase them and kill them if possible. After George Adamson was murdered, his last three lion cubs were flown out of northern Kenya and rehabilitated in Botswana. Their first kill was a leopard.

Dogs have a natural antipathy to foxes. Our farm dogs have never been taught to dislike foxes; they do so naturally, running around growling with their hackles up whenever a fox has been near the hen-houses. Bramble would chase foxes enthusiastically, running alongside them, yapping furiously – a big dog fox was about his size. Because foxes are small and delicate it is quick and easy for a large dog to kill them. One of my foxes, Rusty, was killed by a dog in the next village. She was virtually unmarked apart from two small abrasions on her neck. I was as devastated as usual, but it was clear that she had not suffered.

Similarly, as I returned home from the farm one day Bramble and Rinty the farm Labrador tore into a neighbour's garden. They had caught the scent of a fox and by the time I had run a mere forty yards to sort out the commotion an old vixen lay dead – killed in an instant. Growling, Rinty then picked her up again across her back and shook her as he would a rat. The old vixen had no teeth and had obviously been starving; the two dogs had done her a favour and she had died in an instant.

In exactly the same way the death of a hunted fox is just as quick. The leading hound will grab it across the back of the neck, and it will be over in a flash. Alternatively all the hounds will dive in, like terriers on a rat, and it will be over in a fraction of a second. It will not be pretty to watch, but it will be very quick.

119

THE HUNTING GENE

Because death is so quick, and because I have seen it happen so cleanly, I find the attitude of the RSPCA difficult to follow. It seems to have a fixation on disembowelment. In 1996 the RSPCA ran an advertisement featuring a disembowelled fox, omitting to say that it had been shot. As a consequence it fell foul of the Advertising Standards Agency. In August 1999, Rachel Newman, head of prosecutions for the RSPCA, wrote to *The Daily Telegraph* claiming that hunted foxes died through 'disembowelment'. For this to happen the lead hound would have to catch a fox from behind, release it to turn it on its back, seize it once more, and then release it again in order to bite the stomach – without being bitten itself. All this is of course nonsense. My vixen Rusty and the old vixen next door showed how dogs kill foxes. Why does the RSPCA continue its emphasis on disembowelment? In her letter, Rachel Newman spoke of veterinary post-mortem reports confirming her claim. When I phoned to ask if I could have copies of the reports I was told that I could not have them as they were 'confidential'.

What puzzles me is, if the RSPCA is so concerned about the death of animals, why does it not do more to campaign against real animal abuse? Where are the full-page adverts exposing the outrage of the closure of slaughterhouses and the great distances animals now have to travel from farm to abattoir? For humanely killed, stress-free animals, slaughter needs to take place as close to the farm as possible. Under European directives the reverse has happened; with unnecessary closure, due to ridiculous hygiene regulations and unacceptable costs, farm animals are now being transported many miles to die.

The RSPCA has produced a charter for animal welfare standards, but this does not include a limit on the distances animals may travel. It gives a time limit of eight hours. This means that animals can be transported hundreds of miles and still be sold under the RSPCA's 'Freedom Food' label, a system set up to improve animal welfare. It is beyond my comprehension that a meat-monitoring system designed to protect animals can allow long and gruelling journeys.

But there is worse to come: the killing of Britain's 800 million broiler fowl. Up to 60,000 can be dispatched in a day in one slaughterhouse alone. The birds are shackled, hung upside down on a moving line and dunked into a water bath containing a submerged electrode. Some are stunned, some are killed and up to 2 per cent – 1200 birds – may remain conscious. The RSPCA's *Welfare Standards for Chickens* states: 'Birds that fail to be properly stunned must be humanely slaughtered before entering the scalding tank.' Strange, that: I thought killing by using the 'electrically alive stunning bath' was supposed to be humane. With this method, it seems that some birds are humanely killed *twice*.

Welfare Standards goes on to say:

> The most reliable indicator that a bird is properly stunned by the low-voltage method is the electroplectic fit. The characteristics of this condition are: neck arched with head directed vertically; open eyes; wings held close to the body; rigidly extended legs; and constant rapid body tremors. The physical conditions of the electroplectic fit are shorter lasting and less profound when cardiac arrest is induced at stunning.

120

There is still more; the RSPCA instructions continue:

> Carotid arteries and jugular veins must be effectively severed using a ventral cut. This must be checked by the appointed member of staff, who must be given sufficient time to sever the blood vessels manually, if necessary. No more that 10 seconds must elapse between stunning and neck cutting.
>
> All birds must be checked to ensure that they are dead before entering the scalding tank. Chickens must not be immersed in a scalding tank or plucked until at least 90 seconds have elapsed since the major blood vessels in their necks have been severed.

These birds can then be sold as Freedom Food, approved by the organisation that finds fox-hunting immoral.

There is no doubt that when fox-hunting began, it was regarded purely as a sport. In the fourteenth century some fox-hunting took place, but its popularity did not increase much until the 1800s and it was not until the nineteenth century that the great fox-hunting boom took off. For those who 'hunted to ride' it was regarded as bringing in 'the golden age' as it offered far more adrenalin surges than hare-hunting. The attraction was summed up completely by Jorrocks when he said; 'hunting is all that's worth living for – all time is lost wot is not spent in 'unting – it is like the hair we breathe – if we have it not we die – it's the sport of kings, the image of war without its guilt, and only five-and-twenty per cent its danger'.

Fox control was not an issue; sometimes fox numbers were so low that animals had to be imported from France to ensure good sport. Conservation was not an issue either; the countryside was at its most pastoral with wealthy land owners and newly rich industrialists adding to the rural scene with opulent houses surrounded by parkland and whole new landscapes created and manicured with vision – or vulgarity, depending on their outlook. With the advent of the railways this rural world was opened up. The aristocracy and the *nouveau riche* flooded in to the great shire counties where hunting provided them with thrills,

spills, status and celebrity. When the enclosures arrived the thrills and spills were intensified; hunting country became criss-crossed with quickthorn hedges and a new tradition was born – tally-ho and the devil take the hindmost.

Over vast tracts of land hunting dominated the landscape; spinneys and woods were maintained especially to harbour foxes and new coverts (pronounced 'covers') were planted to attract and hold foxes. Hedges were seen as challenging jumps; for the fainthearted hunt jumps were put in place to allow greater safety and improved access. Rutland and Leicestershire became the Mecca of the fox-hunting set and other top hunts developed in Warwickshire, Oxfordshire and Gloucestershire. Farmers' hunts followed and gradually fox-hunts covered the whole country. In many areas fox-hunting replaced hare-hunting in popularity. Social boundaries were stretched too, until as late as 1962 when the Banwen Miners Hunt was formed. Today the hunting traditions of Wales remain both strong and thriving.

Currently there are an astonishing 196 packs of foxhounds in Britain, 38 in Ireland, 161 in the USA, 29 in New Zealand, 23 in Australia, 12 in Canada and another handful sprinkled throughout the world, including 1 in India and 2 in South Africa.

A sport born out of privilege and wealth gradually became available to anybody who could spare the time and the money. This is not simply a meaningless cliché, for in virtually every hunt in the country boundaries and barriers have been lowered. As a boy I perceived my local fox-hunt to be the preserve of the rich – just as I imagined writing was the preserve of the privileged Oxbridge graduate with contacts. Yes, the Cambridgeshire Hunt did include large land owners, solicitors and accountants; but now it also has working farmers, housewives and country people who simply like hounds, horses and foxes as well as the thrill of the chase. One of its recent Masters was a non-riding farmer who became actively involved only after he retired from village football. He was a good player and for many years we enjoyed kicking lumps out of each other in opposing teams on Saturday afternoons. He became a Master after the hunt had experienced considerable harassment from hunt saboteurs, nearly all of them urban and some with sinister neo-Nazi or anarchist backgrounds. At that time, with the Cambridgeshire Foxhounds being targeted, it was a courageous act for a non-riding farmer to take on a Mastership. 'I wanted to make a stand for hunting, for country people and for the countryside,' he says. 'I've always enjoyed watching hunting and people should be free to do it; it's their choice, it is as simple as that.'

From the very early days of hunting the meet was a spectacle enjoyed by all. Before the age of electricity, television and the Internet any break in routine provided interest and entertainment. A meet of the foxhounds was eagerly anticipated in every village and considered to be a major event. One of the few remaining old inhabitants of my parish was born in the village in 1910. She left school at 14 to go into service and remembers the meets with pleasure:

> We loved it when the foxhounds met at The Hoops. Nearly the whole village would turn out. I loved the dogs, the horses and the red coats. There wasn't much to do in those days and we enjoyed it. We accepted it as part of the village year. There wasn't

The Heythrop hounds – a fine sight.

all the fuss about it like today – it's ridiculous. We had a few hens, but I didn't see a real fox until I saw your cubs. I suppose the people who did it were rich – we hadn't got any money, I still haven't, but we enjoyed it and wouldn't miss it.

With many opponents of hunting it is the rich 'toff' image that has stuck; at the root of their objections is not animal welfare or an affection for the fox, but old-fashioned envy and class hatred. As I write the truth of this is apparently being confirmed by a left-wing Labour MP from Central London who wants to become Mayor of London. He says that he is determined to ban fox-hunting, although how fox-hunting affects the day-to-day life of Londoners is a mystery.

It seems to be beyond the perspicacity of these self-created stereotypes to notice that football has moved in the opposite direction from hunting. Once soccer was an almost totally working-class sport; now to get a prime season ticket to watch Manchester United or Chelsea at home and also watch their away matches is more expensive than joining *two* good fox-hunts.

In fact my most disappointing sporting memory involves cruelty, barbarity and football. I was in Zimbabwe on Wednesday 29 May 1985. Along with a variety of races and colours

THE HUNTING GENE

I went to my hotel's television room to watch the European Cup Final between Liverpool and Juventus. All we could see was hordes of Liverpool football thugs rioting at the Heysel Stadium in Brussels. It was ironic that there I was in the middle of the 'dark continent', in a country that had just experienced years of civil war, watching British yobbo violence on television. The Africans were dumbfounded. I sank lower and lower into my chair. For the first time in my life I was ashamed to be British. Numerous people were killed and injured. Every year private property is damaged, people are maimed and even killed because of football. Are the urban MPs calling for a ban on professional football? Despite the money in football now being more important than the ball, and despite football having become the new opiate of the people, urban socialist MPs prefer to attack fox-hunting, a subject they know little about and never come in contact with.

To see the hunting gene in action at one of Britain's top shire packs, I chose the Heythrop Foxhounds for no other reason than that on one winter's day at dusk, between Stow-on-the-Wold and Chipping Norton, I was suddenly surrounded by hounds, horses and mud-splattered coats as I was making for the West Country. The horses and hounds were steaming, the huntsman was smiling and one rider with side-whiskers and a frayed black coat was looking as if he had just ridden out of the pages of Surtees. He saw me and said,

An interested observer in Stow-on-the-Wold.

alluding to *One Man and His Dog*, 'We don't normally see you in these parts; have you lost your dog?' It was a wonderful scene; even my anti-hunting, leather-jacketed, vegetarian nephew enjoyed it.

Although most people have an opinion about hunting, it intrudes only infrequently into everyday life. I can only remember being engulfed by a hunt on two other occasions. One was years ago near Malmesbury, when I was going to see Elspeth Huxley, one of the CRT Founder-Trustees; the other was in the middle of writing this book. Entirely by accident I came across the opening meet of the Ledbury Foxhounds, which hunts around the Malvern Hills. On each occasion I have experienced a mixture of immediate sensations – excitement, tension, apprehension, fascination – and the back of my neck has tingled, all this in someone who does not hunt. It must be a stirring of the hunting gene.

The Heythrop hounds date back to 1835. Before then the area was hunted by the Duke of Beaufort, whose hunt dates back to 1750. The country covers the heart of the Cotswolds in Oxfordshire and Gloucestershire, running thirty miles east–west and fifteen miles north–south, with the country around Chipping Norton and Stow-on-the-Wold at its heart. The list of former Masters shows a sprinkling of lords, colonels, captains, majors and women – so the hunt is more progressive, and even less conservative, than the Labour Party. The membership is interesting too: a mixture of old money, new money and no money. There are family names that go back generations in banking, investing, tobacco and slaves; and new names of those with smaller pockets: a working farmer, a vet, an agricultural engineer, a national hunt jockey and a groom.

Roger Dancer, farmer and hunter.

For my first hunt, discretion took the better part of valour. I wanted to ride but, seeing the Cotswold countryside with acres of grass, much of it hemmed in with large hedges, I decided that I wanted to finish the book in one piece. Many years ago I had ridden with the Fernie Hunt for *The Daily Telegraph* and fallen off at virtually every jump. From the ground horses look very big, and on each occasion I had to find a fence to climb onto before I could remount. My four-wheel drive Daihatsu was a much safer proposition and was granted a special dispensation to follow the hunt – and the vehicles of the terrierman and fencemender – cross-country.

The meet was to begin in the grounds of a large house. At Lower Swell I asked the way. The cottages were of Cotswold stone and there were daffodils in the gardens; this was the final meet of the season. I heard the sound of hooves on the metalled road and a hunter came into view. He was a lone rider making his way to the meet, a man doing what he wanted to do and what he had been doing for the last sixty years. He was happy, content and whistling. 'Good morning' he said with a rolling Cotswold burr. He had side-whiskers, a frayed coat and he smiled; farmer Roger Dancer was on his way.

The meet was beyond my expectations; there were well over one hundred horses and people were milling around everywhere. There were black coats, red coats, green coats and no coats; there were large horses and small; there were smart clothes and comfortable ones. There was ostentation and modesty, greetings, laughter and hail-fellow-well-met. The anti-hunter's eye would have settled on a 'toff'; the hunting supporter's eye would have settled on

125

The traditional meet of the Heythrop.

a good countryman; my eyes settled on a close-knit but varied community within a community, a living culture surviving in a world that is rapidly becoming cultureless.

My companions for the day were varied: Joe, the hunt fencemender, a social commentator of wit and wisdom; Gary, the terrierman; Dessy, a retired farmworker, earthstopper and ex-terrierman, famous for having once shot himself in the foot; and Bill, a rat- and rabbit-catcher who really does live down Mousetrap Lane.

A pleasant lady's voice said, 'Hello, Robin'. I did not recognise her. It is strange how people in riding clothes seem to change in appearance and manner when sitting above you. It is easy to see how accusations of hunting snobbery arise; it stems from the psychology of the horse rider looking down and the pedestrian looking up. Fortunately Joe had the answer to female identification: 'You wait until they are galloping and standing up in their stirrups – then you recognise their arses.'

Anthony Adams, the huntsman, blew his horn and moved off with his hounds. We drove to the top of a valley side – a deep valley of old grass, sheep walks and gorse. It was like a photograph of a past scene before farming had been turned into a food production process, but this photograph had the smell of rising sap, the sound of birds singing and the warmth of sunlight.

Across the valley the hounds were working a fringe of woodland. Anthony was calling words of encouragement to his hounds. The large gaggle of followers moved along the edge of a field with the sound of hooves muffled by grass and shafts of sunlight picking out the few red coats. A robin sang and a 'saw-sharpener' (a great tit) called high up in the ivy. How is it possible to describe the sights, the sounds, the scents of the day without using clichés? It was a mixture of pageantry and symphony, a mingling of all the senses, given heightened awareness through a combination of anticipation and uncertainty. What would happen?

Would a fox die, would a horse fall, would a fallen rider fail to get up as the birds sang and the old countrymen watched?

This surely was the hunting gene in action, an ancient thread joining countless generations through thousands of years. The distant past was meeting the present through the red fox. The leaves of the trees were a dozen shades of green; a mistle thrush sang from the top of a leafless ash and a brimstone butterfly told of spring. We were standing, listening, watching, calculating – we were hunting too. Only the dulled and insensitive city mind would have failed to appreciate the rhythms of spirit and nature filtering through the moving, changing scene. A hound spoke, the pack was in full cry. We sped off.

Scent is one of the mysteries of hunting; it opens up a world that we cannot understand. Some days scent hangs thick and lingering and the fox has to depend on its wits. On other days it is thin and disperses on the wind; then animals that are hunted by scent know that they are almost safe.

Desmond Lane (Dessy), retired earthstopper and farmworker, 'sick' in the summer and fit in the winter?

There was silence, until suddenly hounds could be heard again. We tore on over farm tracks and suddenly we were with the 'field'. Horses were all around us, hooves were pounding and turf flying – the horses were alert, their ears forwards, they were part of the herd again. Some riders were travelling at an angle to us and we stopped. Horses jumped a hedge and galloped on across our track. One woman performed a delightful somersault almost in slow motion as her horse stopped suddenly, deciding that jumping was not for him. She was unhurt and suffered more from loss of dignity than loss of horse.

The hunt stopped with the hounds nowhere to be seen. Riders and horses were both sweating. Some riders stretched their legs, smoked or sipped from a flask; the horses stamped, snorted and shook themselves. Beanie Hughes, who runs a livery yard, undid her jacket button to flash her naked stomach to Joe – she was so hot she had taken off her shirt.

'I hope it gets even hotter,' said Dessy. 'We'll see something then.'

'Take no notice of him,' Joe said. 'We won't see him again until hunting starts in September – he's always sick in the summer and fit in the winter. What he wants is a good rub down with badger fat.'

THE HUNTING GENE

The wonders of badger fat were then discussed in great detail. Apparently at one time a few badgers were dug out each year for their fat. This was then rubbed onto the joints of race horses – there are several leading stables in the Cotswolds – and it was effective for rheumatism and arthritis too.

'It was so fine,' Joe continued, 'that if you put it in a glass jar in the evening, by morning it would have run straight through the bottom.'

'So it would,' agreed Dessy. It took me several days to realise that I had been taken, hook, line and sinker.

Joe heard hounds again and, anticipating action, we sped off to the corner of a large grass field, the vehicles bouncing as we went. Suddenly a new world opened up; there was a deep-sided valley with the Windrush meandering fast and clear through it. Who would imagine that water so clean and clear would flow through to the Thames and London, the complete antithesis of this small, hidden valley? Hounds were hunting in bracken and trees on the far side and three roe deer ran from their wood to stand looking and listening – the hounds ignored them completely, the scent message was wrong.

A hound spoke excitedly and soon the rest of the pack joined it. The hunt was on again and the deer retreated into the wood. Riders arrived at the gallop to be confronted by the steep grass drop. Determination, apprehension and discretion were the orders of the day. Some went straight down slowly and skilfully; some went slipping and sliding, their lack of

confidence being transmitted to their horses; and others rode on along the valley side, looking for somewhere less daunting. A small boy arrived on a pony; with no thought or fear he headed straight down almost at the gallop, his pony not putting a foot wrong. Fear comes with falls and injuries – from your own, or from witnessing the misfortune of others; the young boy had obviously experienced neither.

The horses and riders splashed through the river, a blackbird and a skylark sang, the deer moved into a clearing and the Windrush continued to flow towards the Thames. Joe again worked out the action and we moved up the valley and across to the other side. There was a breathtaking view of woods and grass, the winding Windrush, longhorn cows, recently pollarded willows, a buzzard mewing high above and one man and his dog putting up a fence.

The hounds were hunting in cover along the valley floor when somebody 'hollered', they had viewed the fox. From our grandstand view we could see the fox; it had broken cover and was running uphill over a grass field, after it came a stream of hounds in full cry. The fox was halfway over the fifty acres, totally exposed, and the hounds were gaining. Suddenly the fox changed direction by ninety degrees, accelerating as he began to run downhill, making for the corner of the field. Scent had been replaced by sight and the hounds were working hard, gaining with every stride. The fox's lead was visibly slipping – fifty yards, forty, thirty. I noticed I was holding my breath; I was about to see a kill – how would I feel? The distance became fifteen yards and the lead hound was closing; the corner of the field was approaching

The two illustrations here, and the one on the following page, show hounds hunting – an ideal subject for the sketching skill of the late Raoul Millais, third generation of a famous painting family.

– the fox leapt the cattle grid, clearing it by several feet, and disappeared into the wood. The hounds poured into the wood followed by the huntsman, the 'music' given a hollow echo by the density of the trees. They were hunting but not finding, and the fox got away; Reynard had lived up to his reputation once more. It is this uncertainly and spontaneity that make hunting so much more attractive to those who do it than drag-hunting, following an artificial trail. In 1977 when researching for *The Hunter and the Hunted* I went on a drag-hunt and found it tedious.

A HUNTING WE WILL GO

There were two fascinating features of this hunt. It was obvious that, although the fox was almost caught, it had remained alert and was still trying, but failing, to create its 'flight distance' until the wood was reached. It showed no signs of stress or distress, and if the leading hounds had caught it the end would have been very quick. For me there was no sense of shock or outrage; death would have arrived in an instant. What, it seems to me, the opponents of hunting cannot cope with is the fact that death would have been so visible. That is not hunting's problem – that is their problem, the problem of urban living and the problem of being separated from nature. Do they see the swallow take the fly, the fly-catcher take the butterfly, the roe deer take the rose, the mink take the dabchick? The answer appears to be no – they only see the hound take the fox.

It was odd that my companions all assumed the fox to be a *dog*; I cannot tell the difference in the wild between a dog fox and a vixen. Nor, according to hunting humour, could one Master.

'Where's the fox?' he asked an old rustic leaning on a gate.

'A large dog fox ran that way, Master,' came the answer.

'How do you know it was a dog fox?'

'As it jumped the gate I heard its balls rattle.'

The old rustic has a busy time with hunting humour. The Isle of Wight is famous for its red squirrels and for being fox-free for many years. When foxes were introduced, hunting switched from hare to fox. One day when the hounds had disappeared in full cry, the Master came across the old rustic, still leaning on his gate. 'Have you seen the hounds?'

'Yes, Master, they were running like the clappers that way, chasing the biggest red squirrel I've ever seen in my life.'

When a Master decided to hunt the pack, he foolishly included his favourite little bitch, although she was in season. All the hounds quickly vanished; again the old rustic was approached.

'Have you seen the hounds, my man?'

'Yes, Master, they were chasing a little bitch who was running like hell; a large dog fox was lying fourth.'

Hunting continued. Another fox ran along the top of a stone wall, narrowly missing a solitary hound coming in the opposite direction, before it disappeared into a spinney.

The landscapes of the Cotswolds are stunning; at every rise, fall and bend there was a new picture, of coverts,

The marbled white butterfly thrives in a hunting habitat.

meadows, valleys and gentle hills. There were lanes overhung with branches and dappled light; wide views patterned with hedgerows and woodland; long views given distance by hilltops, stone walls, of church towers and steeples. I was seeing hunting landscapes: old woodlands and newly planted coverts – a mixture of ancient and modern providing a living for wealth of wildlife in addition to the fox.

At a heap of large round bales, Gary the terrierman was called to see if a fox was present; there is no other practical way of flushing a fox. Terriers are attractive, courageous little dogs and they are used to flush or to hold a fox at bay underground if the farmer wants it killed. When the fox is in its earth the terrierman digs down to where his dog is barking and the fox is shot at close range. Professor Twink Allen says that the foxes involved show little signs of stress. They feel secure underground and the end is quick. Without hunting and the widespread interest in the land and foxes of the hunts, illegal terrier gangs would work, putting dogs into earths and rocky dens and letting the fox and sometimes several dogs fight it out. On a dark January night where would the police be? Where would the opponents of hunting be? It is their lack of knowledge that prevents them from seeing that a ban on hunting would increase fox distress.

From the roadside the hounds could see what was happening, standing on their hind legs by a stone wall watching the proceedings. No fox was flushed and after a few false hunts the day and the season were over. During the course of the season many foxes had been accounted for with no major mishap. Twice the hounds had made headlines, but on both occasions the incidents were blown up out of all proportion. On one occasion two riders rode through Bladen churchyard and the media was full of the possible damage to Churchill's grave. When I visited the

churchyard in midsummer there were no signs of damage and in fact no horse could have been ridden close to Churchill's grave without injuring itself.

Outrage also briefly flared when hounds went close to the main railway line. No mention was made of the fact that at every annual Gamekeepers' and Earthstoppers' Dinner of the Heythrop, a bus load of train drivers arrives and enjoys a good evening. They are sent meet cards and know exactly when the hounds may be near the line. The dinner I attended was very pleasant – the comedian was the local undertaker, who judging by his shape and colour looked in grave danger of becoming one of his own customers.

The anti-hunters missed one horrendous incident, however. Living on a quiet hillside is a well-known writer from London. She knew nothing about hunting before arriving in the Cotswolds and accepts it as part of country life. On one hunting day a hound ran into her kitchen, seized her newly baked sponge cake and continued on its way. She was greatly amused. Sadly this disgraceful example of hunt theft failed to make the BBC's main national news.

Oddington Ashes, owned by the Badminton Trust, shimmers with bluebells.

One problem is that on every hunting day all over the country, hunts are followed by opponents with video cameras and these people seem to have instant access to the BBC and ITV news. The real news is that after days of filming, miles of video tape and dozens of hunts the only horror recorded for weeks on end was two riders riding through a churchyard. If hunting really is cruel, why are real incidents not recorded weekly?

Another horror, apparently, over the same season was that the 196 British packs of hounds accidentally killed 6 cats. There are nearly nine million cats in this country, most of whom wander off the properties of their owners. It is estimated that domestic cats kill up to 250 million birds and animals a year and many of the birds are protected species. If anti-hunt protestors are genuinely worried about hounds occasionally being out of control – what about cats?

Once hunting stops, the hounds rest; they love hunting but it is physically demanding and May and June is a time of little activity. I went back to the south-facing slope of the little valley. It was alive with colour and birdsong; there were spotted orchids, yellow-wort, delicately scented wild roses, devil's bit scabious and banks of wild thyme. It would have made an ideal site for the reintroduction of the large blue butterfly. Along the Windrush there was marsh marigold, ragged robin and yellow iris; willow warblers; chiffchaffs, blackcaps and mistle

One of the many Cotswold Foxes.

thrushes sang and a roe deer browsed in the warm sunlight of a glade. A late orange tip butterfly flew, and almost crossed the path of an early marbled white; all this was on farmed land, hunted land, a naturalist's paradise and a complete contrast to farms where the only interest is production, yield, subsidy and financial return. Throughout the area there are old wet meadows, woods, birds, bees and flowers. Oddington Ashes, owned by the Badminton Trust, was shimmering with bluebells and in five minutes I saw all three types of British woodpecker. Some woods contain artificial earths; just as naturalists provide artificial badger setts and otter holts, some fox-loving hunters put down earths. This is not 'huntsmen breeding foxes' as tabloid newspapers claim. It is huntsmen providing a tempting artificial home if a fox wants to move in; and if a vixen with cubs gets killed by a car, then the cubs can be found, moved in and fed. Whatever the huntsman does is wrong in some eyes. If a vixen were killed and the cubs dug out and dispatched, the headline would be 'Huntsman kills defenceless cubs'. If the cubs are saved it becomes 'Huntsman rears cubs to hunt'.

Throughout the Heythrop country 'cover laying' takes place; the stems of hawthorn and blackthorn are half-cut, as in hedge-laying, and bent over. This provides warm, sheltered conditions for foxes, and even better nesting conditions for songbirds. This wealth of wildlife is not limited to Heythrop country. All over Britain hunting provides thousands of acres of woodland, wet meadow and hedgerow: from the woods and heaths of the Isle of Wight, with its dormice and red squirrels; to the thorn covers and clearings of north Yorkshire with their butterflies and wild flowers.

But hunting is about people and communities too, and the culture of hunting runs deeply through the Cotswolds. Throughout the Heythrop country there are nearly twenty-five pubs and restaurants featuring the fox, many displaying hunting prints and fox brushes which would never be seen in London. In Stow-on-the-Wold The Talbot pub even resurrects the old hound name of a thousand years ago. There are events throughout the year: the Heythrop point-to-point, the Game-keepers' and Earthstoppers' Dinner, the Game Fair, the hunt ball, the hedge-laying and stone-walling awards, the puppy show. There is rugby, soccer, cricket and skittles against other hunts and there are activities involving the hunt or the hunt supporters' club most weeks.

The people too are a great mixture, but because of the shared interests, friendships run deep. There is Sue Knock, a racehorse trainer who had the famous Senor el Buttrutti in her stable; Roger Dancer, the farmer with a beautiful farm; Robert Campbell, another farmer with hunting headlands (grass tracks) around all his fields. These were the forerunners of grass margins and conservation headlands, now accepted as good conservation and farming practice. As a result Robert's farm is full of birdsong and butterflies, skylarks and marbled whites. Past a churchyard containing tombstones showing two hunting deaths is the farm of Ted Townsend and his

The ancient word for 'hound' still in use in Stow.

brothers. Ted often wins the hedge-laying competitions and he attacks his hedge with skill and a craftsman's eye. Although he doesn't hunt he loves it when the riders, hounds and sometimes the fox go by. His farm lies just beyond the house where the football manager/pundit Jimmy Hill once lived. He too hunted with the Heythrop. For this book I wanted to talk to a currently well-known BBC sports commentator about his support for hunting. Sadly a message came back: 'He will not talk or be quoted in case it affects his position with the BBC.'

Tony is an old farmworker who has been earth-stopping for forty years. He stops the entrances of badger setts and fox earths before a hunt to keep the foxes above ground and the badgers below ground; at the end of a hunt the badger setts are opened up again. Liz and Johnny Wills are warm, friendly people who farm, while also having an estate in Scotland. Trigger is so called because he shoots injured and ill livestock to take to the kennels. He is a good, self-taught artist and, with his Cotswold accent, he loves night-clubbing in Oxford; it would be interesting to see him in his clubbing mode.

'What's your name?'

135

'Trigger.'

'Why do they call you that?'

David Russell runs a catering business that takes pride in using English beef and Anthony Gill is a practising vet. The hunting community is broad based, making it important both economically and socially to the Cotswolds.

The kennels are important to the hunt throughout the year. It was a feature of my visits to the Heythrop to see Anthony Adams with his hounds; they looked on him as leader of the pack, and he looked on them with pride and affection. His care showed at the annual puppy show; when Busby won

LEFT: *Hound puppies.*

BELOW: *The Heythrop hounds watch the terrierman at work.*

the stallion class at the Peterborough Hound Show, and when he fed them and settled them on their straw beds after hunting and exercise. He always wanted to hunt and went into the kennels of the Vale of the White Horse as soon as he left school. He has been huntsman with the Heythrop for eleven years. His wife Sue helps out and does the book work; she rides to hounds twice a week during the winter. She was born in London and was training to be a draughtswoman until she gave it up to work with horses. She once started a general arts degree with the Open University. She gave up after attending summer schools, where other students criticised her and Anthony's job: 'I felt persecuted because I was a huntsman's wife. They got stroppy and argued about it so I gave up.' If a person from any other minority had been treated so, it would have been classed as victimisation and discrimination.

Raoul Millais, pictured a few weeks before he died in 1999, aged 98.

With all the activities, summer seems to fly by and soon hunting is resumed. I still wanted to see another hunt for the sake of investigating 'stress', 'distress' and 'cruelty'. I did see pain. The hunt secretary, with one artificial hip, went flying through the air three times, bouncing on every occasion and remounting. Some of the hunt went close to the home of Raoul Millais, the third generation of the famous painting family. He started hunting in 1910 and stopped in 1939 when he broke his neck. He was a remarkable man, travelling hundreds of miles over Africa by foot without ever catching malaria: 'In those days it took us three months just to get to the point of departure.' His godfathers were Frederick Selous and Archibald Thorburn and he remembers meeting Rudyard Kipling, Churchill and many famous writers, artists and politicians. Even in his 90s he had a sharp mind and wonderful laughing eyes: 'I don't understand why some people are so against the country when they don't know anything about it. The whole Cotswold landscape has been created by hunting.' At 98 he was looking forward to his centenary and invited me to his party, saying, 'I've already been a hundred once, by mistake. The Queen sent me a telegram of congratulations ten years early.' Sadly he did not make his centenary and died a few weeks after our last conversation, not before generously providing some hound sketches for *The Hunting Gene*.

THE HUNTING GENE

The hunting went in fits and starts. Two foxes ran out of a wood, dive-bombing crows showing their progress to more woodland. Two ravens were circling high above, themselves being harassed by jackdaws. Late in the day hounds chopped a fox in a plantation beyond our view, and almost immediately a new hunt started with the hounds in full cry. Again, Joe had anticipated the hunt and as we stood by some dilapidated farm buildings the fox suddenly appeared twenty yards away from us. It was in fine condition with a superb winter coat. It saw us and went back into the farmyard. Hounds were streaming along a hedgerow in full cry, approaching the buildings at speed. The fox appeared again before calmly retreating. The hounds were by now running towards us, weaving in and out of the buildings – they must catch the fox. Then I saw the fox again, it was running away from us, along a roof of the old pig sties. Again, Reynard had outsmarted the hounds; it ran over two fields and into the middle of the next village.

It had been another fascinating day; one fox had died and thirteen had been seen. The hounds were loaded up to be taken back to the kennels and the sun set in a beautiful red autumn sky. Dessy sniffed: 'I can smell a frost coming,' he said. A gardener finished his work and loaded his tools into his van before driving away – G. P. Blight is a strange name for a gardener.

Hunting is thirsty work

138

Chapter Eight

THE FARMER'S FOX

The Hunting Gene

Whenever fox-hunting is mentioned – whether to attack it, defend it or simply enquire about it – the type of hunting imagined involves horses, hounds and red ('pink') coats: the traditional fox-hunting scene that adorns thousands of Christmas cards each year. Yet in many parts of upland England, Scotland and Wales the terrain is far too dangerous for horses, and the followers go on foot. During one anti-hunting campaign a Welsh MP accepted an invitation to attend a meet of one of his local packs. In a narrow street in a small village tucked into a steep-sided valley, with scree fields, corries annd sheer rock faces in view, he asked, 'Where are the horses?'

The huntsman and followers of these foot packs are tough, hardy people. The pursuit of the fell and mountain fox reveals the reason for the coloured jackets of the huntsman and the whippers-in. The reason is the same for the red of the Coniston and the Eskdale and Ennerdale as for the green of the Heythrop and the Aldenham. As in a football team, the colours depict the members of the hunting team, the huntsman, the whippers-in and the Masters, all of whom have jobs to do. While the huntsman is in sole charge of hunting the hounds, the whippers-in – normally two or three – help him to control the pack, usually by voice but occasionally by cracking the whip, not actually whipping the hounds. On a cold misty January day the red jackets stand out from the drab surroundings, and the pattern and the direction of the hunt can be followed easily.

One fundamental difference between the foot-packs and the horse-packs is that foxes never had to be imported to the uplands; foxes were always a problem to livestock there. Consequently although horse-packs started as a sport and developed into a way of both controlling and preserving foxes, foot-hunting started as a serious method of controlling foxes, and the social and cultural side of hunting grew from it.

The most famous foot-packs are the six fell-packs of the Lake District. The most well-known huntsman of them all was John Peel 'in his coat so grey' – made from the wool of the Herdwick sheep, the best-known sheep of the Lake District. Through the song 'Do ye ken John Peel', his reputation as a huntsman has travelled the world. Until animal rights began to infiltrate

Edmund Porter hunting over rocks.

some parts of the teaching profession, it was sung in every junior school in Britain.

John Peel was the son of a small farmer with just twenty-five acres; he was born in the autumn of 1776 and died on 13 November 1854. Writing to celebrate his bi-centenary, Melvyn Bragg, then a gifted young writer and now Lord Bragg of Wigton, wrote in *John Peel – the Man, the Myth and the Song*:

Herdwicks, the sheep of the Lake District.

> … And even I can look at the Fells and be impressed by the endurance of somebody who would trudge and trot over them day after day in pursuit of the uneatable. The foot hunting aspect always caught my imagination. A man on foot against nature – that is a fine image. Moreover, as it was on foot, anybody could join in. You did not need to be able to keep a horse. That democratic quality plays an important part in the potency of the John Peel Legend.
>
> Above all though, world-wide, it is the love of the sport which endears him to successive generations of sportsmen. The love of play and the dedication to sport is a profound longing everywhere. John Peel is the epitome of that.
>
> … The names of the dogs and the places, the use of the hunting terms, the colours (long disputed by learned hunting scholars in the heavy shires) of his coat! 'Grey,' gentlemen 'Skiddaw Grey!' From the Herdwicks! It is always back to this particular spot in Cumbria that the spirit and life of John Peel returns.
>
> That is why I call him a 'Very local hero.'

To see fell-hunting as it is carried on today, without the famous grey coat, I decided to follow one of the Lake District's current 'very local heroes'. Edmund Porter is huntsman, Master and owner of the Eskdale and Ennerdale Hounds. A year of visiting the Lake District in all seasons of the year establishes three important features of it: the area is a very special and beautiful place needing special and careful protection; the indigenous people of the Lake District have a way of life and a living culture just as special and in need of protection as their surroundings; and numerous in-comers and visitors regard the area as a rural theme-park that should be set aside for them, their recreation, leisure and amusement. The locals, their farms, their sheep, their sheep trailers and their hunting are an inconvenience.

THE HUNTING GENE

As a result, among the mountains, lakes and fells there are two different life-styles and two different cultures, one looking down on the other. Nearly every village and hamlet has lost half, and sometimes three-quarters, of their traditional stone houses. They have been bought as holiday homes and second homes by in-comers, investment companies and leisure businesses. The money asked for, and received, is way beyond the pockets of the majority of the locals, whose own young people have to move away or rely on the generosity of relatives, council housing or especially built social housing for their accommodation. Even then, at a quarter of the second home price, the 'cheap' social housing is often beyond their pockets.

The newcomers hike and bike in modern, expensive wayfaring wear – colour co-ordinated anoraks and trousers, the latest range of walking aids, water-proof map-holders and an assortment of rambling fashion accessories that confirm their affluence and their second-home status. Yet more special clothes, and mountain bikes, are an even stronger representation of the huge gap between the spending and playing money of the in-comers, and the hard-earned money for living of the locals. It would take hours of washing dishes or pulling pints for a farmer's son to afford a new, top-of-the-range mountain bike; yet it is claimed that 'tourism provides work for the locals' – perhaps, but it is bottom-of-the-heap work for bottom-of-the-heap people.

On bank holidays expensive cars fill the lanes. One afternoon I was held up by a living caricature of an in-comer: a brand-new BMW convertible with the roof down was cruising slowly along the middle of a narrow lane. The driver was desperate not to take his new toy too near the stone walls on either side. He was obviously an over-paid urban paper-shuffler and key-board tapper. As he drove with soft hands, his Fragrance for Men wafted over those behind. The blonde bimbo beside him sat smiling blankly at the quaint rustic scene while he looked with disdain on the mud-splattered shepherds and farm-workers – the peasantry – going about their very basic business on a public holiday. It is astonishing to some that ewes and lambs ignore public holidays and cows have to be milked 365 days a year.

Sometimes the in-comers do more than look. One farmer walking along the road with his dog had a car of youths stop alongside him; a window was wound down and out came 'Ooooh aaaagh, ooooh aaaagh' in what they regarded as an appropriate agricultural accent. They drove off rolling about with laughter at their own cleverness. Strange to relate, after attending a countryside protest at the Labour Party Conference in 1999 I stopped at a service station to fill up my car. A Range Rover pulling an anti-hunting placard on a trailer had also stopped, and a group of people looking affluent and Islington were standing by it. As I walked past a man with the affectation of a male model went: 'Ooooh aaaagh, there goes Farmer Giles.' Similar behaviour with appropriate noises directed at Blacks or Asians would be regarded as racism. Directed against the country's own rural minority it doesn't matter.

One answer to the rural housing problem would be to charge quadruple Council Tax on second homes. In addition, a day-rate admission fee could be charged to all visitors to National Parks – one of which is the Lake District – and a smaller charge could be made for passing through on roads such as the M6. This money should then be earmarked for the local communities and local employers and to top up environmentally friendly farm subsidies. This kind of thing is done successfully elsewhere in the world – why not in Britain?

Life in the Lakes is lived at two levels, with the locals well and truly at base level. When the hounds and followers with their wind-proof coats and gaiters come by, many of the visitors in their coloured anoraks look aghast; occasionally, when a good flight distance has been achieved, an anonymous 'Cruel bastards!' will be shouted. All this is taking place at a time when the incomes of hill farmers have reached rock bottom; when Herdwick wool is being burnt on bonfires as there is no market and when hunting – the one area that provides relief – is under attack from both outsiders and in-comers. To the remnants of the real rural communities of the Lake District hunting is extremely important; it gives a social life, sport, friendship and laughter at a time when there is not a lot to laugh about.

The plight of the upland farmer is tragic. In 1998 the average earnings of hill farmers plummeted by 58 per cent. In 1999 they fell a further 35 per cent to just £2000, way below the Government's minimum wage level for employed people. It is a situation manufactured by the Common Agricultural Policy with its quotas and built-in over-production, exacerbated by an incompetent Government and indifferent Members of Parliament.

From an environmental perspective the quotas of the CAP have led to over-stocking,

Thanks to the Common Agricultural Policy, shearing wool to burn.

which in turn has led to over-grazing and a dependence on chemicals to keep livestock healthy. In addition farmers have tried to produce more grass, so pastures are rolled in the spring, clumps of rushes are cut and damp areas drained, meaning that in the Lake District too the curlew and the lapwing are in steep decline.

To be within striking distance of the main events of the Cumbrian year, I chose to stay in the village of Threlkeld, a few miles from Kendall. It is a village that demonstrates the importance of hunting to the Lake District and to the social life of the people. In the garden of my bed-and-breakfast were the kennels of the Cumbria Beagles, a small private pack owned by John Hume, a retired schoolmaster. He is helped out by a sensible in-comer from London, David Reade, who retired early from running his own small engineering business. 'Before I came up here I would have been classified as an anti,' he says, in almost pure Cockney. 'Then I met John, met his hounds and I was hooked. I go to every meet, I act as whipper-in; I help out in the kennels and have some hounds at home, I love it.'

The lapwing is in steep decline.

Overlooking the house and garden where I stayed are the kennels of the Blencathra Foxhounds, known as the John Peel foxhounds because the ancestry of many of the hounds goes back to Peel's famous pack. It is a wonderful sight to look from the beagles up to the foxhounds, with the brooding Blencathra mountain rising directly behind. The present huntsman of the Blencathra, Barrie Todhunter, has a famous name and one which makes nonsense of moves to ban foxhunting in Scotland as 'an upper-class English import'. In Scotland and northern England the local country name for a fox is Tod, just as in my part of East Anglia it is Charlie. 'Todhunter' was the name that developed for the member of the clan responsible for controlling foxes, and it is particularly associated with the Camerons. The foxhunter or 'todhunter' would take six hounds and an assortment of terriers and deerhounds to catch foxes and was an important member of the clan.

Barrie believes that his ancestors moved to Cumberland and Northumberland at the time of Bonnie Prince Charlie. When the Prince and his followers were driven back north of the border, various noblemen offered the todhunters money to stay behind and hunt foxes for them. Being Scotsmen, they took the money and stayed. In the early 1850s an Isaac Todhunter hunted the Blencathra hounds. He died in 1868 and is buried in Threlkeld churchyard. Barrie does not know whether he is related to the earlier hunter.

144

There are several famous old huntsmen buried in the churchyard, leading to the erection of a hunting memorial just inside the churchyard gate. On it are the famous names of fell-hunting: Richardson, Porter, Nicholson, Todhunter, Crozier and several more. New generations of the same names are still active in hunting today.

Just down the road from the church is The Salutation pub, with hunting murals front and back and an assortment of hunting memorabilia, brushes and fox heads (masks) inside. The interests and way of life of the village are regional, rural and unique. Whenever I visit the Lakes I am always amazed at how London dominates television programmes and how irrelevant London is to most people who do not live there. After one wonderful hunting day I sat down to watch the BBC news. The main item was about the contest to become Mayor of London. I was astonished; what interest could the contest hold for anybody outside London and why should the BBC assume it to be of national importance? To the people of Threlkeld it was about as interesting as watching paint dry and as relevant to their lives as under-water cycling.

The Salutation Inn, Threlkeld.

Beyond the pub, the social life of many farmers and locals revolves around the six fell-packs. There are darts matches, discos, dinners and coffee mornings – 'coffee mornings' not with coffee, rich tea biscuits, the rattle of bone china and the hum of polite conversation; but with soup, filled rolls, cans of beer, hunting stories, gossip and real belly laughs.

There are other events too, big and small, in the social calendar. The Game Fair is important to many huntsmen and hunt followers, a meeting of like minds from all over Britain. More local is the Appleby Horse Fair, just along the A66 from the Lakes, which draws many country people to see its alternative life style. A different class of horse is found at the Lowther Show, which also features a hound show. There I was astonished to meet a genuine Aborigine; he was a full-time Aboriginal rights campaigner, on holiday from Australia. He could see a parallel between what had happened to the Aborigines and what is happening to Britain's rural communities – the result of cultural colonialism backed up by

bad laws and bad politics. The Rydal Show must be one of the best country shows in Britain, concentrating solely on sheepdog trialling, hounds and hound trailing – that Lake District sport in which hounds bred faster and thinner than foxhounds follow an aniseed trail; the first one back is the winner. Shepherds and hunting people from all over northern England attend and tourists mingle with farmers and hunters – admiring the hounds and watching the sheepdogs work. At the end of the day singing often breaks out: hunting songs in the beer tent, old songs and new songs all sung with the required degree of passion, harmony and humour.

A way of life is under threat from bad laws and bad politics. ABOVE: *The Brocklehurst's tent is the focus for a hunting family at a game fair.* BELOW: *Kate and Michael Nicholson with family and friends.*

I heard the best singing in The Three Shires pub after a day's hunting, including old and young, in tune and out, lubricated and alcohol-free. It is almost beyond belief that those who are part of this living culture should have to defend themselves in a society that boasts of its multi-culturalism on the international political stage. The most telling song was sung and written by Kate Nicholson, the wife of the huntsman of the Coniston Foxhounds. Her husband's job depends on hunting; her home belongs to the hunt and her two children live truly country childhoods. For her the rights and wrongs of hunting are more than just an academic debate; they are about her chosen life-style, her husband's livelihood and the future of her children. She is an attractive woman with clear blue eyes, and as she speaks her voice wavers from burning anger to deep despair. Her song, called 'Walk that Road', describes the feelings of many and was written for those who marched down from the Lakes to the Countryside Rally in Hyde Park in July 1997:

From the corners of the Kingdom
United in an aim,
They set off in their masses
Their message to proclaim.
We're marching for our freedom,
Our right, as countrymen;
So long may it continue,
The way of life we ken.

Our lads went from Caldbeck,
They carried John Peel's horn.
Through every fell-pack country
Their heavy boots adorn'd,
And with them went our wishes
In a true old Lakeland way,
To Foster and his hunting Bill
They'd blow 'Gone Away'.

The MPs in Whitehall
Have ideas of their own,
They want a country playground
Just like the Greenwich Dome.
They'll drive out us natives,
Custodians of the land,
And replace us with Park Rangers
In green Escort vans.

When the blood in your veins
Is as old as the land,
And your roots run far beneath
This they'll understand.
Like the solid English oak
We are a country breed
And we'll not be uprooted
By a common urban weed.

Our children are the future,
For them we will prevail;
The countryside is theirs
Whether fell, moor or dale.
Some day they will thank you,
Pleased to be born
To hear the music of the hounds
And follow the hunting horn.

Chorus
Walk that road, lads,
Don't look back;
We're thinking of you,
Our hopes you will carry,
In Hyde Park we'll all greet you.

THE HUNTING GENE

Hound trailing. Get ready – get set.

The show that competes with Rydal as the best country show of the year is held on the last Saturday of September, at the foot of Hardknott Pass. Eskdale is a friendly little show set in some of the Lake District's most rugged scenery. There is hound trailing, hill running, Cumberland wrestling, a Herdwick sheep competition and the foxhound show; the only thing missing is a horn-blowing contest. The hounds of the Eskdale and Ennerdale pack won most of the prizes when I visited, and why not? They were on home ground.

The Eskdale and Ennerdale hounds hunt three hundred square miles of the south-west corner of the Lakes, some of the most spectacular and remote country in Britain. It includes Ennerdale, Wasdale, Langdale and Eskdale; each valley has an appeal of its own and to drop down into the country over the Wrynose and Hardknott Passes is almost like visiting a hidden land, much of it off the main tourist track.

Edmund Porter knows virtually every square inch of his country, as do his hounds, and he has been actively involved with the pack for over forty years. Hounds have hunted the fells and dales for many generations. From 1857 to 1910 they were owned and hunted by Thomas Dobson, a remarkable fellman who gave his hounds to Edmund's grandfather in 1900. William Porter hunted them until 1952, and he handed over to Edmund's father.

Edmund left school at 15 and started whipping-in immediately; then in 1966 at the age of 23 he became huntsman. He has never wanted to do anything else and in 1999 he celebrated his fortieth season following the hounds. He owns the entire pack, all fifty-four of them (they are counted singly, not in couples) and eight terriers. For a day's hunting he will take thirty-eight or forty hounds and three terriers. Despite hunting and owning the hounds, the pack is organised like any other hunt, with his wife Linda acting as secretary. Because of the state of farming, subscriptions are voluntary; but even so the turnover is £22,000 a year, to keep Edmund, his family and his hounds. This compares with the Heythrop's income of about £200,000, it just about breaks even after paying for a staff of ten, occasional part-time help and eighteen horses.

To Edmund, fell-hunting is a total way of life:

> It's very social, but it keeps the foxes down to a reasonable level too. In the old days grandfather used to take the hounds away for three or four days, and the school children in the area would look forward to it. When it was time to return home there would be a dance and it was one of the highlights of the year.
>
> We hunt four days a week from September until Easter, and then from Easter until May I'm on lambing calls. I take the hounds by trailer these days and keep them at the kennels most of the season. I'm 56 now and the hills seem to be getting a bit higher than they used to be. We kill about 80–100 foxes a season. If a fox has killed a lamb there is usually a mark on its neck. If the vixen is feeding cubs, then the lamb will have its insides ripped out. If the cubs are a bit older then the fox will sometimes carry the lamb away. The runs are not so long these days; the foxes' environment is different – they go to picnic sites and stay more local, feeding is easier.

Foxes can be a real problem to some farmers and so the fell foxhounds are important to the farming community. On the League Against Cruel Sports's website is an interesting piece of misinformation. The League says, 'According to the Ministry of Agriculture, predation on lambs by foxes is "insignificant".'

What the Ministry actually says is:

> The Ministry's interest in foxes is as a predator of livestock, especially of lambs. On the basis of current evidence, the Ministry does not consider foxes to be a significant factor in lamb mortality nationally, but it should be stressed that this is against a background of widespread fox control by farmers. Foxes can cause serious problems for individual farmers and the Ministry therefore considers that foxes do need to be controlled to minimise lamb losses.

The League's website goes on to state that 'studies' show that lamb losses to foxes amount to only 0.5 per cent per year. It fails to say that by using even this doubtful figure, it means

THE HUNTING GENE

115,000 lambs are killed by foxes in a single year (based on 1998 figures). The Ministry of Agriculture's experimental farm at Liscombe in Somerset – now closed through Government cuts and a declining interest in farming – concluded that there was a 1 per cent lamb loss to foxes per year – 230,000 lambs. If my understanding is correct, this means that the League Against Cruel Sports is concerned about 16,000 hunted foxes, but is dismissive about the fate of 230,000 lambs.

In the summer, when I first visited the kennels, most of the hounds were out on farms. After a hard season, to rest the hounds and to reduce the cost of keeping the pack the hounds are dispersed to farms all over the area. I came across one, Bellman, outside a farm in a secluded valley once owned and farmed by Beatrix Potter. Like many farmers today, if Beatrix Potter saw the hounds cross her land she would follow them, and her sketchbooks show that she also drew them.

Bellman is a fine hound and each summer he lives with Glen and Dorothy Wilkinson and their two boys, as one of the family. He comes and goes as he likes and acts as if he owns the farm; when he's tired he curls up in front of the Rayburn, and he sneaks onto the settee when nobody is looking. A footpath runs through the farmyard, and when the butcher's van arrives Bellman growls at every passing tourist, just to let them know that the contents of the van are not for them.

Sheepdog trialling at Rydal Show.

The previous February, when hounds had been hunting the valley, the pack broke into a number of small groups. It was a bitterly cold day and a gang of four hunted into the Wilkinsons' farmyard. Strangely, only three were seen hunting out of the farmyard. Bellman had pushed open the door of the farmhouse and was found asleep, curled up in front of the Rayburn. Normally, during a hunt Bellman just sniffs at the Wilkinsons and briefly wags his tail before making off again with the rest of the pack. On the farm he is a member of a different pack, consisting of eight sheep dogs and a terrier.

Like the rest of the Lake District farmers, the Wilkinsons are finding the going tough. They farm 1500 acres with 800 ewes, mainly Herdwicks but also 150 Swaledales. They had just sent some ewes and lambs to market, they made £10 each – the year before they had made £19 each. They estimated that in the previous twelve months their income had fallen by 50 per cent, while during the same period the National Trust had put their rent up by 25 per cent. To cope with the demands of livestock and because they cannot afford hired labour, Glen works 80–120 hours a week. His wife works full-time as well, in addition to coping with the family.

Glen is not impressed with his landlords:

> The National Trust claims that it could get a lot more money for letting the property. The rent assumes that we will have to do bed-and-breakfast or let buildings as holiday lets. Once the National Trust was interested in what we were doing; now they come round in suits. They seem to know nothing about farming and are only interested in money. If we say that we can't afford the rent, they say that there are plenty who can. Visitors and access are considered more important than we are. Yet we are the ones

who have been working the land for generations. We have made the Lake District what it is – yet we are at the bottom of the heap and are treated like dirt.

There is no doubt that Beatrix Potter, who gave nearly 6800 acres to the National Trust, regarded the farmers, the rural communities and her beloved Herdwick sheep as being as important to the Lake District as the mountains, lakes and fells. When I asked the National Trust why rents had been raised when farm incomes had fallen, it was claimed that only one rent had been increased. At the Rydal Show a few weeks later, virtually every other farmer I met claimed to be a National Trust tenant with an increased rent burden. It really did seem to be a case of men in suits with no roots and no culture telling men without suits but with roots and with culture how to run their lives. I understand that the Director General of the National Trust does not have to open his house up for bed-and-breakfast to make ends meet.

The Wilkinsons love hunting and at one time attended every meet in the area; now they go occasionally, when they can get away from the farm. Foxes are sometimes a problem to them, and three years ago a dozen lambs were lost. With farm prices desperate, every loss is important.

I met the Wilkinsons again, with their son George, high up on a rocky crag overlooking a misty valley with bracken, scree and oak woods far below. The hounds and Edmund were walking along the road and into the wood. There had been a hunt earlier, but I had not seen it and the fox had never been under any pressure. Almost as soon as the hounds had moved away from The Three Shires, distant figures had appeared on the topmost crags, like Apaches in an old Western anticipating the arrival of white men. These Lake District natives were anticipating the direction of the hunt. Until I caught up I saw little – clambering over stone walls, walking through birch woods and stumbling over scree is not the easiest activity for somebody who normally lives just twenty-five feet above sea-level.

Despite the lack of a hunt, the Wilkinsons had enjoyed their day. Bellman had briefly sniffed them, wagged his tail and hurried on his way. As we waited for action a famous huntsman stood on my right; he has helped me with this book but I have promised not to give his name. 'Listen to that,' he said suddenly, 'the music of the hounds in the wood.' With that an old Ford tractor spluttered out of a gateway far below. 'Do you want a hearing aid?' asked Stan, one of the Lake District's living legends, to my left. There are so many stories about Stan that they would fill a book thicker than this one. His greatest achievement was to stand at a bus stop after a day's beagling when the hound van refused to start. The bus duly stopped and Stan, followed by twenty couple of beagles, climbed on board. The bus driver eventually evicted Stan and the dogs after one of the beagles had insisted on sitting on another passenger's lap.

On Stan's seventieth birthday it is said that he was presented with some blue pills that looked encouragingly like Viagra. They were tape-worm tablets coloured blue, and he spent the next three days sitting on the toilet. 'He takes one a day now,' said another beagling friend, 'to stop himself rolling out of bed.' A more recent tale suggested that Stan had asked for a ton of granite to be delivered for his drive; when he arrived back from beagling, a large granite boulder had been placed in the middle of his gateway. How many of the stories about Stan are true I have no idea, but I do know that at over 70 he could get up and down the hillsides and scree slopes faster than I.

Two days later, under a warm spring sun, the hunting was little better – but the scenery was spectacular. In crags above Blea Tarn peregrines were mewing, and it was a woman's turn to need a hearing aid. 'Isn't that peculiar,' she said. 'I think I can hear a lorry reversing.' As the sun warmed, eight buzzards circled effortlessly on thermals and jackdaws with less expertise tried to join them. The hounds and Edmund were hunting the steep rocks, high up on the valley side, with distant watching figures perched up on the crags above them. In the valley were patches of juniper bushes and the sun made the leaves of holly shine silver. Juniper is a good plant to have growing in sheep country; the berries take two years to ripen but they are wonderful in lamb casserole.

Again, as hounds began to climb and hunt the higher ground of Pike O'Blisco, I was fascinated. Eight whooper swans were becoming increasingly restless on Blea Tarn; they flew, circled and landed on the water, repeating the routine several times. Then they flew once more, calling louder and flying stronger; they circled once around the tarn and then flew along the valley towards the sun, climbing all the way. Soon they were higher than the valley sides, higher than the highest mountain top, flying straight and climbing all the time. They flew on, still rising, twice the height of the highest peak, then three times higher, small specks at the start of their great spring migration. They would spend their summer anywhere on a line from Iceland, across Scandinavia to the Bering Sea. It was the first time I had seen the migration

The goshawk, an efficient red squirrel killer.

flight of these graceful white birds. Hunting, it seemed to me, was more than hounds chasing foxes, it was about being in contact with the rhythms of nature again.

The regular followers of the Eskdale and Ennerdale are a mixture of farmers, builders, workers from Sellafield, farmworkers and even the owner of an old people's home. Several carry CB radios to keep in touch with what is happening, a development frowned on by purists but welcomed by many – including Edmund. It helps him to keep in better contact with the hounds once they are hunting and running well. On this day the hunt was slow and relaxed and I caught up with the field on a high valley side looking into two large and distant corries. The hounds were tiny specks working among the boulders and scree. There were nearer coloured specks too. The sun had brought out the walkers – the 'crag rats' and 'plastics'. In Cumbria-speak those visitors who fail to get out of their cars are simply 'gawpers'. There were no signs of foxes. The hounds had worked hard and as they cooled off in a stream I wished I could join them.

I returned to the Lakes in the autumn. I really did want to see a hunt after two almost blank days on my earlier visit. The 'cruelty' spoken of so freely by the antis is very difficult to see in reality. As soon as I arrived at the kennels I did see one example of cruelty. A heap of a dozen dead small calves was piled just inside the doorway, brought by farmers who could not afford to keep and rear them. It was the only time I saw Edmund depressed. 'I hate it,' he said. 'I don't mind putting livestock down if it is ill or injured, but I hate putting down these small healthy calves – it doesn't feel right, but the farmers have no other option.' It isn't right – it is just part of the social, economic and farming cruelty of the CAP and BSE.

Passing through pines, I saw a flash of grey wings and was reminded of another cruelty that the antis and conservationists never speak about. Goshawks are back in Cumbria and Northumberland; they are spectacular birds of prey whose killing is so efficient that in some northern countries they are controlled as a conservation measure. It is said that their return to northern Britain was aided by conservationists acting illegally, replacing wild sparrowhawk eggs with goshawk eggs. If a gamekeeper had meddled with a sparrowhawk's nest, howls of outrage would have followed. Because conservationists were involved, a whole series of incidents was hushed up. This conservation master-stroke is reaping a tragic reward; it has been realised that goshawks not only like curlew on their menu, but also red squirrel. Cumbria and Northumberland represent the final stronghold of the red squirrel in England. During the last breeding season the remains of twelve red squirrels were found beneath one goshawk's nest, and thirteen under another.

It was in Wasdale, against a backdrop of Wast Water and of Scafell Pike, complete with a powdering of snow, that I saw my first real fell-hunt. It was the Salvers Hunt, so named because it was the hunt that once celebrated the end of 'salving'. Gangs of salvers would visit the farms applying a concoction of tar, rancid Irish butter and 'salve' (probably lanolin) to the fleeces of the sheep to ensure better weather-proofing for the winter. To celebrate the end of the work a special hunt was held, followed by a

"Viper"

The spectacular hunting country of Wasdale.

Hounds and friend among the rocks.

'tattiepot' and sing-song in the pub. The 'tattiepot' consisted of mutton, black pudding, potatoes, carrots and cabbage, all cooked in the same pot.

Salving stopped many years ago, and the tattiepot and sing-song take place at the opening meet, but the Salvers Hunt still attracts many followers as the road by Wast Water provides excellent viewing. Edmund worked the hounds along the base of Buckbarrow, a high valley side of crags, scree and rockfalls rising to nearly 1500 feet. It was a stirring sight: the hounds keen and eager, Edmund giving encouragement and a panorama of slate-grey cliffs, water and snow-dusted tops. A fox was bolted by a terrier from the scree, and the hounds were immediately in full cry. After the initial burst it looked as if the fox was going to turn towards a small group of hounds, but Charlie or Tod veered away, just in time. He went upwards, almost skipping over the scree, running along pathways and sheepwalks through rock falls and crags that looked impassable. Then, with a brief look away as a buzzard called, I had lost him.

The hounds clambered all over the rocks, standing on crags and looking over sheer drops; they were confident and sure footed. The 'music' ebbed and flowed as scent was followed and lost. It was a remarkable sight, and again I felt a fusion of wonder, anticipation, hesitation and apprehension. As I watched, the large man standing next to me informed me that he was a prison warder; then he made a confession. If ever hunting was stopped he would go to prison for his right to follow the hounds.

The fox had gone to ground deep among the boulders and scree and Edmund's little Jack Russell terrier could not flush it out. It was too dark beneath the rocks to see the fox and Edmund could not shoot it. He moved on, down to the valley floor. Almost immediately the hounds were in full cry, bursting from a small wood and running fast through a dip between Buckbarrow and Middle Fell. On they went towards Haycock, Silver Cove and into

Ennerdale, an expanse of empty ground away from houses, cars and people. We searched but we could find no sign of hounds or huntsman; silence fell as dusk edged in and stars came out. The temperature began to fall, there would be a frost. The Salvers Hunt was over for another year.

From the speed and direction of the hounds it seemed to me that Edmund would take hours to find his hounds, but he caught up with them quickly, Bellman included, and soon they were safely returned to kennels. Occasionally hounds cannot be found for hours or even days. The longest absentee during my period of writing did not occur with the Eskdale and Ennerdale, but with the David Davies Hunt in mid-Wales. Songstress went missing at 2000 feet and all efforts to find her failed. Huntsman David Jones returned with the whole pack to try to find her, but there was no sign and David feared the worst. Then reports came that she had been seen in Snowdonia, which indicated that she was travelling in the wrong direction. Suddenly, three and a half weeks later, she appeared at the kennels. She had been lost eighty miles away as the crow flies and had covered many more on her great journey home; it confirms for me that foxhounds are very remarkable dogs.

In addition to the fell-packs and foot-packs, there are up to fifty 'gun-packs' in Scotland and Wales. The hounds have the slightly lighter features of the fell-packs and

Paul Crofts and his daughter exercise his fine pack of hounds.

they are joined by followers – farmers, keepers and farmworkers with 12 bore shotguns. In woodland the guns line the rides, waiting for a fox to cross, and they will line up on the edge of woodland and moorland to get a shot at a fox making for open country. The packs are needed because of the decline in the number of gamekeepers. In Scotland there were about 6000 gamekeepers in the early 1900s; almost a hundred years later there are between 1000 and 1500.

The Hunting Gene

Stephen Frank air coursing with English pointers and peregrine.

In addition to lambs and sometimes deer calves, the foxes are particularly hard on ground-nesting birds – black grouse, red grouse, ptarmigan, capercaillie, pheasants and partridges. Wildfowl and waders including lapwing, golden plover, snipe and dunlin are all on the menu as well, either as adults or chicks. Because the fox is such a versatile creature and good hunter, it can be a danger to birds in woodland and on the valley floor, and to those that frequent the high tops.

When checking his free-ranging reindeer in the Cairngorms, Alan Smith has seen foxes on the very highest summits looking for ptarmigan. In the valleys the capercaillie has suffered, from a mixture of deer fences and foxes. I visited the RSPB's Abernethy reserve shortly after it was purchased in 1990. Almost the first bird I saw there was a capercaillie. Over recent years the RSPB has been carrying out an experiment of no predator control and the 'capper' population has plummeted. My information is that the culprits are foxes and pine martens; it will be interesting to see if the RSPB blames just the protected pine marten for its foolish experiment. Chris Knights saw what happens with no predators recently at Hudson Bay in Arctic Canada. Arctic foxes had been badly hit by rabies; as a consequence ptarmigan numbers had exploded.

On my way up to Scotland to see Paul Crofts and his Three Straths Fox Control Association, I stopped to see the famous black and tan Dumfries hounds. They are striking dogs from French stock, directly related to the early Gascons. Because they are hunted from horseback their future is threatened by the earnest egalitarians of the Scottish Parliament. One worried Scot wrote to the veteran

Scottish Nationalist MSP Winifred Ewing about his concern. She wrote back with a very brief letter, getting his name wrong, and saying: 'I will vote against "ceremonious" fox hunting but I will allow farmers to kill the foxes when they take lambs' eyes.' Apart from appearing to be unable to tell the difference between the way a crow and a fox kill a lamb, it seems that in her view unceremonious fox-hunting is permissible, which again comes back to the issue of class, not cruelty.

Paul Crofts has a fine pack of hounds, kennelled on the banks of the Findhorn river. In a normal season he will take 200 foxes. Most will be shot and his hounds will kill a number of both healthy and wounded animals. Again they are superb dogs,

RIGHT: *A gun-pack foxhound cooling off.*

BELOW: *An English pointer out hunting.*

running lightly and quietly through the woodland until hitting scent, and then the sound of the pack's enthusiasm reverberates through the trees.

Beyond the kennels of Paul Crofts I travelled further north, to the desolate Flow country. There, within sight of the wild north coast of Scotland, I saw more hunting with dogs. Stephen Frank and friends were using English pointers to flush grouse. Then a country sport arguably as old as hare coursing took place. Falconry is a skilful and spectacular sport. When the hunting partnership of man, dog and bird seeks to catch game, it can be described as air coursing. But what of the pointer? In the course of a day it runs miles, hunting – looking for scent, finding it and freezing until the peregrine or gyr falcon has gained height, sometimes a thousand feet. Then the grouse is flushed and the peregrine stoops with spectacular speed and beauty. Sometimes the grouse is caught and sometimes it gets away. But it is hunting with dogs and some politicians want to ban all hunting with dogs. A falconer, his dog and his bird are usually welcomed at schools as contributing to education, and falconers have offered their services to conservationists and been accepted. Greyhounds and foxhounds are welcomed at few schools, and offers of help from huntsmen to conservationists have been rejected. It is a strange world.

Ennerdale, off the beaten track in the Lakes.

Chapter Nine

THE RUNNING
OF THE DEER

William Garfit.

THE HUNTING GENE

T he red deer is Britain's largest land mammal, and the mature stag, with a fine set of antlers, is also its most magnificent. Although many people immediately associate red deer with Scotland, the area with possibly the oldest and best-managed herds is the West Country – particularly Devon and Somerset. There is no doubt that if the management of the West Country deer by hunting with hounds had been carried out in any other country, with the same long-term success and stability, it would be described as 'the sustainable management of a renewable resource'. Indeed if countries in Africa or South America managed any of their larger mammals in the same way that would be heralded as a major step forward for conservation.

But of course here in Britain things are different. Hunting the red deer is taking place in a country that has lost its rural roots; where the majority of people no longer work with animals, or live with them – apart from pampered pets – and where the Bambi syndrome is activated nearly every day of the week by televised anthropomorphism laced with animal rights. Consequently deer hunting is seen as 'cruel', 'barbaric' and 'totally out of place in the modern world'.

The traditional view: red deer in Sutherland snow painted by Raoul Millais.

Confirmation of the double standards comes from Zimbabwe, where a scheme known as Campfire is being heralded as the way forward for both conservation and indigenous local communities. In areas where traditional African people have been in conflict with wildlife, efforts have been made to give that wildlife community ownership by putting an economic value on it, a value that puts hard cash into the hands of poor local people. Photography and controlled hunting for sport bring in that money. As a consequence the local people protect and look after their wildlife; elephants, lions and antelope are no longer just seen as a threat to crops or a danger to life and limb, they are seen to have a value and to produce an economic return.

The red deer of Exmoor, the Quantocks and the Tiverton areas are regarded as community animals too. They wander

A red deer stag during the rut.

over private land – damaging fences, eating crops and competing with sheep, cattle and ponies for food – but because of the community benefits, even quite high densities of deer are tolerated. The advantages are simple: hunting is a community-based activity that manages the herds for the benefit of all land owners – and the land owners enjoy some of the venison if the deer is hunted over their land. In addition the hunts provide the social hub for rural communities that are isolated and experiencing severe difficulties because of the current farming crisis. Hunting is important as a source of income too, from visitors wanting to follow the hounds, whether on horseback or by car, and it creates a number of rural jobs at a time when rural employment is decreasing.

Chris Huxley (from a remote branch of the famous family) is an ecologist working in international wildlife conservation. For several years he was the key natural resources policy adviser to the countries of southern Africa, excluding South Africa, and he knows all about the Campfire scheme. He says:

> Campfire's aim was to ensure that local people valued the wildlife in their area. If this is achieved, then there will be a big incentive to conserve. This was approached by firstly relinquishing ownership rights on wildlife to the local communities. Secondly, mechanisms were encouraged to provide financial returns from the wildlife.

A stag with his harem on Exmoor.

The parallel with Exmoor deer-hunting is clear. As things stand, the deer are tolerated by farmers and valued by local people because they bring a substantial benefit to them. The West Somerset District Council commissioned report suggested that the deer hunting generated £5.5 million annually for the local economy. The activity also supports substantial local employment equal to over 400 full-time jobs. Set against this is the fact that the red deer can be a serious agricultural pest.

I think that what is more important than all this are the principles involved. Banning hunting with dogs is imposing the views of those who are ignorant (the majority) on the minority practising the sport. The views of the majority are influenced primarily by the media and by an even lesser minority of extreme 'animal rights' activists. It seems that if a small, or even tiny, group of extremists create sufficient of a disturbance, they can become powerful enough to 'create' what is euphemistically known as 'public opinion' (but that is actually what the media wish to present as public opinion). This public opinion is then used as the reason for prohibiting what has been a legitimate activity.

Chris Huxley speaks as someone who does not hunt, has never followed the hounds and has never even attended a traditional Boxing Day meet.

The sustainable nature of hunting red deer is the reason Henry Williamson supported stag-hunting. His book *Tarka the Otter* shows his love of both wildlife and Exmoor. He could see that without hunting there would be no deer – there would be no reason to tolerate the animals. Dick Lloyd, at over 70, still follows the Devon and Somerset Staghounds on horseback and possibly knows more about the history of Exmoor's deer than any other person alive. He has mapped out the ebbs and flows of the red deer population over the last four hundred years. The flows correspond with the times when hunting flourished; the ebbs coincide with little or no hunting. Ted Hughes, the previous Poet Laureate, also loved Exmoor and could see that the hunts and the deer needed each other. At the time of Cromwell and the Civil War, hunting on Exmoor stopped. Ted Hughes explained what happened: 'The West Country red deer population immediately collapsed. By 1660 it was almost extinct. One doesn't have to suppose that social vengeance prompted the massacre. Human nature was quite enough – as with animal populations everywhere. What endangers profit will be exterminated.'

After the Civil War, with the resumption of hunting, the population of red deer increased and was topped up with animals brought in from Germany. Hunting fizzled out again in 1825, whereupon the red deer population crashed once more because of poaching and crop protection. Regular hunting started again in 1850 and the population of the Exmoor herd showed signs of increasing almost immediately. During the First and Second World Wars, hunting again diminished and deer numbers were deliberately reduced to protect crops for the war effort. Since then, management through hunting has seen the red deer flourish and there are now around 3000 red deer in the area. This seems to confirm that hunting the red deer in the West Country really does represent the 'sustainable management of a renewable resource'.

In 1992 the United Nations Conference on Environment and Development, the 'Earth Summit', was held in Rio de Janeiro. Its conclusions confirm and support the form of red deer management practised in the West Country. The aim of the conference was to draw up a number of principles to ensure a sustainable future for the planet – in other words, to fight for its survival. The blueprint for a sustainable future that emerged from the conference is

The Devon and Somerset staghounds out hunting.

known as Agenda 21. Governments and politicians were urged to accept the principles of Agenda 21 and it is the boast of MPs and their equivalents the world over that they support every one of its dots and commas.

Principle 22 of Agenda 21 clearly supports sustainable local traditions and communities. It states: 'Local communities have a vital role in environmental management and development because of their knowledge and traditional practices. States should recognise and duly support their identity, culture and interest and enable their effective participation in the achievement of sustainable development.' The deer management of the West Country would appear to fit not only the international conservation strategy demonstrated by Campfire, but also the principles of Agenda 21.

Despite this, politicians, pressure groups and the media continue to snipe at the three packs of staghounds in the West Country. In 1997, after years of animal rights agitation and infiltration, the National Trust – a conservation charity – banned deer-hunting on its land – even on land donated by land owners who had hunted deer or supported the hunt.

The ban followed a report commissioned in 1995. After years of pressure from the usual anti sources – lobbying as members of the National Trust – an enquiry into deer hunting was set up under Professor Patrick Bateson of King's College, Cambridge. It was an odd appointment as the professor's subject was animal behaviour, not animal physiology. In 1997 Bateson reported back that deer-hunting was unacceptable on National Trust land. The Council of the National Trust banned hunting on Trust land almost immediately. This example was followed by the Forestry Commission (which is so-called here for simplicity as Britain's forestry interests seem to change names and identities at regular intervals, while at the same time they become more remote from the local people in the areas in which they operate). The ban caused inconvenience at some meets of the Devon and Somerset Staghounds and real difficulties for the Quantock Staghounds. Because of this many pro-hunters began to join the National Trust; inevitably when they did so it was called 'infiltration'. When the anti-hunters joined, that was called 'democracy'.

The truth is that country sports should not be an issue for the National Trust, just as they are not an issue for wildlife charities such as the RSPB and the CRT. This avoids division and confrontation on matters that should be left to the individual. The National Trust ought to concern itself with the stewardship of its properties, its land and its rural communities. Because of its remote, bureaucratic and increasingly urban attitude, it has driven a wedge between itself and the indigenous people of Exmoor, just as it has in the Lake District. Fudge shops and fudged policies seem to be more important than people. The resulting frustration shows periodically when anti-National Trust posters appear in hedgerows. Another sign is the emergence of FONT – Friends of the National Trust – an organisation started on Exmoor with the aim of getting the National Trust to respect the people and traditions of the land it owns.

Once more it seems that men in suits with no roots, no culture and no wildlife are telling men without suits but with roots and culture how to look after their wildlife. This appears to be confirmed beyond the issue of hunting. It seems odd that an organisation claiming to be concerned for wildlife has hundreds of hedges on its properties that are cut during late summer, denying birds such as blackbirds, thrushes, redwings and fieldfares berries for winter. And it has hundreds of acres of grassland that are cut for silage during April, May and June, the key months for ground-nesting birds. Hunted red deer are evidently higher on the National Trust's agenda than minced lapwings, skylarks and grey partridges.

The Bateson Report was remarkable. I am a non-scientist but it seemed to me to be bad science; I wanted to know the facts – the report seemed strong on assumptions. It appeared not to compare like with like. It did not compare the physical condition of hunted deer with the physical condition of hounds, horses, race horses, athletes or people running for the bus, so there was little relevant information about blood samples and recovery rates. In addition, as I understand it, the report was not 'peer reviewed' in the normal way – scientific findings are usually submitted to inde-

Riders during an Exmoor hunt.

pendent anonymous experts in the appropriate field for criticism and assessment. Findings are then effectively assessed for flaws.

Because of what seemed to be the flawed science of the Bateson Report, another study of red-deer-hunting on Exmoor was carried out under the supervision of the Royal Veterinary College and the chairmanship of Professor Roger Harris, a biochemist. This was 'The Physiological Response of Red Deer (*Curvus elaphus*) to Prolonged Escape Exercise undertaken during Hunting, also known as 'The Joint Universities Study on Deer Hunting'. The report was thoroughly peer reviewed. The final paragraph of its summary is quite specific: 'Professor Bateson concluded that red deer are poorly equipped for the demands of hunting. In consequence, pursuit by hounds pushes them far beyond normal physiological limits, resulting in severe pathological damage. These conclusions lack any support from the finding of the present study.'

Numerous scientists seem to be both dismissive and cynical about the Bateson Report.

THE HUNTING GENE

Some of Professor Bateson's own colleagues in Cambridge University disagreed with his findings. Dr Douglas Wise from the Department of Clinical Veterinary Medicine has written: 'It has been demonstrated that Bateson was wrong about almost every conclusion he drew and interpretation he made from his behavioural observations and biochemical findings. Contrary to his belief, deer are well adapted to prolonged exercise and do not damage themselves in any significant manner as a consequence of taking it.' Professor Twink Allen says: 'Bateson is an animal behaviourist, a good one, the best in the country. He was, with his panel, interpreting very complex exercise physiology data, making comparisons and conclusions, which in my view he did wrongly and I would say so to his face.'

My astonishment at the professor's findings started on reading the first page of his report. How could a serious report have as its third line the words: 'If you wept as a child at the death of Bambi's mother you *know* what it is like to be hunted'? You don't know; Bambi's mother was shot. On page viii I was baffled again. Deer are animals of flight – that is, retreat. Their eyes are to the side of the head, enabling them to see predators more easily – the eyes of *Homo sapiens* are at the front, the normal position associated with predators. In addition red deer are fast and sure footed – they had to be; their main predators in Britain for hundreds of years were wolves, hunting dogs and people. Despite this, Professor Bateson writes: 'Red deer are remarkably sedentary animals and their distribution suggests that they tend to return to areas they know well.' Red deer sedentary? Masters and Fellows of Cambridge colleges may well be sedentary, but not red deer. Deer have territories in the breeding season and home ranges throughout the year – both may be many hundreds of acres in size. Dr Tim Coulson has studied a variety of deer in Britain and America, including red deer, and he has no interest in country sports. He says with a degree of cynicism: 'Sedentary strikes me as a rather unusual description for a red deer. I would consider trees and reef building corals as sedentary and possibly a red deer hanging in a butcher's shop. Swallows also return to areas they know well – they are not sedentary.'

If Bateson's conclusions were correct, numerous deer that are hunted but not caught would be so distressed and traumatised that they would die. Bodies would be apparent on Exmoor and the assortment of pursuing antis with their video recorders would undoubtedly find them. The facts are that the recovery rate from exercise can be very quick and *distress* may be very infrequent, compared with the more usual occurrence of tolerable *stress*.

'How would you like to be chased?' is a popular question. 'I wouldn't, but I wouldn't like living underground, eating raw hens either; nor would I like to browse birch leaves,' is the easy answer. My serious answer is that as an asthmatic I would not like to be chased, but my condition has given me an insight into exhaustion and fighting for breath. On occasion after exercise I have been attacked by asthma so severely that I could not walk or talk. Strange to relate, in that condition there is discomfort, but the body and mind switch off. I suspect that they do the same in the hunted animal. As an over-weight middle-aged asthmatic I have wheezed my way to the top of Mount Kilimanjaro twice. I imagine that if blood tests had been taken at the top and Professor Bateson's conclusions applied, then wheezing fat men would be banned from climbing high mountains.

Not only have I suffered from total exhaustion, but I have also experienced danger. I have had guns pointed at me and was once arrested as a mercenary by a drunk Zambian soldier with attractive blue socks, simply because I was white. While writing about the bloody civil war in Rhodesia I had several encounters in which I might have been expected to feel fear – while driving into what we thought was an ambush, when observing a nearby 'contact', and when flying in an old Viscount just after two had been shot down. What I experienced was not fear, but great rushes of adrenalin.

Similarly, in Kenya I have had a number of encounters with lions. One of the most memorable was when I was sitting on top of an Landcruiser with a friend in Tsavo East. Joe Cheffings, the driver, was inching towards two male lions at a kill; they were the short-maned Tsavo males, made famous by the book *Man Eaters of Tsavo*. As we pulled nearer their yellow eyes flamed with anger. Their top lips curled back as they snarled and their tails jerked from side to side. Suddenly they charged – one to the front and one to the back – spitting with rage. I shot through the sun-roof at record speed and Michael fell on top of me. Once more I did not feel fear, just a huge surge of adrenalin. All Fiona Silver said as she clicked away for the African pictures now in this book was, 'Sit still – all you need to do is sit still.'

At George Adamson's Kora reserve I also had two more close encounters with wild lions while on foot, described in greater detail in *Dust in a Dark Continent*. On the first occasion two male lions walked right past us when we were out in the open. They must have walked within ten yards of us. Next, when out without George, our Land Rover broke down and we had to walk twelve miles along bush roads back to his camp, in the mid-day sun. On the way, totally unarmed, we had to pass a pride of wild lions on the side of the road. Again, it was adrenalin that took us on our way and it was only afterwards when I paused to analyse the incidents that I felt concern. Do animals analyse and rationalise after escaping from a hunt? It is very unlikely.

Certainly there will be much adrenalin released in the last few minutes of a hunt. Does that reduce fear and distress? It is impossible to measure the mixture of fatigue and perceived fear in a hunt realistically. I believe that just as my mind and body switch off when experiencing an asthma attack, and just as I do not rationalise a potentially dangerous situation until afterwards, a stag at bay or a tired fox experiences a closing down. It is part of nature's answer to a natural process.

The Hunting Gene

A charging short-maned male Tsavo lion.

Away from men in suits, hypothesis, hyperbole, fact, fiction, egos and eccentricity, the hunting of the red deer on Exmoor involves real people and real animals in a beautiful place. The people of Exmoor are warm and friendly and the rolling rrrrrs of their authentic accent can still be heard throughout the area. The various attacks on hunting have come, as in the Lake District, at a time when family farms are suffering and as a result those with their roots attached firmly through many generations feel victimised and discriminated against.

The kennels of the Devon and Somerset Staghounds lie in the very heart of the moor at the picturesque village of Exford. Hunting forms the hub of village life – *Hounds Magazine*, sold by subscription throughout the country, is sold over the counter at the local newsagents in Exford. Visitors ask openly at the local shops where the next meet is and details of various hunt activities can be read in the church magazine.

Although many locals follow the hounds on horseback or by car, visitors arrive too, to stay in the local hotels, pubs and bed-and-breakfasts and to hire horses. Hunting really is important to the local economy, bringing £5.5 million flowing into the struggling area, creating the equivalent of 414 full-time jobs (16,000 throughout the country). Jobs from hunting do not just involve the huntsman, the hunt staff and accommodation. They encompass farriers; saddlers; hat, coat and boot makers; feedstuff suppliers; whip makers;

horn sellers; bridle makers; horse-box manufacturers; vets; breeders; livery owners; magazine publishers and photographers and many more. Some occupations are full-time, some are part-time, but all contribute to the local economy and the local community.

The Masters of the Devon and Somerset are Diana and Maurice Scott, who farm about 1000 acres around Brendon Hill. They both love hunting and Exmoor itself; the deer and the farm are important to them as well. Maurice speaks with the accent of the moor and his ancestry on Exmoor goes back many generations. He started deer-hunting on horseback when he was 5. He reckons that deer eat about 10 per cent of his grass, which means less for his 160 cows and 1400 ewes, including some traditional Exmoor horns. Like all farmers he has been hit badly by falling prices; last year his income fell

All sorts of people follow the hunt through the beautiful scenery of Britain.

THE HUNTING GENE

30 per cent, and the year before 23 per cent. He did not burn any wool this year, but for his Jacob fleeces he received just 2p a fleece – 1p to be paid this year and 1p next. After hearing of the price Maurice was receiving for his wool, I stopped on my way home to East Anglia at a tourist shop in Stow-on-the-Wold. The price for one jumper on sale there was £187.

TB is a problem for Maurice. His farm contains numerous badger setts and he thinks that there is a link between badgers and TB. At the last Ministry test, two of his cattle were confirmed as having TB and had to be sent away for slaughter. The story does not finish there, for one of the bullocks escaped from the abattoir. A dozen police cars tried to round it up and then a police marksman took four shots to kill it. Maurice was not amused. 'Why did they shoot it and why did it take four shots? Then they call hunting cruel. With deer hunting, the hunted deer either stands at bay, and is shot stone dead, or it gets away. There is no question of wounding, four shots, or the wounded deer getting away.' That is yet another mystery linked to the hunting debate.

Curlews are under pressure on Exmoor too.

In deer-hunting, hounds hunt the deer until it stops running; it then faces the hounds and they bark at it – it stands at bay. It is not bitten and it is not torn to pieces, as some antis suggest. With video cameras present at virtually every hunt, the lack of pictures of biting hounds confirms the lack of incidents. What happens is quite straightforward; the hounds are trained to bark at the deer standing at bay, just as the Labrador is trained to retrieve wounded pheasants alive, and the bloodhound is trained to follow an aniseed trail and not wander off after pheasants or rabbits, or bite the runner trailing the aniseed.

The matter of shooting deer as an alternative to hunting also involves a lot of hot air. Stalking will finish the concept of community deer on Exmoor and the Quantocks, and there will be a free-for-all, with night shooting, day shooting, legal shooting with rifles and illegal shooting with shotguns. As a boy I regularly went as a beater at a shoot on Forestry Commission land in the Breckland. Seeing roe deer sprayed with shot, described in some detail in my book *The Decline of an English Village*, stopped my beating and effectively destroyed any interest I had in shooting. I have a gun, Gordon Beningfield's 12 bore, but I simply use it for the odd magpie, mink and grey squirrel; it is a conservation gun.

When I think about the suffering of those beautiful Breckland roe, the images still haunt me – woundings; maimings; deer found days after being shot, hardly able to move but still living and suffering. In the course of a normal hunting season the Devon and Somerset

Staghounds will account for about forty stags and forty hinds. Of those virtually every animal will require just one shot, possibly one animal a year will require two. During the same season the huntsman and a few couple of hounds will be called out to over fifty animals – ones that are road casualties, or wounded by bullets, with horrendous injuries.

Despite this the RSPCA is very enthusiastic about so-called marksmen and expert shots. In 1997 two Tamworth pigs escaped from a market and the RSPCA arrived with experts and a dart gun. It took three shots at each pig to tranquillise them, much to the amusement of friends of mine who manage to tranquillise black rhinos with just one dart each. When I queried this with an RSPCA spokeswoman she said: 'Well they had thick skins, but a vet was present so it was all right.' Didn't the RSPCA 'experts' know that pigs have thick skins, and what use is a vet if the animals cannot be caught? Is the RSPCA working to a different set of standards from everyone else?

To the farmers of Exmoor such as Maurice Scott, what is happening seems to be a form of intimidation and victimisation, evidence of a general lack of understanding. He takes solace from his farm, which is a beautiful one. He has won numerous farming and wildlife awards and he has several wet meadows full of rushes and wild flowers. He worries that Exmoor's wildlife is diminishing. I asked him about the decline in curlews, as noticeable here as in other parts of the country. In 1977, when I visited the moor many times, the bubbling of curlews in the evening was a common sound of spring. While researching *The Hunting Gene* I heard and saw just one bird, at the foot of Dunkery Beacon, which is one of the places donated to the National Trust by an enthusiastic deer hunter that is now barred to the hunt. Maurice believes that the decline of the curlews is because of the usual three culprits – fox, magpie and crow. Badgers have possibly contributed too; the rise in badger numbers would increase the chances of eggs being found and eaten.

Diana Scott also works hard, both for the hunt and on the farm. Her farm enterprise is horse-breeding. Her stallions have bred some of the best eventing horses in the country, and the offspring have won at Badminton and Burghley and have represented Britain in the Olympics. Her favourite and most famous horse was Ben Faerie; she had him at the age of 2 and he died aged 28 in 1996. She had him buried in the garden. 'He was a really special horse and a really special friend, the sort of relationship that you get just once in a lifetime with animals. That's what people don't seem to grasp; we love our animals and that goes for the deer too.' There is no doubt that the local people who live and work on the moor have a special relationship with the deer, and to some the red deer has an almost mystical or even religious significance.

Throughout the year there are numerous events held by the Devon and Somerset Staghounds. At every one, much of the conversation is about the deer. There are dances, dinners and whist drives. There are duck races too. Plastic yellow ducks are raced down rivers, rather like a sophisticated form of Pooh Sticks. With all the ducks bar one being yellow, the winner can only be determined by the number on its underside. The one exception is a solitary red duck, which is auctioned at the start of every race.

The biggest events of the year are the puppy show and the point-to-point. The puppy show is slightly different from other puppy shows, for not only do knowing heads nod at hounds and names such as Chaffinch, Charity, Glider, Deadlock and Dragoon, but all the antlers – called 'horns' on Exmoor – of the hunted stags from the previous season are on display. Each set is marked with where the deer was 'found' and where it was 'taken'. Tanned faces are seen and West County accents are heard while the talk is about each hunt: 'Eee werr a good deerr, tak'n overr the brrow and down by Bullock's End.' Those who follow the hunt have names for every feature of the moor, large or small – names handed down as part of oral tradition, many not on any map: Mother Martha's Meadow, Jellico's Pool, Cuckoo Mountain, Dipper Copse, Sow and Nine Pigs, Birdfield and countless more.

The point-to-point is popular too, attracting a big crowd and a sudden explosion of anti-National Trust posters. Point-to-points are specifically held to raise money for the hunts, but they are also important for National Hunt racing. To qualify for point-to-point racing a horse has to have seven days hunting, each day witnessed and signed for by a Master of the hunt. The point-to-pointers and hunter-chasers then become the national hunt horses of tomorrow. If hunting ever goes and point-to-point racing goes with it, it will be a significant loss to the rural calendar and a huge pool of volunteer labour and enthusiasm will disappear.

Hedgerow protest.

During my time with the Devon and Somerset there was one other important event. Two thousand people, a huge crowd for Exmoor, met on Exford village green to protest at the attacks on farming, hunting and the people of the moor. They were addressed by an assortment of speakers including their local vicar, the Rev. Robin Ray, who spoke passionately about people, rural communities, the need for a living and a working countryside, farming and, yes, the traditions of hunting. If six lesbian lorry drivers, seven one-legged vegetarian Muslim pogo-stick racers, or eight gay left-handed income tax inspectors had demonstrated outside Parliament for any reason, their activities would have been in every national newspaper and on every national news broadcast in the land. Away from London, two thousand country people on Exmoor were totally ignored.

For my first hunt with the Devon and Somerset I rode by ancient Land Rover.

Tom was driving; he had a gravelly Somerset accent that almost required an interpreter. 'Have a drink,' he said to start with, pouring the largest whisky I have ever seen. I managed to reduce it to just a quadruple whisky. Almost as soon as the Land Rover moved off, the movement and the alcohol put me to sleep for half an hour. However, an ice cream van usually follows the hunt, even in mid-winter, and a clotted-cream ice-cream on a bitter morning soon restored me to consciousness. It was a fragmented day of stopping and starting, watching and listening. I found it difficult to follow, but Tom claimed that a hunt was taking place. Late in the afternoon the sun came out and hounds were soon hunting in a low, wet valley with grass, water, sallow, oak and old crack willow.

Roe deer ran from one copse to another but the hounds ignored them. Roe deer have very small home ranges. If Professor Bateson believes that red deer are 'remarkably sedentary', how does the eminent academic describe roe deer, whose home ranges are significantly smaller – 'static'?

An Exford protestor.

Two unofficial roe-packs have started up on Exmoor, hunting roe deer with a mixture of beagles, harriers and Bassetts. I have mixed feelings about that; the roe deer are held at bay by the hounds and shot, but roe-hunting has never been a tradition in Britain. Fallow and red deer, yes; but not roe. On the other hand, roe numbers are rising rapidly and roe-hunting with hounds has always been popular in France. The roe seasons are fragmented, including some summer hunting. Minkhounds quickly pass through an area and do little damage, but roe deer run in circles and are consequently hunted in circles, causing much disturbance to breeding birds and damage to wild flowers. Another concern I have is regulation; I think that all hunting should be registered and approved, so that there is both monitoring and control. This ensures that there are no abuses and also that kennel and hound management meet a required standard. Freedom is an issue with hunting, but responsibility should be part of that freedom.

Suddenly there was a distant shot; the hunt was over. I did not see the finish and it surprised many of those on horseback, who saw as little as the car followers. The horses and hounds went to an open grassy meadow. The hounds sat or rested after a long day. The dead stag arrived in the back of a Land Rover. It was an old animal 'going back', with not very good horns; it had been shot humanely with a single shot to the head.

Donald the huntsman took off his red coat, rolled up his sleeves and paunched the deer. The hounds fed on the innards. There is a theory growing in popularity that hounds are fit because many of them are fed on raw meat – mainly fallen stock. With cancer increasing even in young house dogs, a movement is developing to feed pets with a mixture of raw meat and biscuits to get back to a more natural canine diet.

It is the sight of blood, a knife, paunching and butchering that antis love to photograph, along with descriptions of 'cruelty' and 'barbarism'. It is neither. What the huntsman does is exactly what a butcher or an abattoir worker does. The difference is that the hunted deer is dealt with out of doors, while sheep, cattle, pigs and broiler fowl are butchered behind closed doors. The farmers over whose land the deer has run get joints of venison and the huntsman gives slices of liver to anybody who wants them. The giving of the liver, 'the best bit of the stag', is another old custom that excites the antis.

By coincidence, shortly after following this hunt and seeing a stag cut up for the first time – something that appeared normal and natural – I was watching television. Sport was replaced with a cookery programme, one of a never-ending stream, called *Big Kevin, Little Kevin*. The two Kevins announced that they were going to cook rabbit, so I left the television on. When travelling to Wales, they met three Welsh rabbiters with their ferret. It looked promising. Nets were put in place, the ferret was put down the hole, a rabbit bolted and was netted in next to no time. Little Kevin held it and said words to the effect: 'Oh, isn't it pretty? Much too nice to kill. We'll let it go.' He took it out of the net and released it, with no sign anywhere of Professor Bateson taking a blood sample.

The next scene was in the kitchen, with a rabbit already skinned and prepared and bought from a supermarket. It was no longer an animal, it had become a product. It was the great evasion again – separating the idea of meat from real animals. On a news report about a hunt, the emphasis is on killing and the body, complete with potted outrage. In a cookery programme, extraordinary steps are taken to avoid any glimpse or mention of killing, although the aim is to cook and eat an animal. To cap it all, safe in his kitchen, little Kevin picked up the rabbit's liver. 'Now this is the best bit of all,' he announced, 'a delicacy and good for you.' (At least, that was the gist.) He then ceremoniously put the liver in a blender or mincer. Hunting a deer openly, outdoors, for control, sport and food is wrong; killing a rabbit out of sight for televised entertainment is good.

Yet again this seems to confirm that there is a definite animal rights agenda at the BBC. Some may doubt that the BBC has agendas, but I believe that it has several. After my one-and-only appearance on BBC's *Question Time* I was congratulated by the producer, the presenter David Dimbleby, and told, 'We will want you again.' After announcing my intention to stand for Sir James Goldsmith's Referendum Party at the 1997 General Election, I was informed, 'We do not want you on the programme again. We wanted you as a countryman – not as an anti-European.' The fact that many countrymen are anti-European – having seen that the CAP is the death of British farming, not its destiny – seems to be beyond their understanding. When Salmon Rushdie was banned by foreigners wearing funny hats, the BBC described it as censorship and a denial of free speech. When the men in suits at the BBC ban a Cambridgeshire peasant, there is no way to protest. It is done quietly and efficiently – I was 'Solzhenitsyned'. Fortunately I have not been devastated by my removal. Now *Question Time* has five panellists, not four, and there is no real discussion – just a delivery of sound bites. Perhaps it should be re-named *Sound Bites for Bigots*.

To get a better look at the deer-hunt I again turned to riding. This was shortly after my venture with the Aldenham Harriers. The meet was well attended and my horse, Murphy, was a powerfully built animal from a local livery stable that depends on hunting for most of its income. At 16.2 hands it was again a long way up, and much to my alarm Murphy had had his mane cut, normally a handy thing for an incompetent rider to grab in an emergency. Fortunately, however, he had a neck strap across the base of his neck. In Ireland this strap is called 'the Jesus strap' – when a large unexpected hedge is approached, you say in alarm, 'Be Jesus!' and grab the strap.

Those gathered showed again the variation and different backgrounds of riders and car followers. A smartly dressed barrister was next to a farmer who looked like a mounted hay-stack, with long hair and a flowing beard. Among the car followers was Hope Bourne, a remarkable lady who for years lived in an isolated caravan in the Barle valley. She thinks that she is about 80, but is not too sure. For many years she was almost self-sufficient, growing vegetables, shooting rabbits and walking miles all over Exmoor. As she talks, her eyes shine with enthusiasm for life, for Exmoor, its wild beauty and its wildlife. Her voice is frail but as she describes the places and things she loves her words almost turn into poetry. She says:

> It is the call of the wild, the excitement of the chase, the social occasion, the running of the deer and the hounds coming through the heather and hearing them cry. There is the horn, the red coats, the landscape, a hundred riders on the skyline – where else can you see that? The pageant of the hunt is the pageant of the countryside and *they* want to take it away from us.

Hope Bourne – the voice of Exmoor.

Now she lives in an old people's bungalow in Withypool, but she still spends most of her time walking: 'I don't like being indoors – the air is too dry.'

Jo Scott, the daughter of the Masters, was at the meet too. She is a lively girl with laughing eyes, but it is not easy being the Masters' daughter. 'Everybody watches you and it's stressful too – when you see your mother opening strange packets outside the back door, over a bucket, wearing gloves – it is very worrying.' She loves hunting: 'It's in your blood, it's natural – it's better than sex.' This presumably means that the hunting is very good, or the West Country men are very bad; it weakens one neurotic anti-argument that hunting is all about macho images for men!

She would find a hunting ban difficult to cope with:

It would be catastrophic. What would we do? I can't imagine life without it; I know so many people through hunting and wouldn't see any of them. Every weekend there is a social event for the hunt. It would devastate my life. I have turned down good jobs because I don't want to leave Exmoor and I only work four days a week in winter so that I can hunt. Hunting is not cruel compared with other things – what about halal slaughter? They are allowed to do that but we are not allowed to follow our own traditions; it's mad. We are a minority in our own country.'

For a successful hunt, it is the job of the harbourer to find a warrantable stag. The harbourer goes out at all times and in all seasons, watching the deer and learning their ways. Martin Locke at Hawkridge had been up at dawn and had seen a good stag. It was the beginning of the rut, with the leaves of birch and beech turning to gold and copper and the berries on the holly crimson. Martin is the fifth generation of his family in the village. At one time they were wheelwrights; now he is a builder, hedger and fencer and had just been working on the Exmoor beech hedge banks at Hawkridge. Both he and his wife follow the hunt in their Land Rover and in term time he breaks off to pick his sons up from school so that they can join them. 'I've found a fine stag,' he said, 'there must be some good in hunting with the deer looking so fine.'

Out at all times and in all seasons. ABOVE: *Exmoor ponies.* RIGHT: *Martin Locke (left) working on an Exmoor hedgebank.*

The stag was a magnificent animal. He had been hunted before, apparently putting paid to one of Bateson's theories. The huntsman with five and half couple of 'tufters', the hounds that find the stag and start the hunt, had roused the stag in the Barle valley. The tufters were then joined by the rest of the pack. The scenery was spectacular, with steep valley sides, the river below and striking autumn colours. The hunt had started, we galloped along tracks, rode up steep banks and down others. It was exhilarating and Murphy was loving it. The hunt stopped. Even on horseback it was difficult to see what was happening because of the trees and the terrain. 'Where are the hounds?' and 'Can you hear the hounds?' seem to be the most common questions when out hunting. Diana Scott called me over; the stag had clapped down in the undergrowth after putting up another stag – a ruse to make the hounds switch quarry. Among fallen branches his antlers moved, betraying his hiding place.

The hounds began hunting again and the old stag moved off. The deer of the Barle valley move up the valley sides and over into the farm fields for grazing. This movement to feed over steep terrain appears to make nonsense of the theories concerning fitness and sedentary life-styles. We paused. 'Where are the hounds?'

All was quiet. I was with two farmers, a dentist and a surgeon, so I would be well looked after if I fell off. Charles Collins is a surgeon of national repute, specialising in cancer: 'I've lived here for twenty-five years and come from city life in Yorkshire. My wife comes from here and she taught me to ride – I was hooked. I see no contradiction in saving lives at work and hunting. I hunt for the friendships, the beautiful country of Exmoor, the pleasure of hunting and knowing that we are conserving the herds.'

The Hunting Gene

We had a choice. Most of the followers were going left, but the dentist had a hunch. 'Come right,' he said. We galloped; across the river, along rocky tracks with steep drops down one side and through the trees. We went up and down, ducking to avoid branches – holly dragged across one of my cheeks drawing blood. It was exhilarating, exciting – we paused – the horses steamed, the river murmured as it ran over stones and birch leaves floated down, caught in an eddy of air. A distant shot rang out; we had been galloping in the wrong direction.

Riders and horses, including a lady riding side-saddle, gathered again in a grass meadow. Some dismounted; I stayed on as I would never have got on again if I had followed suit. The hounds were resting and the stag arrived, a fine animal with splendid antlers. He died in the country he knew; among the trees, the wind, the water, the scents and sounds of Exmoor, and at the end, his end was quick. There had been no wounding, no loading up in a cattle truck and transporting hundreds of miles, there had been no loss of dignity. His death had been simply a modification of nature.

Tilly Smith is an animal behaviourist and zoologist with a particular interest in deer and reindeer. She does not hunt and has an independent view: 'Hunting on Exmoor is as near to nature as you can possible get. I think it is acceptable. Hunting is an instinct and part of man's survival over millions of years. There is a hunting gene and it is natural.'

Resting at the end of a hard day.

My visits to Exmoor would have made an excellent television programme. I met some wonderful people and found a community almost under siege. They feel victimised and misunderstood and they are convinced that attempts are being made to culturally cleanse them. I was fascinated by the hounds, the horses and the way of life. I attended two hunts in which two stags died in the country they knew. Deer have to die to prevent over-population, which would lead to disease and unacceptable crop damage.

Perhaps if all this were seen on television as a record of events, rather than as a programme of horror and confrontation, viewers would understand the countryside, its people and its culture more clearly. Sadly, in the present climate of urban political correctness, this seems too much to hope for.

Chapter Ten

THE MENACE OF MINK

William Garfit.

THE HUNTING GENE

ink-hunting is one of the most recent forms of hunting with hounds and there are currently twenty packs of mink hounds operating each summer. New packs are forming almost every year and it is becoming an increasingly popular form of both control and recreation. Although the activity is relatively new, it grew out of otter-hunting. For the old English otterhound the arrival of the North American mink could not have come at a more opportune time; as the otter disappeared, the mink appeared and possibly saved the attractive otterhound as a working dog.

Otter-hunting stopped when the otter was protected in 1978 in England and Wales, and in 1982 in Scotland. It was not an anti-cruelty measure – it was a sensible conservation move to try to save the otter. Although the action prevented the otter being hunted, trapped and shot, the protective legislation itself could do nothing to prevent the pollution by agro-chemicals which was the otter's biggest killer.

Otter-hunting was probably the oldest form of organised hunting with hounds in Britain. An early record indicates that in 1175 one Roger Follo was appointed 'King's Otter-hunter' by a charter of Henry II. Otter-hunting was undertaken for both sport and necessity. Otters were common and freshwater fish were an important commodity. Due to the various religious fasts, feasts and ordinances – such as eating fish on Fridays – there was a great demand for fish from river, stream, lake and stew-pond. Sea fish were eaten by coastal dwellers only because of the difficulties of transportation and storage. It was a pointless exercise trying to breed carp in a pond to eat when otters used the facility as a self-service

Pure-bred otterhounds hunting mink in Pembrokeshire.

fish restaurant. Otter-hunting had a purpose and it also had a season: from 'Shrovetide to midsummer'.

The otter thrived through history until the great agricultural revolution of the twentieth century. It was not hunting that led to its downfall but pesticide poisoning. In fact it was the otter-hunters who alerted the conservationists about the otter's demise. The decline is summed up simply in the Game Conservancy Trust's excellent book, *A Question of Balance*, edited by Dr Stephen Tapper:

> Since the late 1950's organo-chlorine seed dressings (DDT) and, more recently, polychlorinated biphenyls (PCB's), have seeped out of the agricultural and urban environments into English river systems. This appears to have reduced the fertility of female otters and wiped out otters from most

The otter, finally making a comeback in many parts of Britain.

of England and Southern Wales. Geographically, the link between the otter's disappearance and rivers that drain arable and urban areas is clear enough.

It was a science-based ecological disaster; in the countryside chemicals were produced for use with cereal crops and their sale was boosted by the usual false claims of 'good husbandry', 'efficiency', 'progress' and 'profit'. The combination of farming and conservation does need profit, but not profit based on poisoning the world. Some scientists never learn. After the DDT disaster came organo-phosphates, which in my view helped to create the conditions for BSE; again the new chemicals that came with extravagant promises were foolishly greeted with enthusiasm. Now it is the turn of genetically modified crops to be hailed as the great infallible step forwards.

As otter numbers plummeted, their habitat was devastated – driven by the new agricultural mania for drainage and tidiness described as 'efficiency'. It looked as if the otter was doomed to almost certain extinction – at least in lowland Britain. It was during this time of otter decline that the mink population exploded. American mink first arrived in Britain to be farmed for their fur in 1929. Because of their agility – mink can run, jump, climb, burrow and swim – individual animals escaped and North American mink have been living in the wild since the 1930s. The first confirmed breeding of feral mink came from south

Devon in 1956, and since then mink have colonised most of mainland Britain and some of its off-shore islands. Today's population is estimated to be 110,000. Undoubtedly the population boom has been assisted by animal activists, who over the years have raided several mink farms and released hundreds of mink into the wild. Although superficially on the side

of animals, the release of captive mink has turned out to be a wildlife disaster. Supposed animal aid has turned into animal destruction. Many of the mink were shot, killed by dogs or run over. The survivors quickly reverted to the wild and, being carnivores, wreaked havoc on Britain's indigenous wildlife.

The reason why mink flourished in conditions which were unsuitable for otters is two-fold. The otter's diet is about 90 per cent fish, and it is thought that a build-up of chemicals in the otter came through eating contaminated fish. The mink's diet, on the other hand, is roughly one-third fish, one-third bird, and one-third animal; it was not affected by pollution in the same way. Habitat loss was also not so important to the mink. An otter is quite a large animal, often weighing up to 20 lb (old dog otters can weigh much more), and it needs cover for resting and breeding. The mink weighs only just over 2 lb and can find security and concealment in numerous places that are inadequate for otters.

The North American mink, an unwanted and destructive alien.

Some politically correct scientists and conservationists suggested that the alien mink should be left alone; they considered that it caused no problems to indigenous wildlife, that it had found its own niche and that control was unnecessary. Such a view was, of course, nonsense. Countrymen and gamekeepers reported that as soon as mink arrived, water voles, moorhens, kingfishers and ducks disappeared. They believe that our wildlife was easy meat for mink – our birds and animals had no experience of this fierce predator and therefore were too trusting. To make matters worse, mink sometimes engage in surplus killing; there are records of over a hundred hens and a hundred young pheasants being killed in a single night. The so-called experts dismissed all this as 'anecdotal' and 'circumstantial' evidence. They blamed the loss of habitat for the decline of waterbirds and animals.

Most water birds, their eggs and chicks are at risk from feral mink. ABOVE AND RIGHT: *Great-crested grebes.*

I saw my first mink in the early 1980s on the River Otter in Devon. I had gone there in the forlorn hope that the otter could still be found along the river of the same name. Alas, I was too late. Instead I saw my first mink. I have to say that the memory is a pleasant one as the wild mink is an attractive animal. There were a pair of them, both black, hunting in and out of the water. It was not their fault that they were alien animals in the wrong country in a distant continent. Judging by the absence of moorhens they were already having a noticeable effect on the wildlife of the River Otter.

THE HUNTING GENE

My first local mink arrived several years later. I had noticed that both moorhens and water voles had vanished from our little brook, a tributary of the River Cam, but I gave no real thought to their absence. Then early one summer morning, with the dew still heavy, I saw a mallard drake burst into flight, quacking vigorously. I quietly made my way to the bank of the brook, expecting a fox to come into view. Instead a dark mink swam by, totally unaware of my presence. Suddenly the absence of moorhens and water voles was explained. Soon afterwards a neighbour noticed his cattle staring towards the far bank of the brook. As he followed the line of their gaze, he was just in time to see a mink reversing out of a kingfisher's nesting hole with a kingfisher in its mouth.

Gradually reports came from all over the country of a wide range of animals and birds being killed by mink: from rabbits, hares, rats and hedgehogs to mallards, grebes, gadwall, lapwings, grey partridges and even pheasants. The young of many species were particularly vulnerable. It was obvious that the North American mink did pose a serious threat to important parts of our indigenous wildlife population. Even the scientists began to have second thoughts and, behold, soon the anecdotal evidence of country bumpkins was being superceded by the scientific findings of research biologists and zoologists. Of course, they amounted to the same thing – apart from the fact that one set of observations was ignored by the experts, whereas the observations of the scientists were accepted and paid for with research grants.

The threat posed by mink became more apparent when it was reported that mink kills in Scotland had included common and Arctic terns as well as guillemots and razorbills. It was clear that if mink got to certain Scottish islands then a number of Britain's most spectacular and rare birds would be at risk. Since then that is what has happened. Mink have arrived on some of Scotland's most wildlife rich, and ecologically vulnerable, off-shore islands. In just a few years the populations of dunlin, redshank, ringed plover, lapwing and snipe have plummeted on the Hebridean islands of North and South Uist and Benbecula. In addition tern colonies are at risk, along with golden plovers, curlew and common

sandpipers. With predation pressure from mink at its present level, it is unlikely that the rare red-necked phalarope will breed again there in the foreseeable future.

On the Uists the damage being done by mink is topping up that already done by hedgehogs. I like hedgehogs and am worried about their decline in my area – possibly caused by a combination of pesticide poisoning, road casualties and their being eaten by the rapidly expanding badger population. The story elsewhere is different. In 1974 seven hedgehogs were foolishly released on South Uist, an island with no hedgehogs, to control garden slugs. Now over five thousand of them have spread through to North Uist, eating the eggs of vulnerable birds as they advanced. A few years ago, after hearing a gamekeeper talking of the damage done by egg-eating hedgehogs, I asked the RSPB if this did happen. They were scornful and claimed that a hedgehog's jaws were not strong

Seabirds do well where predators are absent: gannets in Pembrokeshire.

enough to break an egg. Now even the RSPB is anxious about the threat from both hedgehogs and mink on the Uists. The scientists got it wrong again – twice over.

Scientists are not the only ones to get things wrong. On our farm we began improving the habitat along the brook several years ago, despite the protestations of the inappropriately named Environment Agency. Although fish numbers appeared to be good and cover came back to the banks, I was convinced that otters would never return. I believed that although the otters were much bigger and stronger than mink, they simply found the little aliens too aggressive and belligerent. In 1993 I was proved wrong; otters returned to the brook and they have been there ever since. It is interesting to record that, despite the views of some scientists, the otter's return to my part of Cambridgeshire was almost certainly the result of a successful reintroduction programme carried out by Philip Wayre of the Otter Trust. When another reintroduction programme was launched, on the Thames in 1999, the BBC blamed the otter's original decline on 'blood sports' and agriculture. By using the words 'blood sports' the BBC signalled its bias. As usual it had got some of its facts wrong – otter-hunting played no part in the otter's demise, a fact that is accepted by most informed conservationists.

It is odd how many non-scientists have shown the scientists what needs to be done and how to do it. Philip Wayre is not a scientist, yet he has led the field in the captive breeding of otters. George Adamson was not a scientist, but he pioneered the rehabilitation of lions. In Kent the remarkable non-scientist John Aspinall is successfully breeding some of the world's rarest mammals, from bongos to gorillas. An extraordinary untrained housewife, Dot Eaton, had a more successful dormouse breeding programme in her garden shed than some scientists managed to achieve at London Zoo. Similarly, a teacher in Norfolk is captive-breeding red squirrels and another Norfolk man, Bill Makins, is currently trying to breed corncrakes. Miriam Rothschild is almost self-taught and has set the standard on countryside restoration. I am glad to say that the Countryside Restoration Trust (a group of anxious amateurs inspired by the unqualified Laurens van der Post and the equally unqualified Gordon Beningfield) was instrumental in triggering assorted experts into action over the wildlife disaster taking place in the general farming countryside.

I have never been so happy about being totally wrong as I have about the return of the otter; we now have both otters and mink on our little brook. I believe that if we can remove the mink, moorhens and water voles will come back and the kingfisher population will also improve. The mink is bad for bio-diversity and it should be controlled whenever and wherever possible. If the Government were serious about conservation, MAFF would be instructed to launch a mink eradication programme, just as it did for the coypu in East Anglia. The coypu, of course, damaged agricultural crops and drainage schemes – causing economic damage – so action was taken. Mink only damage wildlife, game birds and domestic poultry – so no action is taken whatsoever.

Logically, mink-hunting is a pastime that should be welcomed. But yet again, because mink hunters dress up (a practical necessity), use hounds (very suitable dogs) and enjoy their sport, mink-hunting is considered by many to be unacceptable. It is a strange view. If one of the crimes of mink-hunting is that the hunters enjoy their sport, then presumably every pest control officer in the land must be encouraged to dislike his or her work and radiate surliness and misery. If the issue of enjoyment really is high on the agenda of the anti-hunt lobby, then it does confirm that many antis are a joyless, ignorant, interfering, intolerant, self-important group of people. Perhaps the collective noun for them ought to be a 'gloom' – a gloom of antis.

In an attempt to feel the same sense of gloom, I arranged to watch the Northamptonshire Minkhounds at work. They are housed at the kennels of the Woodland Pytchley Foxhounds in Northamptonshire, where the kennelman, Tim Taylor – a smiling, happy man – is glad to have them. He has been in hunt service ever since leaving the army as a lance corporal. In fact, he was in hunt service before leaving the forces as he was huntsman of the Purbeck and Bovington Beagles, then one of the army's packs of beagles. He started following hounds as a boy with his grandfather, on bikes, and before moving to the Woodland Pytchley as huntsman, he was a whipper-in with the Fitzwilliam Foxhounds.

Nearly all the Northamptonshire Minkhounds are retired foxhounds or foxhounds drafted in especially for mink. One or two have the best of both worlds, hunting foxes in winter and mink in summer. The pack has no traditional otterhounds, but otterhound blood can still be found in many packs. In Pembrokeshire there is a pack of pure-bred otterhounds;

with no terriers they catch few mink, but they make a wonderful sight hunting the rivers and streams of west Wales.

The followers of the Northamptonshire Minkhounds are a most un-toff-like group of people, but the huntsman wears a red waistcoat and the Masters and whippers-in yellow waistcoats – thus revealing themselves as toffs to the eyes of the unknowing. One of the Joint Masters is inevitably a vet. He sees no contradiction between saving animals and hunting animals: 'It's the hunting that I enjoy, not the killing, and many vets go hunting. It is not cruel, it's all over too quickly. The reason Tony Blair wants to ban it is that he has simply plucked something out of the air to try and get some instant respect and easy popularity.' Another Joint Master, David Fortescue, hunts the hounds. He is a down-to-earth working farmer and a countryman through and through:

> We farm sheep and cereals, but I've been hunting since I was 6. My grandfather used to take me with the Fitzwilliam, on my feet. Now my daughters ride with the Fitzwilliam, but I still hunt on my feet and I have been involved with the minkhounds for fifteen or sixteen years [the pack started in 1982]. I love the relationship with the hounds. Tim feeds them and exercises them, but as soon as they hear my voice they are up and they know me; it is a very special relationship. I feel I am doing a service to the countryside killing mink; the more mink we kill the better. If Blair stops it, I shall carry on. There is no way I can put hounds down that I have bred and have always been in kennels. If we have to go inside, then we will go inside.

A pastoral scene – mink-hunting.

Huntsman and hounds anticipate action.

Another Dave, a warehouseman approaching 60 years old, is a whipper-in. He too sees hunting mink as a conservation plus:

> Mink are such destroying little sods that you have to get rid of them. I used to watch water voles, kingfishers, moorhens, grebe chicks and ducks – now they have all gone. Mink-hunting is sport and conservation all rolled into one. The threat of a hunting ban is bad; not all the townies are against us, it's the media that feed them rubbish. When my dad came home from the war, he told us that we would have freedom for the rest of our lives; now look what they are doing. They are chopping it off.

Matt Allen, an articulate and enthusiastic glue salesman in his 40s who lives in St Ives in Cambridgeshire, is another Joint Master. He says:

> Yes, I sell glue, it kills time between weekends. I chose mink-hunting because it is a form of hunting I could afford. All I need is a pair of boots, a stick and £2 in my pocket. I am a country boy living in the town because I was priced out of the

countryside. I love every aspect of hunting; the people I meet; the countryside; watching the hounds work and I love being beside the river. Hunting is everything to me – next to my children's health. It is a tragedy; everybody in this hunt is working for their living; Labour should be an ally, but nobody here will vote Labour now because of its stance on hunting. If hunting is banned I shall break the law and continue to hunt. It will make me a criminal when I have never broken the law before, and I would go to prison. It has become a way of life – it is not simply a pastime, like golf. I am not prepared to sacrifice a way of life and I would not be prepared to see the hounds all shot – you can't drag hunt mink. If the politicians were honest they would know that most people never think about hunting. One per cent want to ban it; one per cent care passionately about it and 98 per cent are more concerned about where they are going on their next holiday.

My first hunt with the Northamptonshire Minkhounds was on the River Chater at North Luffenham in Rutland. It was a beautiful day of early summer with a variety of lush and dripping greenery, and birds singing. Two wet hounds sang too, on touching an electric fence – the water ensured an excellent earth. As a boy I once saw two unsuspecting men relieve themselves over an electric fence; they jumped even higher than the hounds.

The hounds hunted keenly, but there was little scent or perhaps no mink. Occasionally a hound would speak, setting off a short chorus amongst the others, but there was no prolonged hunt. At willows the hounds and the huntsman watched with interest as Frank the terrierman and his two terriers investigated various cracks and crevices with no luck. Even with no mink the appeal was clear; a walk by water, along an unfamiliar river in the company of hounds. Anybody who likes walking along river banks with a dog would have liked hunting along the River Chater with the Northamptonshire Minkhounds.

Matt's son Hadley was with his 10-year-old friend Ben. Ben has cystic fibrosis and following hounds has been his passion since he was 4. Despite his chest condition he hunts with the South Herts Beagles in the winter and the minkhounds in the summer.

Hilary Chasteauneuf gets her leg over – the fence.

THE HUNTING GENE

His mother is convinced that the interest in hunting and the exercise help him to lead an almost normal life. One lady from Hertfordshire follows the hounds because of the wildlife she sees; when she is not hunting she is holding coffee mornings and opening her garden for the benefit of her local wildlife trust. I was astonished to discover that there was even somebody who had spent several years of her childhood in my own village. Since going to my old primary school, Hilary Chasteauneuf has become a qualified interior designer. She has no doubts about the morality of hunting: 'There is nothing wrong with it; it is not unnatural; better to be wild and killed by hounds than reared in cramped conditions and sent to an abattoir, or be squashed on the roads.'

We walked through grassy meadows; waded through stinging nettles, climbed through or over barbed wire fences and saw no mink. There was little disturbance as hounds and followers moved upstream, certainly less than that caused by fishermen – who in a competition can cause disruption to wildlife for a whole day along miles of river bank. The only damage to wildlife that I saw had been committed by the Environment Agency: a stretch of the river had been cleaned out and turned into a drainage channel.

Environmental damage courtesy of the Environment Agency.

At the next hunt there was an even bigger blot on the landscape – Milton Keynes. Nobody seems interested in the number of bee orchids, badger setts and butterflies displaced or killed when this twentieth-century architectural and social folly was designed and created. When animals are killed by hounds there is a public and media outcry; when wildlife is destroyed by development, cars and the industrialisation of agriculture there is public apathy and media silence.

The valley of the River Ouse to the west of Milton Keynes makes an astonishing comparison with the social engineer's dream; in just a few miles modern urban fantasy land is replaced by rural pastureland and water-meadows where again hounds, huntsman and followers enjoyed a fine summer day. At a concrete bridge the hounds spoke and over the next few minutes their volume did not fall. There was a hidden mink living in the cracked concrete support of the bridge. The hounds were called away as Frank and Matt arrived with their dogs. The concrete cracks were too tight for the two Jack Russells and two Border terriers, and the mink could not be flushed. The farmer was asked if he wanted the mink removed – he did. A crowbar was fetched and efforts were made to get into the cracked support from the top, by breaking the surface of the farm road. The mink evidently did not like the banging and stuck its head out of a crack just below the roadway to see what was causing the disturbance. Just as it did so, a Jack Russell stuck its head over the edge of the roadway to see what lived in the crack. The terrier jumped at the mink and they crashed down five feet to the water's edge; at the commotion three other terriers piled in immediately and the hunt was soon over in a mêlée of growling and snarling. The mink's end was almost instantaneous. It was not a pretty sight but it was not torn to pieces and it would have felt and known next to nothing.

The hunt resumed. Suddenly ahead of three swimming hounds there was a swirl of water, then a bird surfaced behind them. It had dived and swum beneath them. I was astonished; it was a female goosander or red-breasted merganser – they look very similar to me. These saw-bills (birds with serrations on their beaks for holding fish) are normally associated with Scotland and the north. Whether it was a stray bird or whether they are increasing their range in the same way as cormorants, I cannot say.

'Has anybody seen the mink?'

Another hunt started and finished at a fine old willow tree with a hollow trunk. Hounds went inside and outside the tree, but were again called off until suddenly an adult mink was seen moving through the top branches of a clump of hawthorns. As the hounds were called, it scrambled to the ground and disappeared, showing the versatility and speed of these remarkable little animals. The terriers found seven young mink among the roots of the willow.

Further along the river hounds spoke again, but no more mink were found. Eight alien carnivores had been accounted for – which in conservation terms meant that a variety of indigenous fish, small mammals, birds, chicks and domestic fowl would survive the summer and a number of eggs would hatch. The stretch of river was not keepered and trapping mink is too time consuming for most working farmers with no game interests. The minkhounds had performed a service; they had shown that they could locate mink and that they did provide an element of control. In the normal course of a year the twenty minkhound packs in Britain account for about seven hundred mink.

Because of the control element in mink-hunting, the combination of minkhound and terrier could be one of the ways to combat the spread of mink in the vulnerable Scottish islands. In the summer of 1999 some conservationists gave serious thought to the possibility

of taking minkhounds to the Uists; unfortunately a resurgence of political anti-hunting rhetoric led them to develop cold feet. Political correctness and expediency triumphed once again over conservation.

The effectiveness of minkhounds in Scotland was demonstrated to me by the Northamptonshire Minkhounds when they were invited to the upper reaches of the Tweed. Despite the area being keepered, a mink was caught on both days. One was killed by the hounds in the water, and one was killed by a combination of hounds and terriers at the end of the second day. It was rather like a rat-hunt, with the mink running from tree roots to grass clumps until several dogs jumped on it.

The fact that it finished like a rat-hunt raises another important issue. If politicians ever decide to ban mink-hunting with dogs, does this mean that rat-hunting with dogs is also cruel and must be banned? There is little significant difference between them. When we get too many rats in our deep litter shed (a hen-house with a deep straw floor), we dig them out and a variety of dogs dig and dive enthusiastically alongside. I have never liked rats, but with rats scurrying, dogs pursuing, and people shouting the politically correct would see ratters and dogs enjoying themselves. Oh dear, what will happen if someone blows a horn and wears a red waistcoat as well?

The Hunting Gene

Is there really a difference between a dog chasing a rat and a dog chasing a mink? Or between a rabbit and a hare? The anti-hunters claim that rabbiting and ratting will never be banned, which confirms that animal welfare does not seem to be the real issue. Certainly killing rats and mice with dogs is kinder than any alternative. It is estimated that up to twenty million rats and mice are killed each year with anti-coagulant chemicals, and that it can take as long as a week for some of the animals to die. Most of the deaths are underground and unseen and so they are acceptable – out of sight, out of mind; another moral evasion.

To make yet more of a mockery of the issue, some opponents of hunting with dogs want to classify rabbits as rodents. The idea is that legislation would allow dogs to be used to control rodents. A rabbit is a *lagomorph*, the same family as the hare. This is the stuff of George Orwell's *1984* – the thought police and the assertion that two and two equals five. Here is piece of almost Orwellian wisdom: 'If you call a horse's tail a leg, how many legs has a horse got?' The answer is simple – four. You may call a horse's tail a leg, but it remains a tail. Those who want to stop toffs hunting at any price may want to call a rabbit a rodent, but it is still a rabbit and still a *lagomorph*.

Hunting with dogs? The author (right) and friends ratting.

Chapter Eleven

FACT AND FICTION

william Garfit -

THE HUNTING GENE

To reach the last two chapters of a book is usually a relief. It signifies the last leg of an emotional and physical effort in which a project is at last completed. On this occasion it is different; I have finished earlier than originally planned and have not been able to take the time I wanted to meet every last contact and see every aspect of the hunting year. The book is thorough, however, and I have seen the hunting process in its entirety and at closer quarters than before, although I would have liked to have attended the Boxing Day meet of the Heythrop in Chipping Norton and there was no time to go with the harbourer on Exmoor to see deer in the snow.

The choice to finish earlier than first intended was my own. During the course of writing about the various hunts, I have met many good people, seen hounds in a completely new light, and been fortunate enough to have travelled in some of the most beautiful parts of Britain. Consequently, with hunting under renewed attack, I feel obliged to bring the book out as early as possible. If hunting is still taking place when *The Hunting Gene* appears, I hope it will help to keep the sport in its place in the countryside. If hunting has been banned already, then I hope it helps to alert people to the injustice that has been done – an injustice to our long traditions of individual freedom and an affront to the whole concept of civil liberties. Banning hunting represents an attempt to 'culturally cleanse' the countryside, and with agriculture forced into desperation it is within a whisker of becoming 'ethnic cleansing'. It was ethnic cleansing, we are told, that our Prime Minister and President Clinton of the United States found so morally unacceptable in Kosovo. By a whisker, banning hunting would be cultural cleansing rather than ethnic cleansing; but economic desperation and anti-cultural legislation lead to exactly the same result: rural communities shedding their indigenous populations, families being driven from the land and a wave of suicides – killing by mental anguish and hopelessness rather than as a result of outside physical violence. Their double standard shows Blair and Clinton to be two of a kind; they are, it seems to me, insubstantial men, morally bankrupt, high on veneer and low on substance.

The whole anti-hunting saga is a sorry one, based on distortion, misinformation, ignorance and money. As far as wildlife, conservation and the environment are concerned, hunting and the concerted effort to ban it are a distraction diverting attention, time and millions of pounds away from the real issues. It might make a few people feel good to give their fortunes to 'saving our beautiful wildlife', it might assist ego-tripping politicians with their self-promotion, and it might make several animal welfare organisations extraordinarily rich – but it does nothing to stop global warming, the depletion of the ozone layer or the pollution of our air, our soil, our rivers and our seas. It does nothing to stop the frightening deforestation or the over-abstraction of water; it ignores the ever-increasing use of fossil fuels and has no relevance for over-population. It is not involved with stemming the current mania for development, and the Common Agricultural Policy remains unreformed – turning food production into an industrial process, slowly killing our wildlife, driving old farming families off the land and killing our rural communities. The Common Fisheries Policy continues to kill billions of fish a year in the name of conservation; while globalisation has been turned

A traditional countryman – a member of an endangered species.

into the acceptable face of unsustainable food production, unsustainable industry and unsustainable trade.

In the cause of the global market-place the rural populations of the world are being destabilised as never before. While politicians and pop stars recite platitudes about the plight of Rainforest Indians, Aborigines and 'native Americans', these same people do not appear to give a thought, yet alone a tear, for the rural cultures of other countries, including the country people of Britain. Those who live, work and play in rural Britain, as part of traditional communities, have become members of an endangered species.

But in the lexicon of disaster and folly all this is only a start; there is the growing problem of genetically modified crops, the lingering madness of BSE – and there are other nightmares now emerging, such as the over-use of antibiotics. There is the damming of rivers, the destruction of eco-systems, the mounting number of 'food miles' for every meal eaten and the ignored scandal of the harm being done to the outer limits of our atmosphere by air travel. The growth in the air industry totally disregards the huge amount of damage being done by high-altitude pollution; expanding business is considered to be far more important than long-term sustainability. So activities that threaten the very life-support system of the

THE HUNTING GENE

What is the problem – over-population, deforestation, pollution, global warming? No, chasing foxes.

planet are accepted, just so long as they stimulate economic activity and promote political popularity. In answer to all this, what does Tony Blair – thinker, philosopher and leader of men – decide to do? He wants to stop people chasing foxes across muddy fields. What courage, what vision, what intellectual genius!

Why will politicians never learn? We know that the disappearance of the dinosaur, and possibly the demise of the wild horse, was caused by rapid climate change. Those who rule us know that the same threat is the greatest one to our current way of life. In my school days we were told that global warming would be a fraction of one degree per hundred years; already that estimate is way out of date. Government departments have data on a new warmer world, but they do nothing to stop it; they need the oil taxes to keep up their fantasy spending and life-styles and nothing must be done to hamper the global market-place. In the face of all this, urgent and obvious, to focus on fox-hunting is not only one of the greatest evasions of all time, it also turns most of our politicians into a new generation of Monty Python characters.

Even the assumption that a ban on hunting will save innocent wild animals is wrong. It is ironic that a ban on hunting will actually lead to the loss of more foxes, deer, hares and mink. It follows, too, that the alternative ways of killing will cause an increase in suffering, not a reduction; the simple pluses for hunting are that it is nearer to nature than any other form of control and that the hunted animal is either killed or it gets away to run another day. It is not wounded, maimed or left to die a slow and painful death. As a non-participant in country sports I find it much easier to defend hunting than certain aspects of shooting and fishing.

A ban on hunting would simply lead to many thousands of acres going over to pheasant shooting. From these areas the permanent fox population would be wiped out through the use of gun, trap and snare. Incoming foxes would receive the same fate when they move into the vacated territories. Then, when pheasant shooting is banned – when, not if – the illegal lurcher and terrier men would move in for those foxes still surviving the effects of 'land improvement' through chainsaw and plough.

The fate of the red deer would be simpler. The Exmoor herd, the oldest and possibly the healthiest herd in Britain, would quickly be decimated. Deer are the property of the land owner whose land they happen to be visiting for feeding. At the moment they are tolerated because the land-owning and farming communities of Exmoor look forward to seeing the deer; they enjoy welcoming the hunt and most of them have a taste for venison. Because the hunt has turned the red deer into a community animal, the West Country deer are in the main tolerated, although there is a low level of poaching. One deer eats as much as four sheep, but that loss is not a problem to those who follow the hunt. With hunting banned every deer would be seen as a loss, with no community benefit or advantage. When that factor is added to a deep resentment at the perceived vindictiveness of a ban, the red deer of Exmoor will be shot in

The future for the red fox and the red deer is secure while hunting continues.

unprecedented numbers. Without Government intervention and compensation, their status as a common animal in the south-west will be in danger.

When I told an anti-hunt campaigner this, her reaction was interesting. 'Who cares?' she said. 'We just want to criminalise the bastards.' There, in a nutshell, the anti-hunting case was put simply and concisely. The truth is that banning hunting is not about cruelty or a concern for wildlife; it is a political desire 'to criminalise the bastards'. It is the old class war: 'toff bashing', them and us, privilege against the working man.

The Devon and Somerset Staghounds expose this fraud; 75 per cent of those who ride are locals who are normally found with mud on their boots and smells on their hands. They are ordinary, hard-working country people experiencing great financial hardship because of the fall in farm incomes, who now find their sport to be politically incorrect although it is a model of sustainable use and good management. 'Criminalise the bastards' says more about the anti-hunting fraternity than the hunters.

The 'Criminalise the bastards' anti was interesting for another significant reason. Campaigners against country sports claim to be 'fighting for wildlife'. In reality they usually know very little about it. This particular one lived in East Anglia and was ranting about red

deer in Scotland and Exmoor. 'But,' I said quite innocently, not trying to catch her out, 'the biggest red deer live in East Anglia.'

'There aren't any red deer in East Anglia,' she replied instantly, showing the true depth of her knowledge. In fact the red deer of Thetford Forest and some areas of Suffolk are the largest and most magnificent specimens in Britain because of the favourable habitat they live in.

The fate of the brown hare will be no better. Although it is the subject of a special Biodiversity Action Plan, intended to double numbers by the year 2010; that is most unlikely to happen if hunting and coursing are banned. The hunters and coursers are in fact the hare's best friends; they want hares and they ensure that they have a healthy population through both the creation of habitat and, in shooting areas, control of predators. With that interest gone, farming will intensify, destroying hare habitat, and many farmers will be less likely to tolerate hare damage.

The brown hare flourishes alongside hunting and legal coursing.

Barn owl hunting headlands, painted by Robert Gillmor.

But there is a larger threat to the hare than this. If hunting and legal coursing were banned, the hare would be at the mercy of illegal coursing gangs. These men will not be deterred by laws – their activity is illegal already. They defend themselves with catapults and steel ball bearings, and their life-styles are often very different from those of normal society. Land owners approach them with caution and most police forces already tend to turn a blind eye to them to avoid violent confrontation and possible injury. With hunting gone, the gangs would move onto new land and there would be less control and regulation. Even if they were caught, what would happen? Many illegal coursers are diddicoys or travellers; they will claim that they have no money and no address and that they are merely tired, hungry people catching hares for the pot in the traditional way. A court case and conviction will actually cost money and achieve nothing. Over recent years, despite the existing legislation, illegal hare-coursing has increased substantially. If legal coursing were banned, illegal coursing would become out of control and illegal coursing is about dogs catching and killing hares. Sadly, the illegal coursing would surely widen to include foxes and deer.

Some farmers are now taking action to avoid conflict – they are actually shooting all the hares on their land in order to prevent the arrival of the illegal coursers. Already thousands of acres in Essex and Cambridgeshire have been almost cleared. Consequently, in the name of animal welfare and conservation the hare will have to suffer the horrors and suffering of hare shoots, and will face local extinction. Again the simple hypocrisy and double standards of the anti-hunting lobby seem to make them unwilling, or unable, to face the facts; and the actual welfare of the quarry species seems to take second place to ego-tripping gesture politics.

Even the mink will get no respite. Support for mink control with hounds and terriers comes from some of Britain's leading conservationists. With hunts and hounds gone, trapping and shooting will be the only ways of control. Just like a trapped fox, the trapped mink cannot create its required 'flight distance' and so it suffers stress. Unlike the trapped fox, however, the trapped mink is often not shot; the cage, with the mink inside, is thrown into deep water and the mink drowns in a cruel, unacceptable way. But who is going to be

A small copper on a hedgerow in hunting country.

policing the river bank – Messrs Blair, Foster and Lord 'call me Mike' Watson? Here is more of the usual evasion and distortion, coupled with a refusal to acknowledge the facts.

So, ironically, a hunting ban will actually be anti-animal welfare for all the quarry species. Similarly, a hunting ban will be anti-conservation and anti-Green, making the Green Party's opposition to hunting quite astonishing – I write this as someone who has voted Green in a European election. Britain has thousands of acres of woodland, grassland and wetland, and hundreds of miles of grass margins and hunting headlands, and it is clear that hunting makes a tremendous contribution to conservation in the general countryside. When added to land and water managed for shooting and fishing, then the acreage of wildlife-friendly land increases even more. The simple truth is that the land managed for fox, pheasant, fish, hare and deer provides the ideal habitat for a wide range of flora and fauna – barn owls, otters, orchids and many more – and this at a time when commercial farming is becoming more of an industrial process. Away from areas involved with country sports, most farmland wildlife is under pressure. The CRT farms in a sympathetic way for wildlife, but we are the exception rather than the rule.

In a world claiming to encourage bio-diversity, hunting habitats do exactly that. All over Britain, not just in the Heythrop country, it is possible to tell where land owners have a country sports interest; the land changes from intensive cereals in large fields or high density, over-grazing livestock – the system favoured, encouraged and financed by the Common Agricultural Policy – to a patchwork of woodland, grass and smaller cultivated fields surrounded by grass tracks and hedgerows. Birdsong increases and there are flowers and butterflies. It really does become a living, working countryside, featuring the traditional and wildlife-rich beauty of rural Britain.

With hunting gone there will be no reason for a landowner to have 10 per cent or even 20 per cent of his land out of production. If pheasant shooting is not chosen as an alternative and farming continues in its present decline, then for the sake of 'efficiency' and cash-flow grass will be ploughed, woodland felled and wetland drained. Once again the environmental illiteracy of the antis, and of those who rule us, will have triumphed over wildlife, landscape, rural communities and conservation.

In many parts of the world no conflict is seen between conservation, hunting and shooting; it only seems to be a problem in over-populated, urban-dominated Britain. Again Dr Tim Coulson has a practical view:

> Hunting is an integral part of North American culture. For example, in recent years approximately a quarter of a million white-tailed deer are shot on the first day of the hunting season in Pennsylvania alone. As well as supporting managed hunting of some species, the United States has developed some of the best wildlife management strategies of any country in the world. The success of these strategies can be seen by looking at the increase in the size and range of populations of many diverse species over the past fifty to a hundred years: successes include white-tailed deer, mule deer, black bears, wolves and bison. Of course, not all of these species are hunted, but the United States demonstrates how good conservation and wildlife management strategies can co-exist with a culture that accepts hunting.

In an open and honest world there would be numerous conservation bodies standing up and explaining the facts. Sadly, we live in a politically correct world, where most conservation organisations want to curry Government favour, court subsidies and grants, and to humour

No hunting, no habitat – anti-hunting, anti-green.

THE HUNTING GENE

'Where there are woodlands, where there are hedgerows and where there are field sports.'

their own membership – even if a proportion of that membership does not fully understand the issues. Consequently the subject of killing for sport or control must not be mentioned. Fox-hunting is almost a taboo subject and, as we have seen already, rather than explain the need to control predators, some conservation bodies seem willing to sit back and watch the demise of the red squirrel, the curlew and the lapwing – anything rather than risk political or conservational incorrectness.

There are a few personalities and conservationists willing to speak their own mind for the sake of principle and wildlife. The late Johnny Morris, the former television naturalist, attended the Countryside Rally in 1997. Professor David Bellamy spoke at that rally. I hope it is simply a coincidence that since then his appearances on television seem to have diminished. What he had to say was simple conservation common sense, linked to honesty. He is a man who has probably done more for the cause of conservation than any other of his generation. He is passionate about the natural world and angry that it is under such pressure. He does not hunt, shoot or fish and has never done so, but at the rally, after extolling the countryside he visited from London in his youth, he said this:

Now what do I see? The whole of the British Isles has been turned into a factory, a factory in which wildlife really has no place. And if you fly across the British Isles you can see where there are meandering streams, where there are hedgerows, where there are woodlands, and where there are field sports. Now I think you're bloody cruel. I couldn't do it myself, but I'm very glad you're there doing it! Because the real cruelty is the battery hens and veal crates and the whole factory farming … Now please, Mr Blair … keep this countryside bio-diverse and sustainable.

It seems that one of the main objections to hunting that many people have is that it involves cruelty and distress or, at least, perceived cruelty and distress. We are back to *Bambi* again, with the hunted animal once more becoming a little furry person. Not only does it become a little person, but it is also given the reasoning powers of Einstein.

I have actually heard someone say, 'the fox must be terrified knowing it is going to die'. How can a fox know it is going to die and how can it possibly contemplate death? I have seen a family of domestic pigs fed in a field; three, including the sow, were shot as they fed, later to be butchered and put in the freezer. The remaining piglets continued to feed greedily without turning their heads; the thought of death and the meaning of life meant nothing when compared to the taste of food. If fear is such a perceived force in a hunted animal, then why have foxes and mink been seen to hunt while they themselves have been hunted? Similarly, if hares and deer can rationalise about a hunt and a sticky end, why are they seen regularly stopping to feed when hounds are in the next field?

The problem with fear and imagined suffering is that we see them entirely through our human eyes. Consequently, the cruelty and distress in hunting are to be found mainly in the minds of those separated from nature and separated from the realities of life and death. Often, cruelty is mistaken for the image of death. Hounds fighting over the body of a fox are not a pretty sight, but the scene is not cruel – the fox is already dead, just as the cow, pig or sheep is already dead as it is 'torn to pieces' on the butcher's slab and the turkey is dead when 'ripped apart' at Christmas dinner. In reality, the cruelty arises only from the deliberate misuse of language.

Similarly, the sight of a dead stag may be unpleasant to some, but it is not cruel. The sight of hundreds of dead animals in a modern slaughterhouse would be much worse, but we are sheltered from that. The situation is summed up perfectly by the Rev. Jack MacDonald: 'People don't like to see an animal broken up. But it is dead already; it is the aesthetics of the scene they don't like.'

In everyday life there are far greater cruelties that individuals and society choose to ignore. As Professor Twink Allen points out:

Stopping my car and catching a blinded and myxamatosed rabbit that has been like that for three weeks – it must be in real terror as it can't see. It's full of pneumonia, starving to death and we have inflicted that on it. That is distress; that is cruelty. The ewe on the Welsh hillside probably carrying twins, with a soaking wet fleece, and with foot rot – is starving and cold and it may die of pregnancy toxaemia – that is distress. The gypsy pony staked out on the side of the road eating rubbish and with no shelter and not able to seek shelter from the wind and rain. Cold, wet and miserable – that is distress. Equally, and much more distressful, is the 14-year-old fat poodle living in the sixth-floor flat. It is much loved but has developed cancer. It should be put down, but it is put through serious surgery and all the complications – on an aged pet that doesn't understand why it hurts and why it is feeling awful; just because the owner will not take the responsibility to put it down. That is what I call cruelty and distress. When the animal can't understand what is happening and can't do anything about it.

But there are other cruelties too, far worse than fox-hunting, that our Members of Parliament deliberately choose to ignore. Often they are the very same members who want to ban hunting. One of the greatest animal outrages in Britain today is halal slaughter, the traditional Muslim method of killing animals to eat, simply by slitting their throats. It is

cruel; there is no need for it; some Muslims themselves, particularly from Iran, condemn it. Yet through political correctness and inverted racism, no Labour MP will raise a voice against it. Once, in the hot climates where Islam started, slaughter by throat cutting was understandable. The throat was cut and the still-pumping heart of the dying animal forced most of the blood out of the body, which meant that the meat would keep fresh longer. Now, with refrigeration, there is no need for such a process. Yet halal slaughterhouses are booming, many of them concealing cruelty, poor hygiene and an almost non-existent standard of animal welfare. If Environmental Health Officers or inspectors from the Meat Hygiene Service question unacceptable practices, the owner simply shouts 'Racism' or 'You are attacking our religion' and the food police are imme-diately in full retreat. If a farmer treated and killed animals on his farm in the same way as they die in some halal slaughterhouses, he would be arrested and sent to prison – and quite rightly too.

The red deer stag – under greater threat without hunting.

208

An inspector in southern England told me: 'Some of the halal slaughterhouses are unbelievable. The cruelty is appalling, hygiene standards are almost non-existent and we can do nothing about it. If the public knew, there would be an outcry, but nobody is allowed to talk about it.'

Another, from the north of England, is just as damning. He says:

> It is appalling. Simple arithmetic tells you what is going on in some establishments. Sheep, for instance, are supposed to bleed for twenty seconds before being moved once they've had their throats cut. The truth is that they are whisked away, bleeding, dying, upside down on the production line as soon as the knife has been used. Most of the slaughtermen don't seem to have the same view of animal suffering that we have. The Labour Party supports this, it seems, for 'cultural reasons' – it respects the cultural reasons from Mirapur, but it does not accept the cultural reasons from Exmoor.

Hounds apparently 'rip apart', whilst butchers merely 'joint and slice'.

Traditional Jewish slaughter is similar, but the standards of cleanliness and welfare are considerably higher.

One of the largest animal welfare scandals of our time concerns ordinary slaughterhouses. To ensure stress-free animals, the nearer the slaughterhouse is situated to the fields where sheep and cattle graze, the better. Similarly, the smaller the slaughterhouse the better, then animals will not be faced with unfamiliar livestock and there is less chance of stress. Yet, because of absurd European hygiene rules – rules that only Britain seems to observe to the letter – hundreds of slaughterhouses, particularly small local ones, have closed down on account of extra red tape and prohibitive costs.

In 1980 there were 1047 slaughterhouses throughout the country. Now there are a mere 416, 40 of which are involved with the slaughter of cattle and the incineration of perfectly healthy cattle under the rules of the BSE fiasco. Alarmingly, as the overall number of

Sheep – some go from pastoral delight to halal horror.

slaughterhouses has decreased, so the number of large abattoirs has increased. In 1980 there were just 44 units with a killing capacity of 50,000 cattle or more a year; now there are 78. Indeed, I don't regard them as abattoirs; to me they are inhumane killing factories.

It seems likely that well over four hundred of the closures were caused by the EU Fresh Meat Directive of 1991. The rules were so absurd and the Ministry of Agriculture, Fisheries and Food was so vigorous in its implementation that I believe there was another agenda. The intention was to 'rationalise' the killing industry and maximise the throughput at a number of large centres, the theory being that the fewer the number of abattoirs, the easier they are to control.

It is bizarre that the two great prizes resulting from 'efficiency' and 'rationalisation' in the cattle industry have been BSE and E-coli. In fact the way in which the small slaughterhouses have been ousted could almost be seen as an exercise to maximise E-coli, in which case Brussels and MAFF should both be congratulated on their foresight and achievement.

Cattle being carted further, and slaughtered younger, and in large numbers have meant a dramatic rise in the stress levels of the cattle being killed. This provides ideal conditions for E-coli. Once killed, the best beef, and naturally produced beef, is hung and any E-coli dies off. Mass-produced beef is rapidly refrigerated and the E-coli is held in suspended animation. What a wonderful achievement – there must be an OBE in there for somebody.

The correct way forward would have been to encourage humane animal slaughter in small slaughterhouses as close as possible to where the animals lived their lives, so reducing the amount of stress to both animals and the owners who reared them. The opposite has happened. As a result we have a massive animal welfare scandal that nobody seems interested in and which, by comparison, makes hunting foxes and deer seem like a Sunday School tea party. The lid is kept on this outrage because of the money involved in the livestock industry and the way in which the present system favours the all-powerful supermarkets. Currently the supermarkets seem to be creating a monopoly on food production and sales, with the connivance of the Government. To make matters worse, several of the largest food chains make large financial donations to the political parties.

It is obvious that the average customer does not want to hear how his or her meat arrives on the table – fox-hunting and other people's business, yes; personal responsibility for humane livestock production, no. What is needed is for people within the Environmental Health Service and the Meat Hygiene Service to be free to tell the public what is actually happening to its livestock and its meat, but their conditions of service forbid them to speak out. As one Meat Hygiene Officer says: 'The service is run like a secret society.'

Astonishingly, none of the charities that are anti-hunting appears to have run a major campaign condemning what has happened to our farm animals – there is evidently not a lot of political capital, or financial capital, to be made from campaigning about slaughterhouses. My astonishment is compounded by the fact that animals can be transported hundreds of miles along British motorways – much further than the distance between Dover and Paris. They can then be killed in a huge killing factory and the meat can appear in a supermarket

BSE and E-coli – tributes to 'efficiency' and 'rationalisation' – now affect the cattle industry.

as the RSPCA's 'Freedom Food'. The morality of the whole thing is simply beyond my comprehension.

Incredibly also, this drift into industrial livestock farming and killing has been allowed by a Labour government which claims to be interested in animal welfare. It almost goes without saying that Labour's first Secretary of State for Agriculture was the anti-hunting Jack Cunningham and his junior minister was Elliot Morley, a staunch anti-hunting MP from Scunthorpe.

Morley is an interesting man. Away from the hunting issue he is the most knowledgeable minister about conservation and the environment in an environmentally illiterate Government. Before Labour was elected, he visited the land owned by the CRT and in the general discussion he condemned industrial farming. I mentioned the eight hundred million broiler chickens raised every year; he agreed it was disgusting. When I asked him if a Labour government would ban broiler houses, he stunned those present with his answer. 'Oh, we couldn't do that,' he said, 'some of the biggest broiler houses in the country are in my constituency and to close them would cause unemployment.' (There are twelve thousand people directly employed in the broiler industry.) Closing down broiler houses in Elliot Morley's constituency is out of the question, on the grounds of employment; yet banning hunting, which would put in excess of sixteen thousand out of

The author's golden Sebright bantams – a world away from broiler 'production'.

work, is permissible. So we have one set of values for people in his Scunthorpe constituency and another set for the countryside.

In reality this means that Labour politicians are deeply concerned about the death of 16,000 foxes each year, but they turn a blind eye to the death of 800 million broiler fowl and 39 million turkeys. Halal slaughter seems not to bother them at all.

In the past I have been a vegetarian. Today, because of the scandal of our killing factories, I only eat meat from traditional butcher's shops, where I know the source of the animals. I feel happiest, however, eating game or our own home-produced and killed poultry. I will not allow my own lambs to be transported long distances or in large lorries. I sell to a specialist butcher who has access to one of the last remaining local slaughterhouses.

I gave up being a vegetarian years ago, and although I would still find it easy not to eat meat, it would be another evasion. We were hunters, we did eat meat and the hunting gene is still part of us. Some of our wildlife such as most of the blue butterflies depend on grazing and several of our endangered ground-nesting birds – the lapwing, the snipe, the curlew and the redshank – thrive in grazing marshes. We need grazing and hay meadows for conservation and bio-diversity, and the production of meat is part of that process. What is needed is for livestock to be reared in environmentally friendly conditions and to die humanely without suffering fear or stress, and without travelling long distances. Only an aware and an interested government can achieve this.

Modern vegetarianism itself is based on a number of evasions. The 'food miles' involved in the average vegetarian meal mean the whole ethos is based on affluence and not on sustainability. In the main it has become a trendy political statement rather than a question of personal morality. There are twenty million acres of Brazil down to soya monoculture, either using high chemical inputs or genetically modified plants – some political statement. Acceptable vegetarianism would mean using seasonal vegetables, frozen vegetables and/or dried peas and beans in winter for added protein. How many of London's fashionable, affluent vegetarians in Islington, Kensington and the House of Commons would sit down to a delicious meal of wholemeal bread and dried peas?

The catalogue of accepted cruelty goes on. Each year I suffer anguish at the huge number of birds and animals killed on our roads. Well over 50 per cent of barn owl mortality arises from road deaths and the recolonisation of Britain's waterways by otters is being slowed by road casualties. During the summer breeding season the slaughter is horrendous as fledgling birds, badger and fox cubs are killed on the roads in thousands. Some die instantly, but many crawl or flap away to die slow and painful deaths. When a fox or a hare lies, still living, with shattered limbs, it is the practical countryman – yes, the farmer or the hunt follower – who is asked to do the final deed. Then it is not 'You are a cruel bastard, will you kill that screaming hare?'; it is 'The BMW didn't bother to stop – we know you'll put it out of its misery humanely.' Two years ago on a road near me there was such a catalogue of dead birds and animals that a friend described his journey along it as like driving through a dead zoo. The mayhem and suffering caused by motor-car madness – selfishness – extends to domestic

Blue butterflies thrive on sensitively grazed land.

animals too. Thousands of dogs and cats are run over as well as other domestic stock. In the New Forest alone about sixty ponies, cattle and sheep are killed each year, despite numerous warning signs and restrictions. As a local councillor says: 'Each year we are presented with figures for animal accidents in the forest. We tut-tut every time, but nothing ever seems to happen.'

In 1999 the CRT asked the anti-hunting John Prescott, the Secretary of State for the Environment, if he would put an automatic 50 m.p.h. summer speed limit on country roads to stop the carnage of young birds and animals. Lower speeds would also lower fuel consumption and reduce pollution. He did not answer personally and his official seemed most uninterested. So much for a genuine concern for animal welfare.

There are less obvious examples of cruelty too. Bird ringing is one that always astounds me. Sometimes mist nets (fine nets) are hung up to catch the adult birds. Yet most facts about migration patterns and population movements are already known. Why do it? The wild birds experience great stress; sometimes they are injured and occasionally they die, but it still goes on. Over 650,000 birds are ringed each year and approximately 1 per cent are injured as a result. The way some people go about bird ringing seems to have more in common with train spotting than conservation.

'Twitching' too can cause stress. A poor rare bird, blown off course in migration, can be pursued by armies of bird watchers once it arrives at its first available landfall. Twitching of course is also a form of hunting.

One of the major hypocrisies in a society that claims to be against chasing foxes is the way in which that same society condones abortion. In Britain there are currently an astonishing 175,000 abortions a year (nearly 500 a day). Foxes, hares and deer have rights; unborn babies have no rights at all and abortion has become just another form of contraception. The reality of this situation is clouded once more by political correctness and doublespeak. The feminist lobby argues that abortion is a civil right and that every woman has the right to make her own choice about her life, and about the life of her unborn child. It is that very freedom, the freedom of choice for their own lives, that some lobby groups and politicians want to deny to the hunting and rural communities – we have freedom for some, harassment and legislation for others.

Chapter Twelve

LIBERTY! EQUALITY! LUNACY!

William Garfit

THE HUNTING GENE

I t is the principle of personal choice that is at the core of the hunting issue. Yes, there is a hunting gene that makes hunting as natural and normal as eating, sleeping, breathing and procreating, and the roots of that particular survival mechanism go back at least two million years into our past. But times have changed, and we have changed and we are no longer forced to hunt. Similarly, we can choose whether to eat meat or be vegetarian, whether to have sex or abstain; personal choice is at the root of how we live our lives, and that personal choice is linked to moral choice. Unhindered moral choice is only possible in a free society and personal freedom is usually linked with the word 'democracy'.

So, the decision to chase a hare, fox, deer or mink is based on freedom, in exactly the same way as various other choices are made – whether or not to eat one of the eight hundred million broiler fowl; whether or not to eat soya beans from the twenty million acres of soya monoculture in Brazil; whether to fly to Majorca for a holiday; whether to set the thermostat on the central heating at 80°F for the duration of winter. They are all moral choices too. I have decided not to eat broiler fowl because of cruelty; I try not to eat soya on the grounds of environmental responsibility and sustainability; for the same reasons my house is heated to a temperature of 60°F rather than 80°F. I prefer to wear an additional woollen jumper than use more atmosphere-heating electricity.

Hunting should be a matter of personal choice and civil liberty.

Countries, we are told, that do not respect personal freedom – 'civil liberties' – are the direct opposite of democracies; they are invariably described as dictatorships, centralised states and even tyrannies that have little in common with the traditions of freedom and democracy found in Great Britain.

Sadly, it seems that the principles, struggles and sacrifices that helped to create Great Britain are being discarded in New Britain. We are told that we live in a multi-cultural society based on freedom and civil liberty, but at every turn fact is being turned in fiction as everyday life is dominated by regulation and political correctness, leading to harassment and social exclusion.

Hunting is quite simply a matter of personal morality that should be left to freedom of choice. Instead, it finds itself threatened with discriminatory laws, based on vindictiveness and intolerance, in a society which for several generations has boasted of its tolerance.

Recently a junior health minister was asked on the radio whether the Government would ever ban cigarette smoking because of the health risks to the smoker and the passive smoker. 'We would never do that,' the minister replied. 'Smoking is a matter of personal choice and has been legal for several hundred years and so it would be quite wrong to make it illegal.' Strange, that; hunting has been legal for hundreds of years too, yet politicians from the same political party wish to make it illegal.

The guarantor of individual freedom and civil liberties should be Parliament; after all, virtually every Member of Parliament claims to be a libertarian. Where are the current threats to farming, hunting and the country way of life coming from? From Parliament itself.

It is an astonishing situation. When Labour was voted into power with a huge majority in 1997, many, including myself, breathed a huge sigh of relief. They had ousted a Tory government that had become arrogant, devious, incompetent, inept, dishonest and sleaze ridden; at the same time they had removed a political leader who could not lead, who had no vision and no charisma and under whose leadership the Tories had stumbled into oblivion. Tony Blair became Prime Minister with an immense amount of goodwill behind him and his victory was welcomed by town and country alike.

In his New Labour manifesto for a 'Better Britain', he promised:

> We have no intention or desire to replace one set of dogmas by another. I want to renew faith in politics through a government that will govern in the interests of the many, the broad majority of people who work hard, play by the rules, pay their dues and feel let down by a political system. And I want, above all, to govern in a way that brings our country together … I want a Britain which we all feel part of … We are a broad-based movement for progress and justice. New Labour is the political arm of none other than British People as a whole. Our values are the same; the equal worth of all, with no one cast aside; fairness and justice within strong communities … I have no time for the politics of envy.

THE HUNTING GENE

In any Third World country or tin-pot dictatorship such cant and hypocrisy would be funny. In Britain, the alleged home of freedom and democracy, the only response can be a mixture of anger and contempt. In no time at all the Labour Government has shown itself to be just as devious, dishonest and sleaze ridden as its predecessor and, rather than bringing the country together, Blair has driven a wedge between town and country, rural and urban, freedom and democracy. As a direct consequence a large section of the community feels totally disenfranchised with nobody representing them in Parliament and nobody to vote for. What can they do and who can they turn to?

Quite cynically New Labour has attacked Britain's rural communities. Agriculture is being decimated and the lives of many farming families are being ruined as a result of political decisions set in motion by the Tories, under the direction of the EU, and eagerly adopted by the present Government. Huge rural development is being allowed for no other reason than short-term economic and political advantage, and rural traditions are being swept aside and legislated against in a way that smacks of dictatorship. This is not simply a reference to hunting, but applies to everyday traditions such as cheese-making, brewing, cider-making, meat production and many, many more. They are all being knocked out one at a time by bureaucracy. The Blair vision for rural Britain seems to be a mixture of cultural cleansing, urban colonialism and European regulation.

This is all the more peculiar since the Prime Minister appears to love the regional rural differences of Italy and France – but he seems to despise the rural traditions and people of his own country. His big wish, it seems, is for everybody to become a homogenised, sanitised, pasteurised, Euro-clone.

In the Labour Party manifesto there was a promise to allow 'a free vote in Parliament on whether hunting with hounds would be banned by legislation'. When Michael Foster's Bill arrived, the threat it presented led to the Hyde Park rally on 10 July 1997, when 125,000 people assembled in London to demonstrate their objections. I had the privilege to be one of those to address them. The Metropolitan Police were amazed at the good humour, the good manners and the subsequent absence of litter. This was followed by the Countryside March on 1 March 1998, again in London, and numerous marches and protests at Labour's attitude have taken place since. Officially over three hundred thousand people marched – although Home Office figures suggest it was more like a half million. When the Bill ran out of time it appeared that the Government had got the message: in a multi-cultural society you do not attack the culture of your own rural people. Again, the march had amazed the police and the ordinary people of London on account of the good nature and the orderliness of those taking part. Regardless of Labour's claim that its anti-hunt stance is based on animal welfare, it is clear that the real issue is still one of class – Old Labour and New Labour hate 'toffs'. The March march should have shattered that illusion for ever.

The Countryside March was not 'toff power', it was a complete cross-section of the countryside from dukes to dustmen and from peers to postmen. My abiding memory of the march was in the Underground afterwards: a group of ear-ringed, windproof-jacketed young

Rolf Harris? No, the kennel huntsman checks his hounds after a days hunting with the Portman.

men, all obviously in London for the first time, were enjoying their ride in the Tube. When the train arrived at their station and they wanted to get off, panic broke out. They pushed and pulled desperately at the doors until somebody kindly showed them the button: 'Push to Open'.

The view across the countryside – in the village pub, at the earth stoppers' dinner and at the hunt ball – was that the argument had been won and for a time hunting would be safe. I took a different view. After the election, because of his disdain for the farming community, I quickly lost my trust in the Prime Minister. My old farming father was a simple countryman, but many of his words were wise. He always said: 'Never trust a public schoolboy or a Socialist'; with Tony Blair we had the two untrustables in one.

It seemed to me that sooner or later his political halo would tarnish and he would have to do something to improve his popularity. With his policy on Ulster floundering, the Kosovo tragedy magnified out of all proportion by NATO's premature and ill-thought-out intervention, and the nurses and the teachers rumbling with discontent, it was obvious that a diversion would have to be created to win back popularity. So in July 1999 a bit of 'toff bashing' was the answer, and fox-hunting again galloped into the political arena. Ironically, if hunting is banned in Britain the 'toffs' will be the least affected. This hunting minority will buy houses in Ireland or go hunting in America or Australia – they can afford to. It will be the hunting majority – the ordinary hunt followers, the 'non-toffs' – who will suffer, since they cannot afford to hunt abroad.

One thing is certain, Tony Blair's stance on fox-hunting has nothing whatsoever to do with animal welfare or an interest in conservation. As the farming crisis intensified and the loss of farmland wildlife accelerated, virtually all the main conservation charities in Britain said one thing of Tony Blair – off the record: 'He is not interested in the countryside.' The only time the countryside briefly appeared on his agenda was at the time of the Countryside March. It was thought that at the Berlin summit of EU leaders in March 1999 he would have to consider farming and the reform of the Common Agricultural Policy. The pundits were wrong; the summit was totally concerned with Kosovo and our leaders' main decision was to bomb Belgrade – the first time that Belgrade had been bombed since Hitler; appropriately the decision was taken in Berlin. Needless to say, the CAP was not reformed and is unlikely to be in the foreseeable future.

The truth is that Tony Blair is not interested in countryside matters and has hardly any

experience of them. There is even a rumour circulating within farming and conservation circles that suggests he has said, 'I will not be interested in farming or the countryside until there are 50 per cent fewer farmers.' And what about animal welfare? In 1997 when President Chirac of France was a guest of our Government he was treated to *pâté de foie gras*. This is obtained by force-feeding geese so that their livers swell up; a practice that is both unpleasant and cruel. Then, shortly after his anti-hunting declaration, Tony Blair took his whole family to the famous and notorious Palio – a horse race in the Tuscan city of Siena that makes the Grand National look like a donkey derby by comparison. Jockeys race horses bareback around the huge cobbled square and every year animals are killed and injured. Between 1970 and 1998 forty-three horses were killed in the race. Apparently the Blairs enjoyed the spectacle and the excitement of this Tuscan tradition. What next? Watching a donkey thrown from the top of a Spanish church?

One of the numerous countryside marches.

It is regrettable that the Prime Minister chooses Italy and France for his summer holidays; it would perhaps aid his understanding of rural concerns if he took his children on holiday in Britain and saw some British rural traditions.

For fox-hunting to reappear on the political agenda when it did was in very poor taste for political and humanitarian reasons; the Prime Minister and the Labour Party were showing concern for sixteen thousand foxes when their policy of bombing Kosovo had helped to create eight hundred thousand human refugees. What several journalists on the ground tried to say was that the ethnic cleansing of Kosovo was *caused* by NATO's intervention, it was not the *reason* for it. This simple but obvious message was sidelined by the constant stream of Government propaganda.

The simple truth about Kosovo was that Slobodan Milosevic, the Serbian President

Toff? No, a man in a top hat who supports tradition.

of Yugoslavia, did behave unforgivably, but the problem was made worse by the Kosovo Liberation Army, trained and equipped by German civil and military intelligence. Milosevic's original 'ethnic cleansing' was planned in order to remove villages where the KLA had been active, rather like Britain's policy in Kenya during the Mau Mau uprising. Once NATO's bombing started, then he obviously wanted to move everybody with Albanian/Muslim loyalties – just as those with German or German-sounding names were shipped away from Britain and put into internment camps at the start of the Second World War. If Blair knew that eight hundred thousand refugees would result from NATO's bombing, he was callous; if he did not know, then he was incompetent. Either way it exposed him for what he really was – a leader driven more by froth and sound-bite than by understanding.

Ulster was another problem for Blair; to raise the issue of fox-hunting when the Ulster peace process was failing showed appalling judgement. At a time when former IRA terrorists, murderers and men who had access to Armalites and Semtex were being released from prison as part of the peace process, he was announcing his intention to outlaw chasing foxes – ironically an act that would criminalise several serving policemen, justices of the peace and judges. Hypocritically, he claimed to want to unite the communities in Ireland; in the rest of Britain he was driving a wedge between communities.

THE HUNTING GENE

A point-to-point – traditional British horse racing.

At the 1999 Peterborough Royal Foxhound Show, Anne Mallalieu, the pro-countryside barrister and Labour peer, addressed the large crowd. She described how she had felt betrayed by recent events and then told a remarkable story. She had just received a letter from a man whose son had been killed by the IRA in the Bishopsgate bombing in London. His son's convicted killer had recently been released after only sixteen months in prison. The man's daughter is 15 years old and loves hunting; her brother's murderer has been made a free man, and her hobby could soon make her a criminal. That, it seems, is British justice in New Britain.

Tony Blair's call to arms against hunting came suddenly, on the television programme *Question Time*. It is interesting to note that in just a few sentences he managed either to lie or to forget the facts not once, but twice. He claimed that the Foster Bill was defeated by the House of Lords, when in fact the Bill did not even reach the House of Lords. Then he implied that he had eagerly voted for the Bill when he had been absent from the House of Commons for the vote. It was a fascinating, if appalling, reflection of his standards, and it is hardly surprising that he is such a close friend of President Clinton.

What followed was pure farce. Scotland, it is claimed, has been waiting for its own parliament for three hundred years. One hundred and twenty-nine members now sit in the new Scottish Parliament, each drawing over £40,000 a year. Fifteen of them continue to sit in the House of Commons, allowing them to vote on English issues also; three can sit in the House of Lords; and one also sits as a Member of the European Parliament – so now Scotland has its very own gravy train, or Scotch broth trough. After three hundred years it could be assumed that there were a number of burning Scottish issues – housing, drugs, hospital waiting lists, child poverty, rural poverty, the farming crisis in the Highlands and Islands, the destruction of the fishing industry through the Common Fisheries Policy, inner-city deprivation and so on. But, no – enter Lord Watson, 'call me Mike', from that well-known fox-hunting region of Glasgow Central. His Lordship, virtually unknown outside Glasgow, had spent the bulk of his life in urban and trades union politics until he was elected to the House of Commons in 1989. Sadly, he was not selected for the 1997 election, but he was then made a Labour peer and he was later elected to the Scottish Parliament.

So, on being elected to the Scottish Parliament what did His Urban Lordship do? Still showing remarkable loyalty to his Westminster leader, he announced his intention to introduce the first Private Member's Bill to the Scottish Parliament, a Bill to outlaw fox-hunting in Scotland. Rather than dealing with the homeless, the drug addicts, the sick and the unemployed of Glasgow, the burning issue for him was nine packs of hounds chasing a few foxes. The situation was made even more bizarre when His Lordship was joined for his Bill by another virtually unknown urban Scottish Nationalist, Tricia Marwick – who had previously worked for Shelter. It appeared to some that homeless foxes had become more important in Scotland than homeless people. Political ambition had, it seemed, become more important than social division.

The situation failed to surprise me, despite my Scottish roots. Ancestors of mine, two brothers, became Scottish prisoners of war at the Battle of Dunbar (3 September 1650). They were marched south – eating raw cabbages as they went – before being put to work under the famous Dutchman, Cornelius Vermuyden, draining the Fens. Desperation must have followed, as the brothers fell in love with two Fen girls, so giving a new branch to my family tree.

Marchers make their feelings clear.

At the time of the referendum to decide on a Scottish Parliament I suggested to Scottish friends that the whole process was misleading. Although the Scottish Nationalist Party and Labour were claiming the issue was democracy and the unwanted domination of Scotland by London, the real issue for rural Scotland was the domination of urban Britain over rural Britain. It would make no difference if that urban majority were based in London, Manchester, Edinburgh or Glasgow – it would still be urban domination of rural issues and rural culture.

THE HUNTING GENE

The whole idea of the Scottish Parliament and the Welsh Assembly being based on greater democracy was in any case a fraud, and the way in which the two deciding referendums were held on separate days was an example of blatant political manipulation. The two assemblies were, and are, all to do with the regionalisation of Europe under Brussels, not the democratisation of Britain under Westminster. Under the Brussels master plan, Scotland and Wales continue, England disappears into regions and the Channel Islands become part of France – as the map produced by the European Commission in 1995 clearly shows.

The notion of hunting being a big issue in Scotland is absurd. As one rural Scot said:

> The whole idea of targeting hunting is ludicrous. The Scottish Parliament and decision making is no nearer rural Scotland than the Westminster government. There is a huge urban majority from the industrial belt – they are not interested in us. The Scottish Parliament is just a rather inferior talk shop – jobs for the boys.

Another highlander thought he had the answer:

> It's all to do with the red hunting jackets. These second-rate Scottish politicians are still living in the world of the 'redcoats'. They think they are fighting the English – they have visions of *Braveheart* – they are pathetic, they are bullies, they are fascist bastards.

He may have hit the nail on the head. An element of anti-English racism has been deliberately allowed to seep through Scottish politics, leading to a spectacular decline in 1999 of one of Scotland's most important money earners – tourism. The mixture of nationalism and socialism pervading the Scottish Parliament also has an unsavoury air about it. Its proposed land reform seems to the casual observer to be almost Stalinist by nature and the attitude to the English seems racist. The driving force behind the anti-hunting movement appears to be class and 'toff bashing'. It should be remembered that the rise of the Nazis in the 1930s came under the banner of 'national socialism' and Hitler's anti-hunting stance stemmed from his dislike and envy of the German aristocracy.

In fact, the highlander's mention of fascism is interesting. Certainly the Britain apparently wanted by some parts of New Labour is the same Britain that was wanted by Oswald Mosley at the end of the Second World War. Mosley wanted Britain to be part of a united Europe with one currency, one parliament, one tax system, one defence force, one foreign policy and so on, and for his trouble he was called a fascist. Hitler, the great vegetarian and animal rights thinker, banned hunting in the 1930s, and – surprise, surprise – he was a fascist too. With the centralisation of power, the erosion of democracy, the regulation of lives and the restriction of civil liberty, I believe that Britain and Europe are again experiencing a form of fascism. In the years after the Second Word War it was the popular boast that 'fascism could never happen here'; a look at Mosley's European dream

Devolution? No, the regionalisation of Europe by the European Commission (1995 version). Scotland and Wales remain, England disappears and the Channel Islands become part of France.

225

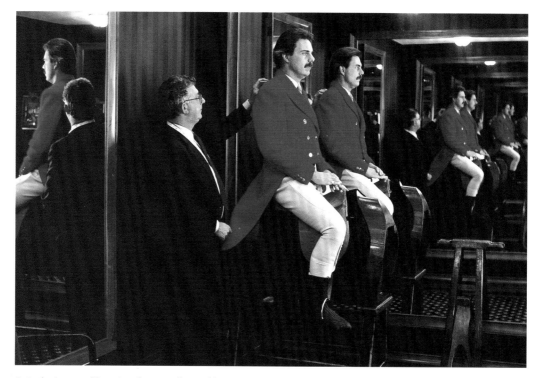

It is the image of hunting that is still a problem.

seems to indicate that it could be here already, with numerous political and bureaucratic quislings to help it on its way.

Just like all people who use and abuse the political system, Tony Blair and his acolytes state that their anti-hunting stance is based on democracy. One often-repeated claim is that a ban on hunting with dogs is a manifesto commitment. If all legislation and political action has to be a manifesto promise, then where in the last Labour manifesto is it mentioned that there is the intention to sell off half of Britain's gold reserves? I have scoured the document and can find no reference to it. Similarly, I have found no mention of the fact that the sale of our gold would be in stages and preannounced, thus guaranteeing a drop in the value by at least half a billion pounds.

The politically devious also support claims for political action by quoting public opinion poll support. It is an interesting concept, government by opinion poll. One thing is certain, it would often work against the freedom of minorities, and the safeguarding of minorities should be a fundamental part of any democracy. Almost certainly most opinion polls show a majority against hunting; just as those same polls would show a majority wanting the return of the death penalty for terrorists and a cessation of gay recruitment in our schools. Will they too become Government policies?

For those who support the opinion poll view on banning hunting, a recent National Opinion Poll survey carried out for the Countryside Alliance throws up some fascinating views. It shows conclusively that an opinion poll will give whatever results are wanted, depending on the questions. Hence, if it is true – as the antis claim – that over 70 per cent of the population want to ban hunting, at the same time 68 per cent believe that it is wrong for a government to ban everything the majority is against. Better still, 68 per cent of the population are in favour of a pay freeze for MPs, so will the Government take action? When we read a list of topics ranging from drug abuse to hunting, we find that only 5 per cent regarded hunting as a topic that should go before the next session of Parliament, 52 per cent believed that foxes needed controlling and 42 per cent believed that anti-hunting activists were keener on attacking the upper class than on saving foxes. In answer to another question, 57 per cent believed that the decision to allow hunting on private land should be made by the farmer, rather than Parliament, while 85 per cent would not change their vote at an election because of hunting. And 89 per cent agree with the Home Secretary that fox-hunting is not uppermost in the minds of more people.

The most alarming reply came to the question 'Where does your knowledge of hunting mostly come from?' Showing clearly that British society has lost its rural roots, 57 per cent claimed to get their information from newspapers and the broadcast media and 38 per cent obtained their information from radio and television alone. With animal rights and anthropomorphism clearly part of television's agenda, it is hardly surprising that a majority of the population is 'against hunting'. With rural and urban Britain drifting steadily apart, this dependence on an unreliable – and at times hysterical – source of information will cause the great rural/urban divide to become even greater.

The gap between town and country is very real, as earlier chapters in this book have shown. It is clear to see in the general population, and it is even more obvious in Parliament itself. In his book *A Walk with a White Bushman* (1986) Laurens van der Post wrote: 'Western Europe was once governed by a country mind – even city states had a keen country awareness – but the country mind has greatly diminished. People who know nothing about the land suddenly sit and rule like gods over the fate of other men.'

Unfortunately, today the cause for concern is not simply the fact that our MPs 'know nothing about the land' but that they are not interested in it either. In November 1998 the CRT was so concerned about the fate of the family farm and our rural communities that it wrote a letter to every MP at the House of Commons. To 659 letters, it received just 18 considered replies (2.75%). In addition it received six personally signed acknowledgements and fifteen circular acknowledgements. The salary of MPs is over £47,000, plus generous allowances for expenses.

The truth is that our present political system has turned democracy into a farce, encouraging mainly career politicians rather than conviction politicians. The situation will not change until a residential qualification is put on all parliamentary candidates, requiring them to have lived or worked in their constituency for five years before being allowed to stand for

Parliament. This would ensure a fairer representation and mean that rural areas would be properly represented. Under such a system neither the present Prime Minister nor his predecessor would have been allowed to stand for Parliament in their present constituencies. Apologists for the current unsatisfactory and unsavoury system maintain that a residential qualification would prevent many 'brilliant' people from entering politics. If such an assertion is true, where are they?

The fact is that the urban/rural divide does affect political outlook and political decisions; it was identified by Laurens van der Post as the 'town mind' and the 'country mind'. The difference was shown clearly when Tony Blair sang the praises of genetically modified organisms (GMOs). To him it was all a matter of 'progress' – New Labour, New Britain and the New Technology for the New Millennium. He was singing the meaningless mantra of the uninformed, for as the personification of urban man he could not see that genetically modified pollen from insect-resistant or spray-resistant crops could cross with wild plants, raising again the spectre of *Silent Spring* (Rachel Carson's best-selling book, published in 1962, which directed attention to the problems caused by pesticides). It follows that he seemed unable to grasp that the driving force behind GMOs was the wish of multi-national companies to make heaps of money and not a humanitarian vision to feed the world.

It is thought that some GMOs could be beneficial, but he was picking the wrong ones. Genetic modifications to allow cereals to fix their own nitrogen from the atmosphere could have enormous agricultural advantages. Similarly, genetic modification to give wheat the drought-resistant genes of sorghum or millet would have huge benefits for developing countries. But these were not the advances Blair was supporting; he was supporting work with toxins and chemicals that could have dangerous environmental consequences.

In Britain the gap between town and county has become greater than in virtually any other European country. In Britain – according to *The Economist*'s *World in Figures* – the urban population is 89 per cent, in France it is 73 per cent, Italy 67 per cent, Greece 65 per cent, Ireland 58 per cent and Portugal 36 per cent. It is hardly surprising that country issues get short shrift in this country. In France, Italy and Ireland many urban families still have brothers, uncles and grandparents on the land and so they have links with nature and rural culture. In Britain those links were broken several generations ago in many families and the countryside is almost like a foreign land for them. As a consequence, when people from the towns move into the country they transport their urban and suburban dreams and values with them.

One example seems to be Sir Paul McCartney. This is sad. I have happy memories of Beatlemania in the 1960s and he seems to be a pleasant, reasonably well-adjusted man. But I think it would be fair to say that he made much of his enormous wealth by celebrating in words and music his Liverpudlian, urban background and roots – his *urban* culture. So why, as an incomer to the Sussex countryside, does he attack *rural* culture? In a document entitled 'Deadline 2000 – the Campaign to End Hunting with Dogs' there is a black-and-white photograph (gelatine free?) of this vegetarian pop singer below which he is quoted using all the usual clichés: hunting is 'barbaric', it must be banned before we can be called 'civilised', we must emerge from the 'dark ages' and so on. To me it is a litany of misunderstanding, misinformation and misuse of English. If he attacked a foreign culture in the same way – say Rainforest Indians or Australian Aborigines, both of whom hunt – he would be regarded as an intolerant racist. Why does he move into a country area and openly attack the culture he moves into?

Campaign 2000 is being master-minded by three organisations: The International Fund for Animal Welfare, The League Against Cruel Sports and the Royal Society for the Prevention of Cruelty to Animals. In a democracy, organisations such as these should be free to put their points of view and argue their case openly and freely, but should they be allowed to give money to political parties and exert pressure on governments?

Here the story of the Labour Party's wish to ban hunting becomes murky. When the Conservatives were in power there were

'I hope you're not collecting money for the Labour Party'

allegations of 'sleaze' and 'cash for questions'. New Labour promised new standards and a new sleazeless morality, but as regards hunting a tangled web of donations and links between some anti-hunt organisations and Labour ministers, ex-ministers, MPs and relations and friends of MPs appears to have brought the return of sleaze. Indeed, many observers believe the situation to be so outrageous that it could almost be called 'cash for legislation'.

It transpires that in the weeks before Mr Blair's dramatic anti-hunting announcement the International Fund for Animal Welfare (UK) had been lobbying hard. It had been sending glossy brochures and a not very impressive video to all MPs, threatening to mount a massive anti-Government advertising campaign if action were not taken. In addition, it had written to a number of celebrities requesting that they write to Mr Blair asking him to ban hunting. The letter, based on the Bambi syndrome, started: 'I am writing to ask for your help for an important and ongoing initiative on behalf of Britain's beautiful wild creatures'.

What the letter did not spell out clearly was that IFAW (UK) is not a charity but a company limited by guarantee that made a special resolution not to have 'Ltd' added to its name. Neither did the letter say that just before the election the Political Animal Lobby – an organisation with close enough links with IFAW (UK) for the latter to have lent it

THE HUNTING GENE

£600,000 – donated £1 million to the Labour Party. Since then a further £100,000 has followed. When Labour were given £1 million by Formula One car racing, the money was returned; the money from anti-hunting sources has been retained. Several MPs have long-standing links with IFAW; they include Elliot Morley, who shortly after the election was made a junior agriculture minister. He did not attend the East of England Show that year, as would have been expected, as he was hosting an IFAW reception at the House of Commons. Now, it is said, a lot of money, effort and propaganda has already found its way to Scotland.

When the Tories behaved badly, that was rightly called 'sleaze'. If the money going to Labour had been uncovered in the political life of Italy or Greece, it would be called 'corruption'. Apparently under New Labour, in one of the world's oldest democracies, it is regarded as acceptable practice.

Some politicians claim that hunting is the only target for abolition. They are wrong. As a co-convener for the Green Party's Animal Rights Working Group says:

> I am pleased to let you know that we are fundamentally opposed to all blood sports. We have supported, and will continue to support, campaigns to abolish all forms of hunting with packs of dogs. We are opposed to all forms of shooting for sport. We also share the view of the RSPCA that angling causes unnecessary suffering and would support laws to alleviate that suffering when an opportunity arises.

Already, as I understand it, various animal welfare organisations have the next campaign already targeted, to follow when hunting is banned. It is aimed at game shooting and involves figures on wounding rates together with film footage of wounded birds flapping about. Then, beyond that, fishing is the target. It is all well thought out, aimed to provide continuity and a steady flow of money through emotive advertising.

It is regrettable that in both animal welfare and environmental issues cash flow often appears to dominate policy. Recently I met a conservationist from France who once worked for the old World Wildlife Fund in Geneva. She left because she believed that emotive subjects were often used to raise money, in preference to promoting serious conservation.

As a result of all this, many true country people see a huge tide turning against them; they believe that the Government is not interested in their plight and that it is accepting money to legislate against them. They see Labour cynically killing off the small farmer, with whole regions of the countryside being turned into theme parks. Anti-hunting legislation is the last straw. The real countryman feels isolated, victimised and discriminated against. As one old farmer told me: 'If only we were black, one-legged lesbians we would be all right. Farming would be prosperous and they would be giving us grants to hunt.'

His mention of lesbians is significant as the Government seems far more interested in gay rights than in rural rights. Obviously what can only be called 'the terminator gene' is more significant to our politicians than the hunting gene. At a time when one of the big issues is lowering the age of homosexual consent for males to 16 – making it a grope away from paedophilia – the same politicians want to ban other men chasing foxes. It is so bizarre that one frustrated huntsman is threatening to get a new T-shirt printed: 'Beagling or Buggery? Ask Tony Blair'.

While driving back from the Lake District one day I heard a scientist talking on the radio. He was worried that homosexual behaviour had been seen for the first time in a species of seagull in the Pacific, and was concerned that the change in behaviour may have been caused by chemicals in the water. Perhaps he had better test the water in London or the Cabinet Office; or are there different biological and chemical rules for humans and seagulls? But, regardless of individual hormone counts, it does seen incredible that a homosexual minority should have their rights defended by politicians when a numerically larger minority comes under attack from the same politicians.

What is clear is that cultural cleansing of the countryside is currently taking place. What the Labour Government did not

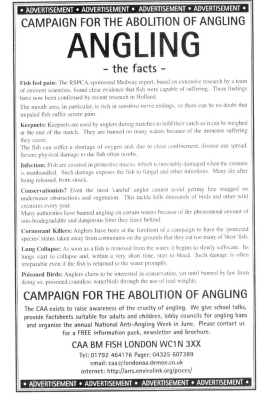

Despite constant assurances to the contrary, fishing and shooting are also under threat.

accept in Kosovo, they are imposing in their own country. Some people believe that the attack on farming and hunting can actually be called 'ethnic cleansing'; the *Concise Oxford Dictionary* definition of 'ethnic' is '(of social group) having common national or cultural tradition'. That of 'ethnic cleansing' is '(euphemistic) expulsion or murder of people of ethnic or religious group in certain area'. If farmers are deliberately being financially bled into bankruptcy at the same time as they and others are being criminalised; surely this constitutes ethnic cleansing?

The protection of minorities from persecution, discrimination and cleansing of either a cultural or ethnic kind should come from Parliament. In August 1999, the Home Secretary, Jack Straw, reaffirmed on television his belief that civil liberties were one of the most important obligations for a Labour government. 'The Government,' he said, 'is very fussed about individual liberties.'

If Labour persists with its discrimination then international help will have to be sought. The Universal Declaration of Human Rights was adopted and proclaimed by the General Assembly

A traditional farmer – no longer wanted.

of the United Nations on 10 December 1948. It is clear that present farming policies break the declaration, as would any anti-hunting legislation. Apart from protecting assorted freedoms of action, work, culture and expression, there are other more specific safeguards. Article 7 states: 'All are equal before the law and are entitled without any discrimination to the equal protection of the law.'

Hunting people, whether following on horse, foot or in cars, get virtually no protection from the law. They are physically and verbally attacked, often by people wearing balaclava helmets and wielding baseball bats, and there are numerous examples of the police standing by and simply watching. It is rural terrorism of the very worst kind, usually carried out by visiting and violent urban gangs.

When the black teenager Stephen Lawrence was tragically murdered and the police took inadequate action, politicians, lawyers and the media demanded and obtained action. In the case of Rod Wilson, mentioned in Chapter 6, he and his family have been totally forgotten. Each week numerous country people face violence and insults in exactly the same way.

At the Waterloo Cup I was shocked by what I saw when the antis arrived. A serving police officer summed up the situation:

> The antis in the main are just a bunch of anarchists wanting a punch-up. We should be allowed to sort them out. They blatantly break the law and we are not allowed to get stuck in. There is one law for some people in this country and another for everybody else. That is a very dangerous situation and it is wrong.

Article 27 of The Universal Declaration of Human Rights is also important. It states: 'Everyone has the right to freely participate in the cultural life of the community.' A law against hunting would be a law against the cultural life of the hunting communities in the Lake District, the Cotswolds, Exmoor, the Scottish Borders and elsewhere.

It seems that throughout history, in almost every society, there have had to be minorities for politicians to attack; they divert attention away from political failings. Hitler had the Jews and the gypsies; there have been immigrants and religious sects. Now, in a politically correct world, there are only huntsmen and smokers left to hate and Labour is eagerly joining the ranks of the political bullies and ethnic cleansers in doing just that.

As farming dies and hunting is threatened with extinction, what should those people under attack do? As I write there are two groups of responses developing. One is disillusioned and despondent, without hope; while the other is angry and threatening to fight for their rights, with civil disobedience. Some are even stating that they are at war and that as far as they are concerned Tony Blair could see a civil war in Britain – the first one since Oliver Cromwell. I do not know what will happen. What I do know is that the Prime Minister promised 'to govern in a way that brings our country together'. He has done the exact opposite.

The British normally have a reputation for tolerance, but victimisation does not breed tolerance – it breeds anger and despair. The despair is frightening. I asked one huntsman's wife what her husband would do if hunting were banned. She suddenly looked shaken and, with tears welling up in her eyes, she said: 'Robin, don't mention it. He says he will hang himself the next day.' If hunting is banned I believe that there will be a spate of suicides by people who love their horses, their hounds and their way of life and cannot face the thought of being without them. If this happens, then any MP who votes for such a Bill should be liable to a charge of constructive manslaughter. If dictators such as Slobodan Milosovic and General Pinochet are held accountable for the deaths of people under their control, why should not the same rules apply to British politicians?

So what should people who feel under threat do? Laws that are discriminatory and vindictive do not represent law in its truest sense; they become articles of political persecution. As a direct consequence, civil disobedience ceases to become a crime; it becomes almost a moral duty. I am a non-hunter and someone who has a financial cushion (provided by my pen) to avoid the worst hardships of the farming crisis; nevertheless I, like many more, will be prepared to face the threat of prison if the present Government continues on its course. The moral argument, the intellectual argument, the social and cultural arguments, the conservation argument and the animal welfare argument have all been won; but the political argument takes no account of these factors since it is driven by prejudice and political opportunism.

The traditions of freedom that run through many generations of British life and history are far too great to be swept aside by anti-democratic, politically correct politicians who do not understand country life. My countryside and my rural culture are worth defending. If Parliament will not defend us, what can we do? Perhaps the Countryside Alliance should become a political party or the old Country Party should be resurrected? Whatever happens, it is rural Britain that is at the heart of the hunting issue; the countryside, its people, its wildlife and its way of life must be protected.

If traditional farming and hunting are lost, then we lose many precious things: we lose woods and water-meadows, wildlife and wild flowers, bluebells and birdsong; we lose the brown hare, the red fox and the red deer, horse and hound, shepherd, farmer, blacksmith and huntsman. We lose a living, working countryside; we lose our culture and our way of life – but above all we lose our freedom.

REFLECTIONS

The Hunting Gene is my twenty-third book. It may sound impressive in just thirty years of writing, but it is not – some of the volumes have been extraordinarily thin. This book, however, is very different from the others. Two years ago an English publisher approached me and gave me the offer to write a book of my choice. At that point I could not spare the time since I was totally immersed in the work of the CRT as well as work on the family farm and my journalistic commitments.

Although still working many hours a week for the CRT (and quite properly receiving no payment for it), when the necessity for *The Hunting Gene* emerged I contacted the publishers concerned, fully expecting them to take up the idea enthusiastically. Their recent titles have included books about poachers, gamekeepers, fishing and shooting; the publishers pride themselves on the strength of their 'countryside list'. Quick as a flash, a reply came back stating, 'I have considered your proposal carefully but regret it is not suitable for our list.' Another mainstream publisher explained that they were only interested in highly illustrated books with a potential overseas market. I will let readers come to their own conclusions as to the quality of the illustrations in this book and simply say that the popularity of hunting in Ireland, the USA, Australia and New Zealand is growing apace.

A friend in a leading bookshop, who disagrees with hunting but is a libertarian, gave me the benefit of her experience: 'You will never get it published properly today – the book is too politically incorrect. You will actually have problems in getting it into bookshops too. I'll fight for you to get it in here – but you will have major problems.' Consequently I wrote to three large book-selling chains: one said that it would consider the finished book, the other two failed to reply.

So, at a time of unparalleled interest in the whole issue of hunting and after having written numerous books in the past, I could not get a publisher. When Salmon Rushdie had problems with his book in Muslim countries there was an outcry. When one English writer has problems in England the political and media establishments are unconcerned because they have caused the problem.

Consequently the only reason *The Hunting Gene* has appeared is because I have published it myself, with invaluable help in distribution from Merlin Unwin Books and a number of pre-publication subscribers who have helped to provide part of the funding since the whole venture has been far and away beyond my pocket.

Sadly, Britain's reputation for free speech and the 'publish and be damned' ethic has taken several further knocks during the writing of *The Hunting Gene*. Two prominent naturalists

234

who both support country sports felt unable to contribute, as did a well-known sports commentator. They all work for the BBC and felt that an association with hunting could jeopardise their future employment. One, with a young family and a mortgage to support, felt that he could not take the risk with animal rights and anthropomorphism-loving editors and producers. Off the record, he was prepared to say that he thought the BBC's attitude to wildlife, conservation and the countryside was based on 'bunny hugging', and that in his view an animal rights agenda permeates the whole of the BBC from its Countryside Unit to the Natural History Unit and Current Affairs; but he felt that his responsibilities towards his family outweighed his desire to become an out-of-work martyr.

Indeed, from what he said it seems to me that one of the reasons for the threat against the BBC's *One Man and His Dog* television programme could be animal rights. After all, sheep dog trials are only held because there

Bramble – he got me onto television.

is livestock farming and we eat sheep; a fact that no doubt appals 'green' Brazilian-soya-eating, television-pet-watching, gelatine-using vegetarians.

But unfortunately the story of *The Hunting Gene* does not end here. When the idea first formed, it seemed obvious to me that because of the political temperature of hunting, the beautiful areas in which it takes place and the wide range of people, animals and issues involved, it would make a wonderful television series. With my television experience it seemed to make good sense; but at the time of writing most television companies, including the BBC, appear to think it makes bad sense. When the BBC wanted to kill off *One Man and His Dog* inhumanely, I was approached by a London company providing ideas for Channel Four. 'You are a natural for television,' they said, 'give us some ideas, Channel Four will love you.' Oh, what a surprise! I gave them *The Hunting Gene* and hardly heard another word.

So in one of the oldest democracies in the world, when the boast is that we have free speech and access to the media I could not get mainstream publishers or broadcasters interested in *The Hunting Gene*, or persuade them to look at the hunting issue from a country perspective. Regrettably I believe that this censorship – for that is what it is – goes beyond 'political correctness' and into an area that can only be called 'emotional correctness':

235

hunting is 'barbaric', people who hunt or raise livestock are 'cruel'; 'pass the tissues and let's watch *Bambi* on video or the latest TV pet programme'. All this as our climate heats, our farmland wildlife disappears and poisons gush into our rivers, seas, soil and air.

A few years ago I wrote this simple poem:

> The rain falls,
> The spring rises,
> The stream flows,
> The river winds,
> The sewage seeps,
> The acid burns.
> The poison bubbles,
> The fish die,
> The trees sigh.
> The dolphins weep,
> The gulls cry,
> The rain falls;
> The cycle of despair.

This is the real message of our age, not hunting, not the purification of the countryside, not watching old dogs in animal hospitals on television. If those who rule us and try to manipulate our minds cannot recognise the real issues soon, then those generations who survive into the future may actually be grateful that there is a hunting gene.

SUBSCRIBERS

The following hunts, individuals and organisations have subscribed to *The Hunting Gene*. We are very grateful to them for their generosity and support towards the publication of this book. Without their help *The Hunting Gene* would not have materialised. There were also a number of people who wished to remain anonymous; thank you all.

HUNTS
The Aldenham Harriers
The Atherstone
The Bedale
The Belvoir
The Berwickshire
The Brocklesby
The Cumbria Beagles
The East Cornwall
Forest and District Beagles
The High Peak Harriers
The Hunsley Beacon
   Beagles
The Hursley Hambledon
The North Cornwall
The North Dartmoor
   Beagles
The Oakley Hunt
The Pembrokeshire
The Pipewell Foot Beagles
The Quantock Staghounds
The Ross Harriers
The South Notts
The Towy and Cothi
**The Vale of the White
   Horse**
The Warwickshire

The Waveney Harriers
The Wealden Mink Hunt
The Weardale and Tees
   Valley Beagles
The West Norfolk
   Foxhounds

INDIVIDUALS AND
   ORGANISATIONS
Mr and Mrs M Abel Smith
ADL Tack Repairs
Ian Alexander QC
Mrs Mary Allen
R C Ames
The Earl of Arundel
Ian Askew
John Austen
A Baillie
Baily's Hunting Directory
Althea Barclay
M J Barclay
A J Barnett
Lt Col. Sir John Baynes Bt
David Bell
Jane Bell
Graham Bendall
Christopher Bennett

Mrs Sue Bentley
Sigi Bergmann
R J Berkeley
Best Nest Hatcheries Ltd
William Bishop
Bill Blevins
R P T Boughen
Colonel D Boyd
David Bragg
Robin Bramley
John Brocklehurst
Brocklehurst's of Bakewell
Broombrae Boarding
   Kennels
R J Brunsdon
Mrs P Burnett-Brown
Sir Richard Butler
Sam Butler
L R Campfield
Simon Clarke
John C Cook
Peter Cook
William Cross
J Crowhurst
Mrs A Darling
M Davies
Mark Davies

Mrs J M Dixon Smith
N R Elwes
Brian Fanshawe
Diana Fernsby
Robin Fleming
Richard Fortescue
George Fowles and Cassy
    Lawson
S Frank
Ken Gifford
Anthony Gillam
Charles Gordon-Watson
George Goring – Goring
    Hotels
Michael Griffith CBE
M Grimes
Henry Gwyn-Jones
Mary Hambro
Daniel T C Hanbury
R C Harbord
Hardwick Farms
Tim Hart
Sir Stephen Hastings
Mrs M Heseltine
Michael Hoare MFH
P J Horsburgh
James Hough
R Howe
Mr and Mrs H Hurrell
J L Jervoise
D E Jones
Lt Col. J R D Kaye
Mrs Ursula Kennedy
A J Kiddy
Knights Solicitors
Mrs J Latham
Bruce Lawson
Mrs E Noel Layton

Martin Letts
Dick Lloyd
J Lloyd
J W Lockwood MFH
T Lockwood
Andrew Love
Mrs C Luzi
Guy L Lyster DL
James Mackaness
Mrs S Mannell
John McCall
J McCulloch
Diane McDougall
Mrs A McGhee MH
Roderick Moore
His Honour Judge Morrell
Sir Philip Naylor-Leyland Bt
Dr J Outhwaite
Miss R J Page
Mr and Mrs J Partridge
Pegasus Horseshoes Ltd
Harry Pemberton
Mr and Mrs A Pinsent
David Pitfield
Mrs H Pocock
Michael Poland
R W F Poole
Liz Powell – Hunter Liveries
Sir Mark Prescott Bt
P Presland
Paul Rackham
Dr Simon Rees
David Reid Scott
David Reynolds
Mary Sanderson
Mrs L Schuster
R D Schuster
Mrs F Silcock

Gillian Simmonds
T W Simpson
M T Smith
Robin Smith-Ryland
C W Smyth-Osbourne
Miss A Squarey
P L B Stoddart
M J C Stone
R J E Stops
Tattersalls
M N B Thompson
Penelope Thornton
R P Tinsley
R C Tomkinson
Mrs Olivia Townshend
H W Turcan
John Tylor
Liz Verity MFH
The Earl of Verulam
E H Vestey
Nick Viney MFH
Badger Walker
A D Wardall
Mrs E Watters
M H S Webber
A H Westropp
Miss Miriam Wiedman
Margot Wiffin MH
Sir Watkin Williams-Wynn Bt
Michael Willett
Mrs John Wills
C Martin Wood III MFH
Mrs Carolyn Wright
Tom Yandle
Lt Col. D J Younger
Mrs E Younghusband

INDEX

239